Promoting Resilience

Promoting Resilience offers a fresh perspective that views resilience through a sociological lens, emphasizing the significance of loss issues and highlighting a range of practice implications across a wide range of fields.

Drawing on the expertise of a wide range of contributors, the book provides a solid foundation for developing a fuller and more holistic picture of the many challenges associated with promoting resilience. Chapters present a range of sociological perspectives that cast light on trauma and vulnerability. Combining theoretical richness with practical insights, chapter authors bring a sociological lens to enrich understanding of loss and adversity.

This volume offers a bedrock of understanding for students, clinicians, and researchers who want to extend and deepen their knowledge of the sociological aspects of overcoming life challenges.

Neil Thompson, PhD, DLitt, is an independent writer, educator and adviser based in Wales (UK).

Gerry R. Cox, PhD, is a professor emeritus of sociology/archaeology at the University of Wisconsin-La Crosse, director of the Center for Death Education and Bioethics, and a member of the board of directors of the National Prison Hospice Association (USA).

"In *Promoting Resilience* Thompson and Cox offer insight into a wide range of contexts in which resilience is relevant. They uniquely apply both a sociological perspective and a practice focus to the study of resilience and in so doing significantly deepen understanding of this complex topic."

— *Susan E. Wright, PhD, professor emerita of sociology,*
Drake University, USA

"*Promoting Resilience* fulfills the lofty objective of its title, bringing together a truly global team to prepare essays that draw upon each other's work. We learn practical ways to be more resilient and to help those in our communities and social networks to thrive the crises that come with life. The contributors draw upon examples from the everyday workplace to locales ranging from a schoolyard in Scotland to the Outback in Australia. The reader is left with insight into the role of community and social capital in overcoming adversity, vulnerability, loss, and grief."

— *Richard T. Schaefer, Department of Sociology,*
DePaul University, USA

"Thompson and Cox have assembled a team of scholars that have collectively applied the concept of resilience in concise and thought-provoking ways to a range of situations that produce ontological insecurity. In so doing, they have succeeded in addressing the challenge posed by Joel Best in his foreword, which is to prove the value of this relatively new concept."

— *Peter Kivisto, Augustana College, USA*

"*Promoting Resilience* makes an important contribution to the literature on bereavement, loss, death and dying and is a valuable addition to the field of mental health more generally. It will engage students, practitioners, professionals, as well as scholars and anyone else interested in how we as humans confront and survive adversity. The book's main point, presented in an excellent and thorough introductory chapter, is to challenge the common understanding of resilience as an individual trait or achievement. In contrast, the book re-positions resilience as a complex, multi-dimensional, socially constructed product of communities, families, institutions, and cultures, plus myriad care professionals and informal helpers. Throughout the book's 30 chapters, a range of contributors elaborate on this perspective with sociological theory and compelling examples from some of the most troubling societal problems and crises of our time. Seeing resilience as a social-cultural phenomenon adds a significant dimension to the discussion of how we respond to tragedy and adversity and helps point the way forward toward better preparation and outcomes. As such, this book is a fresh and welcome addition to the literature."

— *Mary Zimmerman, professor of health policy and sociology,*
University of Kansas, USA

Promoting Resilience

Responding to Adversity,
Vulnerability, and Loss

**Edited by Neil Thompson
and Gerry R. Cox**

Routledge
Taylor & Francis Group

NEW YORK AND LONDON

First published 2020
by Routledge
52 Vanderbilt Avenue, New York, NY 10017

Simultaneously published in the UK
by Routledge
2 Park Square, Milton Park, Abingdon, Oxon OX14 4RN

Routledge is an imprint of the Taylor & Francis Group, an informa business

Library of Congress Cataloguing-in-Publication Data
A catalog record for this book has been requested

ISBN: 978-0-367-14560-6 (hbk)
ISBN: 978-0-367-14562-0 (pbk)
ISBN: 978-0-429-05729-8 (ebk)

Typeset in Goudy
by Apex CoVantage, LLC

For Whitney Gordon and in memory of Ron Barrett

Contents

Preface

The topic of resilience is one that is receiving considerable attention these days. However, the primary focus of the growing literature base is a narrow, psychological one that pays little or no attention to wider social factors. Our view is that this provides too narrow and distorted a view of resilience, giving the impression that it is simply a personal characteristic of individuals, rather than a complex multidimensional phenomenon that merits a more holistic approach. This book is intended to provide the foundations for this more holistic approach by incorporating sociological insights to complement and counterbalance the psychological ones.

In addition, much of the literature is written in a highly technical style, drawing on a great deal of depersonalized academic and technical jargon that (i) does not capture the very *human* nature of resilience (for example, its spiritual dimensions) and (ii) is less likely to appeal to students and practitioners who will be interested in how the insights offered can be of value to them in their professional roles. Such roles will include social workers; counselors and psychotherapists; community workers; probation and prison officers; clergy and chaplains; and various other caring or helping professions.

Furthermore, we are aware of significant links between loss and grief on the one hand and resilience on the other, an important set of linkages that rarely feature in the mainstream literature. Our book highlights the importance of considering the interrelationships between these two areas of practice.

What makes this book distinctive from the existing literature base is its holistic approach and practice focus. The multiauthor approach, with a wide range of short, clear chapters is also distinctive and will help get across the key message that resilience is a much broader and much more complex phenomenon than it is generally assumed to be.

Foreword

We seem to be in the Age of Resilience. A check of *Sociological Abstract's* database reveals that a total of two journal articles published between 1971 and 1980 had titles that contained the word "resilience." This rose to eight in 1981–1990, again to 67 in 1991–2000, then to 428 during 2001–2010. Between 2011 and the end of March 2019 (when I wrote this), 902 scholarly journal articles with resilience in their titles had been added to the database— on pace to reach nearly 1,100 by the time the decade ended. No doubt we could find similar increases in the databases for journals in education, social work and so on.

Some of this increase no doubt represents old wine in new bottles. Disciplines and their members often update their terminology in an effort to seem more contemporary and more enlightened. During the late 1950s and early 1960s, educators described problem students (often poor and members of ethnic minorities) as "culturally deprived" or "culturally disadvantaged"— labels that seemed more or less objective, while apparently avoiding blaming students for their poor performance. Within a few years, these terms were being rejected after critics began asking: "Who decides that some cultures are disadvantageous?" So, educators turned to a new, wonderfully vague label—"at risk"—that also carried connotations of scientific objectivity (surely risks could be measured), while not actually declaring what the risk—or their cause—might be. But, beginning sometime in the new millennium, at risk also began to fall out of favor, and the literature began talking about resilience.

Resilience's appeal is apparent. Culturally deprived or at risk emphasized deficiencies, or at least problems, if not with the students themselves, then with the circumstances under which they lived. In contrast, resilience could be seen as a virtue, a strength; it appeared upbeat and emphasized the positive. Resilience was a desirable quality, something to cultivate.

At about the same time, resilience began making inroads into a variety of other specialties in the social sciences and the helping professions. Within the sociology of disasters, for instance, scholars argued that, after a hurricane struck a Caribbean island, some villages recovered more quickly than others and that they could be understood as resilient.

Scholars and professionals are familiar with this sort of conceptual progression; new vocabularies are applied to old phenomena so that those once labeled feebleminded are defined as mentally retarded, who in turn are renamed intellectually disabled. The old terms—once cutting edge and used as evidence of professionals' special understanding—become tainted as evidence of a less-enlightened age, just as using the new terminology reveals sophistication and superior understanding.

In *Learn to Write Badly: How to Succeed in the Social Sciences*, the social psychologist Michael Billig (2013) warns about the temptation of inventing nouns and treating them as explanations. Why did this village recover from the hurricane? It had high resilience. Note that tautology lurks here. How can we tell which villages have high resilience? They are the ones that recover quickly from hurricanes. What seems to be an explanation threatens to turn out to be just another new label in a chain of circular reasoning.

Part of resilience's appeal may be that we live in a culture that celebrates individualism and favors concepts that suggest the importance of psychological processes. In this respect, resilience resembles another trendy term: grit. If some people have acquired grit or resilience, then perhaps we can train others to have these same personal strengths.

Sociologists, of course, tend to emphasize the social context within which strengths are displayed. Villages—not just individuals—can be resilient. However, it often turns out that the villages that are more resilient tend to have more resources—more money—so that more prosperous villages tend to recover from disasters more quickly than their poorer counterparts. This raises the awkward possibility that resilience is more closely related to—possibly just another name for—social class.

New concepts—such as resilience—should not be dismissed out of hand, but it is also true they must prove their value. They need to add something to our understanding. Their value can only be determined by people trying to apply them. The chapters in this volume are part of this process. They offer a wide-ranging overview, examining the relevance of resilience to understanding contemporary social problems and institutions. These range from episodes of extreme drama—experiencing disasters, terrorism or criminal violence—to continuing challenges that people must confront, such as ethnic hostility, sexism and poverty. The chapters also explore how resilience is relevant throughout the lifecourse, from childhood to old age. And, of course, many of the chapters address death, grief and bereavement. Running through the book is an effort to treat resilience in sociological—as opposed to merely psychological—terms and to suggest ways that the concept can help those in the caring professions. The breadth of coverage and the sensitivity to the issues being addressed will allow readers to assess the value of the idea of resilience. To the degree that readers find these chapters useful, so that they realize that the idea of resilience adds to their understanding, allows them to devise better explanations and can improve their practices, this concept can assume an enduring place in our thinking.

Joel Best
University of Delaware

Reference

Billig, M. (2013). *Learn to write badly: How to succeed in the social sciences*. Cambridge, Cambridge University Press.

Acknowledgments

Neil would like to thank Dr. Sue Thompson for her unstinting support and her helpful feedback on his published work. He would also like to thank Anna Thompson for her practical support and assistance.

Also worthy of mention are the many colleagues, clients and caregivers who have taught him firsthand what resilience is all about.

Gerry would like to thank all of the members of his family, his special friends, the many teachers who have taught him and the many students who have questioned and inspired learning and growth.

Both Neil and Gerry would like to acknowledge the benefits gained from being part of the annual University of Wisconsin-La Crosse International Death, Grief and Bereavement Conference held each June, a conference that never fails to bring together so many warm, committed and inspiring people. Likewise, we wish to express our thanks to colleagues in the International Work Group on Death, Dying and Bereavement (IWG) for the support, camaraderie, stimulation and learning that they so readily offer.

Finally, we would like to thank Anna Moore at the publishers for her support and her belief in the quality of our work.

Editors and Contributors

Editors

Neil Thompson, PhD, DLitt, is an independent writer, educator and adviser. He has held full or honorary professorships at four UK universities. He is a well-published author with over 200 publications to his name, including 44 books, several of which are bestsellers. He has been a speaker at conferences in the UK, Ireland, Italy, Spain, Norway, the Netherlands, Greece, the Czech Republic, Turkey, Hong Kong, India, the United States, Canada and Australia. He is a Fellow of the Chartered Institute of Personnel and Development, the Higher Education Academy and the Royal Society of Arts, and a member of the International Work Group on Death, Dying and Bereavement. He was formerly the editor of the US-based international journal *Illness, Crisis & Loss*. He is a sought-after conference speaker, consultant and facilitator. He runs the Avenue Professional Development Programme, an innovative subscription-based online learning community for the people professions (www.apdp.org.uk). His personal website and blog are at www.NeilThompson.info.

Gerry R. Cox, PhD, is a Professor Emeritus of Sociology/Archaeology at the University of Wisconsin–La Crosse. He was the Director of the Center for Death Education and Bioethics. His teaching focused upon theory/theory construction, deviance and criminology, death and dying, social psychology, and minority peoples. He has been publishing materials since 1973 in sociology and teaching-oriented professional journals. He is a member of the International Work Group on Dying, Death and Bereavement, the Midwest Sociological Society, the American Sociological Association, the International Sociological Association, Phi Kappa Phi, the Great Plains Sociological Society, and the Association of Death Education and Counseling. He served on the board of directors of the National Prison Hospice Association.

Together Drs. Cox and Thompson have co-edited the Handbook of the Sociology of Death, Grief, and Bereavement (Routledge, 2017) and, with Robert G. Stevenson, the Handbook of Traumatic Loss (Routledge, 2017).

In addition, they both have extensive publication records and impressive credentials within the higher education field.

Contributors

Barbara Adam is Emerita Professor at Cardiff University's School of Social Sciences and currently Senior Fellow at the Institute of Advanced Sustainability Studies (IASS), Potsdam. Social time has been the intellectual project throughout her academic career, resulting in five research monographs and a large number of articles in which she sought to bring time and the future to the center of social science analysis. Her theory is always contextual storytelling and presented in a variety of forms. On the basis of this agenda-setting work she has been awarded several Economic and Social Research Council research grants and fellowships. As part of the commitment to social time she founded the journal *Time & Society*, which she edited for 10 years and has been supporting as Consulting Editor ever since.

Tashel Bordere, PhD, CT, is an Assistant Professor of Human Development and Family Science (HDFS) and State Extension Specialist in Youth Development at the University of Missouri–Columbia, where she teaches Black Families, Childhood Death and Bereavement, and Lifespan Development. She is a past board member of the Association for Death Education and Counseling, past chair of the Multicultural Committee, and past editor of the ADEC Forum. She has specialized training as a certified thanatologist (Death, Dying and Grief). Dr. Bordere's research focuses on African American youth and family bereavement, suffocated grief, and resilience through loss. Dr. Bordere has done numerous workshops and consultations and has published works relating to diversity and resilience through loss including her recent co-edited book/co-authored book (with Darcy L. Harris), *Handbook of Social Justice in Loss and Grief* (2016). She has been featured on NPR broadcast "Teens and Grief," Hospice Foundation's Live National Webcast "Living with Grief: Helping Adolescents Cope with Loss," and Open to Hope Cable Show's "Saving At Risk Youth." Dr. Bordere was recently awarded the Ronald K. Barrett Award from the Association of Death Education and Counseling for her research on African American youth grief. She developed SHED Loss and Grief Tools Training (MU Extension).

Wendy Bowler has a PhD in sociology and a Bachelor of Arts (Hons.) from La Trobe University, Melbourne, where she has worked as a lecturer in journalism and sociology. She is currently a research associate with La Trobe and is undertaking a Master of Art Curatorship at the University of Melbourne. Her doctoral thesis *From Terror to Tragedy: A Review of the 9/11 News Images* (2008) is a work of cultural sociology that interprets the media's "tragedy" of the September 11, 2001, terrorist attacks, using Nietzsche's theory of tragedy. Her work combines interests in the cultural psychology of social life, the arts and art history, with substantial prior work experience as a journalist and senior editor. Following the sudden death of a child in 2012, Dr. Bowler has been following her love of visual art and doing research into the sociology and culture of trauma and bereavement.

Michael Brennan is Senior Lecturer in sociology at Liverpool Hope University, UK. His recent work has explored the material practices and identificatory dynamics surrounding public mourning; the narrative practices of the self invoked in "pathographic" accounts of public dying; and the productive uses of creativity triggered by absence and loss. He is the author of *Mourning and Disaster* (2008) and editor of *The A-Z of Death and Dying* (2014).

Shirleen Campbell is a proud Town Camper who currently lives at Hoppy's Town Camp in Alice Springs. Shirleen is a well-respected community member and is a strong voice for women and children who have experienced, or are experiencing, family and domestic violence. In 2014 a group of Town Camp women advocated to government about the issues surrounding family and domestic violence. Shirleen has been pivotal to the development of the Tangentyere Women's Family Safety Group. The group undertakes family violence training, community engagement, consultation regarding the issues for women, children, men and communities regarding violence and are now the governance group for the Tangentyere Family Violence Prevention Programs.

Amy Y. M. Chow, PhD, is an Associate Professor with the Department of Social Work and Social Administration and Honorary Associate Professor with the Li Ka Shing Faculty of Medicine, the University of Hong Kong. She is the Co-Director of the Jockey Club End-of-Life Community Care Project and Associate Director of Sau Po Centre of Ageing. With a background as a registered social worker specializing in bereavement counseling, she is the founder of the first community-based bereavement counseling center in Hong Kong. She was the first Fellow in Thanatology awarded by the Association of Death Education and Counseling in Asia. She was elected as the chairperson of the prestigious International Work Group on Death, Dying and Bereavement, the Secretary of the Association for Death Education and Counseling as well as a board member of the Asia Pacific Hospice Network in 2016. Her achievement in bereavement research is well recognized locally and internationally. She received the Association for Death Education and Counseling 2005 Cross-Cultural Award, Cadenza Fellow in 2008, Distinguished Alumni Award 2013 of Department of Social Work, CUHK, 2013 Rainbow of Life Outstanding Individual Award, 2014 Outstanding Social Worker Award, 2014 Outstanding Teaching Award and 2017–2018 Outstanding Research Output Award of the University of Hong Kong.

Maree Corbo has worked with both victims and perpetrators of domestic and family violence for over 10 years, and is currently the manager of the Tangentyere Community Safety programs at Tangentyere Council in Alice Springs. Programs under the community safety umbrella include the

Tangentyere Family Violence Prevention Program (FVPP), Night Patrol, a tenancy support service as well as an alcohol harm minimization program. Tangentyere Council is the primary service provider for a service population in excess of 3,300 Aboriginal people living on, or visiting on, the 16 Alice Springs Town Camps. Maree works closely with the Town Camp residents who have local knowledge, experience and, importantly, a key understanding of the cultural strengths of their community. As a result, all aspects of the FVPP take a "ground-up approach" to working within the community. In 2013 Maree won the Department of Human Services— Robin Clarke Award for her work with vulnerable children, young people and families in Victoria: *Making a Difference with Children, Young People and Families*.

Charles (Chuck) A. Corr, PhD, is Professor emeritus, Southern Illinois University Edwardsville. Chuck currently serves on the board of directors of the Suncoast Hospice Institute and is Senior Editor of the ChiPPS (Children's Project on Palliative/Hospice Care) E-Journal, a free, quarterly publication of the National Hospice and Palliative Care Organization. Chuck is a long-time member (and former chairperson) of the International Work Group on Death, Dying and Bereavement (IWG) and of the Association for Death Education and Counseling (ADEC). In addition to 37 books, his publications include 130 chapters and articles in professional journals. His most recent book, co-authored with Donna M. Corr and Kenneth J. Doka, is the eighth edition of *Death & Dying, Life & Living* (Cengage, 2019). Chuck's professional work has been honored by awards from ADEC (1988 and 1996), Children's Hospice International (1989 & 1995), the Center for Death Education and Bioethics at the University of Wisconsin– La Crosse (2007), the Musculoskeletal Transplant Foundation (2008), and IWG (2016).

Christopher Cox previously served for 16 years as a Catholic priest in low-income, immigrant communities in the US and Latin America. He provided direct service to immigrants and refugees. Today, Chris engages in systems change as the associate director of Seventh Generation Interfaith Coalition for Responsible Investment (SGI). Chris leads faith-based, institutional shareholders in engaging companies around issues concerning climate change, corporate governance, food justice, health, human rights and water stewardship. Through the lens of faith and the promotion of human rights, SGI builds a more just and sustainable world for those most vulnerable by integrating social and environmental values into corporate and investor actions. Chris also led the Human Thread Campaign, a Catholic effort to raise awareness, direct action and build solidarity with international garment workers. Chris graduated from the University of Notre Dame with a Bachelor of Arts and, later, a Master of Divinity. He resides in Milwaukee, WI. His wife, Patricia, is a native of Peru, and their son, Gastón, was born in Chile.

Vivienne Dacre, PhD, is Senior Lecturer at Wrexham Glyndŵr University in Wales. She is a program leader for therapeutic childcare and teaches across social work and criminal justice programs. Her teaching interests focus on trauma and attachment. Vivienne gained her Professional Doctorate in Health and Social Care from the University of Wales in 2015. She has an MA in Therapeutic Child Care from the University of Reading in the UK. Vivienne was previously employed as a qualified social worker for many years and, as such, has extensive experience of working with children and families in England. Before joining Wrexham Glyndŵr University she was a senior manager in the private care sector with lead responsibility for therapeutic services. For a number of years, she worked within a local authority children and families social work team. As a social worker, she has managed a local authority family center and children's residential homes. Her practice experience therefore has covered both the investigation of child abuse and therapeutic work with children and adults impacted by trauma and loss.

Signe Dobelniece graduated from the Department of Philosophy, Latvian State University, completed the master's program in social work at the University of Gothenburg (Sweden), and received her PhD in social work from Tallinn University (Estonia). Currently she works as Associate Professor at the Institute of Humanities and Social Sciences, Faculty of Economics and Social Development, Latvia University of Life Sciences and Technologies. Her main research interests include social problems, particularly poverty and homelessness, social exclusion/inclusion; social policy; and social welfare. She has carried out several research projects (latest are INTERREG project "Social empowerment in rural areas" and "Methodological guidelines for work with NEET youth") and published a number of articles including: "Social inclusion challenges of refugees", "Social assistance: Comparative analysis" and "Housing security in Latvia: Regional differences."

Kenneth J. Doka, PhD, is a Professor of Gerontology at the Graduate School of The College of New Rochelle and Senior Consultant to the Hospice Foundation of America. A prolific author, Dr. Doka has authored or edited over 30 books and over 100 articles and book chapters. He is editor of both *Omega: The Journal of Death and Dying* and *Journeys: A Newsletter to Help in Bereavement*. Dr. Doka was elected President of the Association for Death Education and Counseling in 1993. In 1995, he was elected to the board of directors of the International Work Group on Dying, Death and Bereavement and served as chair from 1997 to 1999. ADEC presented him with an Award for Outstanding Contributions in the Field of Death Education in 1998. In 2000 Scott and White presented him with an award for Outstanding Contributions to Thanatology and Hospice. His alma mater, Concordia College, presented him with their first Distinguished Alumnus Award. He is a recipient of the Caring Hands Award as well as the Dr. Robert Fulton

CDEB Founder's Award. In 2006, Dr. Doka was grandfathered in as a mental health counselor under NY State's first licensure of counselors.

Ronnie Egan, PhD, is Associate Professor of Field Education in Social Work at RMIT University, Australia. She has specialized in research about supervision and practice for social workers and students, has published widely in these areas and has extensive and active networks in the human service sector. Her relationships with the field span her career as a practitioner and academic, and this has enabled the development of innovative ways of understanding and facilitating the nexus between universities and the community. Her relationship with Tangentyere Women's Family Safety Group began five years ago when a student placement project began where up to 10 final year social work students now undertake their project placements, which have been identified by the women. To date, over 30 students have completed their field education in Alice Springs, a number of graduates continuing to work in the Northern Territory when they graduate and finding employment in Aboriginal organizations in Melbourne.

Darcy L. Harris, RN, RSW, PhD, FT, is an Associate Professor and the Thanatology Coordinator at King's University College in London, Canada, where she also maintains a private clinical practice specializing in issues related to change, loss, and transition. Dr. Harris developed the undergraduate degree program in thanatology at King's University College. In addition, she is a faculty member of the Portland Institute for Loss and Transition, dedicated to postgraduate training in grief therapy, leading toward Certification in Meaning Reconstruction in Loss. She has served on the board of directors of the Association for Death Education and Counseling and is a current member of the International Work Group on Death, Dying and Bereavement. She is series editor for Routledge Publishing Company's *Death, Dying, and Bereavement Series*. Her publications include *Counting our Losses: Reflecting on Change, Loss, and Transition in Everyday Life* (Routledge), *Grief and Bereavement in Contemporary Society: Bridging Research and Practice* (Routledge), *Principles and Practice of Grief Counseling* (Springer), and *The Handbook of Social Justice in Loss and Grief: Exploring Diversity, Equity, and Inclusion* (Routledge). Her latest book is *Non-Death Loss and Grief: Context and Clinical Implications* (Routledge).

Andy Hau Yan Ho, PhD, MFT, FT, is Assistant Professor of Psychology and Joint Honorary Assistant Professor of Medicine at Nanyang Technological University, Singapore. He serves as a Board Director of the Association for Death Education and Counseling (ADEC) and the International Work Group on Death, Dying and Bereavement (IWGDDB). Andy's research and teaching focus on psychosocial gerontology, palliative and bereavement care, arts and creative aging, holistic therapy and community empowerment. He is the founder of a number of innovative and acclaimed psychosocio-spiritual interventions that promote capacity building. These include

Mindful-Compassion Art Therapy (MCAT) for preventing burnout and cultivating resilience among caregivers; Family Dignity Intervention (FDI) for advancing holistic end-of-life care; Narrative e-Writing Intervention (NeW-I) for enhancing pediatric palliative care and parental bereavement support services; and Aspiration and Resilience Through Intergenerational Storytelling and Art-based Narratives (ARTISAN) for citizen empowerment and loneliness alleviation. Andy has produced numerous public health campaigns and short film documentaries; authored over 70 top-tier journal articles, books, chapters and research reports; as well as presented in over 130 keynote, plenary and competitive conference presentations. He is the first Asian recipient of the prestigious 2018 ADEC Academic Educator Award, while his scholarly contributions are recognized with distinction by professional bodies around the world.

Rozana Huq, PhD, is an organizational behaviorist, leadership coach, conference speaker, lecturer, author and philanthropist. She is based in the UK and specializes in leadership, employee empowerment, psychological empowerment, building resilience and stress management. The growing trend for downsizing and merging means that employees are expected to make decisions. However, burdening employees with this responsibility without empowering them does not deliver results. Dr. Huq identifies the problem as a lack of knowledge regarding the implementation of employee empowerment. In response to this problem, she offers a solution and has made a notable contribution to knowledge by creating a framework enabling organizations to implement employee empowerment, titled Huq's Model D.

She has taught at Queen's University, Belfast, on the Leadership course at the School of Management and has also provided teaching on the MSc Strategy and Leadership course at the School of Social Sciences, Education and Social Work. She has wide experience in teaching and management training as well as providing services as a community worker, educational consultant, chairperson, board director, lecturer and workshop facilitator. Dr. Huq's research is acknowledged in the UK and abroad. She is a well-known international keynote speaker and lecturer. www.rozanahuq.com.

Wulf Livingston is a Reader in Social Sciences at Glyndŵr University, Wrexham, Wales. He is a qualified and registered social worker, with 25 years plus of practice experience in alcohol, drugs, mental health and criminal justice sectors. Wulf's current research and writing focuses on alcohol, mental health, recovery, participation and policy. His most recent research activity is concerned with the evaluation of minimum pricing of alcohol for both the Welsh and Scottish governments.

Celeste Medina, who identifies as an intersectional feminist scholar, is the Research Coordinator for the Gender SEAMS (Sexuality, Embodiment,

Movement, Affect, and Space) Research Team and a lead teacher at Children's Orchard Academy in Lubbock, Texas. She graduated from Texas Tech University in May 2018 with a BS in Human Development and Family Studies and a Minor in Women's and Gender Studies. She has presented in college classrooms and at multiple conferences and symposiums. She is co-author of a media review published in the *Journal of Family Theory and Review* and is currently working on a project examining space, embodiment, and romance of Black women at a predominately White institution.

Bernard Moss is Emeritus Professor of Social Work Education and Spirituality at Staffordshire University, UK, where he helped to educate and train social workers. His principal teaching areas were communication skills; death, dying and bereavement; and developing understanding of spirituality and its relevance to professional practice. He has published widely on this theme for which he was awarded his PhD. His teaching excellence was recognized by the Higher Education Academy, UK, with the award of a National Teaching Fellowship in 2004 and subsequent acceptance as a Principal Fellow. He also received a Quality Award for GP Training and Education from the Royal College of General Practitioners, UK, for the contribution that he and his wife, Sheila, continue to make to the enhancement of communication skills for trainee doctors and psychiatrists. The various strands in Bernard's career, including work as a probation officer, relationship counselor, family mediator and faith leader, have enriched his appreciation of the importance of resilience for human flourishing. More recently he has been developing his interest in the use of labyrinth walks to encourage a greater awareness and appreciation of resilience. As Associate Minister of St Mary's Church in Nantwich, Cheshire, UK, he is also deeply committed to best practice in pastoral care within the local community.

Paul C. Rosenblatt is Professor Emeritus of Family Social Science at the University of Minnesota, USA. His research interests include couple and family systems, qualitative research, individual and family grief, cultural influences on families and researchers, the impact of oppressive systems on families, and family theory. He has published 14 books and more than 200 journal articles and book chapters. His recent books include *The Impact of Racism on African American Families, Knowing and Not Knowing in Intimate Relationships* (with Elizabeth Wieling), and *Shared Obliviousness in Family Systems*. His current academic projects include research on love letters, on couples who have a child in cancer treatment or who have lost a child to cancer, on the grief of faculty members when a student or former student dies, and on the experience of learning striking things about a close family member after that family member dies. Rosenblatt also writes for literary magazines. Included in those writings is a work of creative nonfiction about his research on spiritual healers in Mexico and a short story arising from his experiences interviewing bereaved couples that focuses on a child who eavesdrops on his bereaved parents being interviewed.

Ros Scott, PhD, is an experienced practitioner and researcher in the field of volunteering, palliative care and bereavement. An Honorary Research Fellow at the University of Dundee, she is also an independent voluntary sector consultant. She is passionate about the importance of communities and volunteers in supporting people with palliative and end-of-life care needs and those experiencing loss and bereavement. Her work involves her in supporting and advising hospice, palliative and bereavement organizations to assess and develop volunteering strategically and operationally, developing learning and practice resources, as well as supporting sustainability through the involvement of volunteers. Research interests include the role and impact of volunteering in hospices, palliative care and bereavement, bereavement in schools, volunteering ethics, and governance. She is the author and editor of a range of papers, chapters and books and is a national and international presenter in her field. Ros is co-chair of the European Association for Palliative Care Task Force on Volunteering, vice-chair of Cruse Bereavement Care Scotland, a member of the Scottish Advisory Board for Marie Curie and formerly a trustee of Hospice UK. She received a lifetime achievement award in 2013 for her work in palliative care volunteering.

Elizabeth Sharp, PhD, is Professor of Human Development and Family Studies (HDFS) and Director of Women's and Gender Studies and Director of the Gender SEAMS research team at Texas Tech University (TTU). She is the past-interim Vice President of Diversity, Equity and Inclusion, the past chair of the President's Gender Equity Council, and co-founder of the Women's Faculty Writing Program at TTU. As a scholar-activist, she incorporates intersectional feminist framings in her research to focus on ideologies of romance and families and how these cultural ideologies interface with gender, sexuality, race/ethnicity, and socioeconomic class. Her work has been published in HDFS, sociology, psychology, and family therapy journals and has been cited by media worldwide, including the *New York Times*, the *Toronto Star* and *ForbesWomen*, and her work with choreographers and dancers was featured on the London School of Economics website.

Gerry Skelton is the Director of Treadagh House and has a number of roles, including lecturer, social worker, counsellor, practice teacher, trainer, consultant, facilitator, mediator, peace and reconciliation worker; with occasional writing, ministry and pastoral work. He has been involved within the caring profession for almost 40 years in a statutory, community, voluntary and private capacity. Gerry has gained a highly respected reputation for specializing in, and subsequently animating, a plethora of often marginalized social justice issues, including homelessness. He is the creator and director of the annual Belfast Homelessness Awareness Panel Event, drawing the health, social care, social work, journalism and other broadcast media (and affiliated professions) attention to "the spectre of homelessness." This is complemented by his work in education, training, conference addresses, participation in various initiatives, lobbying of decision makers, and work with and alongside a variety of organizations and groups, including those with current and former experiences of homelessness. In Britain's 2019 New Year Honours, Gerry was awarded an MBE for his outstanding campaigning work and service in Northern Ireland. The internet has a number of readily available links to his work and associated resources; one such example is www.youtube.com/watch?v=KA3Cdw4usMM. He can be contacted at gskelton@belfastmet.ac.uk.

Lorna Stabler is a research associate working in Children's Social Care research at Cardiff University in Wales. She has worked on a number of projects in social work research, directly with social workers, families, young people and children and also drawing together international literature on interventions to evaluate social work practice and its potential to improve the lives of families. The uniting aim of these projects has been to improve service delivery for families, young people and children that need social welfare support. She is particularly keen to understand and incorporate the lived experience of those who have experienced services into service development, implementation and evaluation by taking a participatory approach to research. Lorna herself grew up in foster care so brings this perspective to her writing and research. She was selected as Winston Churchill Memorial Fellow in 2019, which reflects her commitment to learning from the experiences of people from different cultures and social environments across the globe.

Paul Stepney, PhD, is Adjunct Professor of Social Work and Social Policy at the University of Tampere in Finland and Visiting Professor at Chydenius University Centre, University of Jyväskylä in Kokkola, Finland. Prior to this he taught at four UK universities and, during the 1990s, combined teaching at Exeter University with a hospital social work post. Paul's research interests are in the area of critical practice and prevention, and he has published numerous articles and contributed book chapters on this. He recently completed research with mainstream practitioners in two European welfare states to identify the most effective strategies of prevention that can be integrated into protection plans. He is currently working with a partnership manager to evaluate the effectiveness of mental health services in one National Health Service mental health center in the South West of England. He is co-author or co-editor of four books: *Social Work Models, Methods and Theories: A Framework for Practice* (with Deirdre Ford, Russell House Publishing, 2nd edition, 2012); *Social work and the Community: A Critical Context for Practice* (with Keith Popple, Palgrave Macmillan, 2008); and *Social Work Theory and Methods: The Essentials* (with Neil Thompson, Routledge, 2018).

Robert G. Stevenson is a Professor Emeritus of the Graduate Counseling Program, Mercy College, NY. He helped start the master's programs in mental health counseling and school counseling. He has edited/authored a dozen books and over 70 articles and chapters in the areas of grief and loss, as well as in living history. He is a graduate of the College of the Holy Cross (BA), Montclair State (MA) and Fairleigh Dickinson (MAT, EdD). He helped found the Center for Help in Time of Loss in Hillsdale, NJ and created the first independent high school death education course, teaching it for 25 years. He is the recipient of the Wendel Williams Outstanding Educator Award, the ADEC National Death Educator Award, and Founder's Award from the Center for Death Education and Bioethics for outstanding university teaching, research, publication and professional service in the field of death, dying and bereavement. He is also a certified high school counselor and coached championship high school teams in four sports (cross country, track, bowling and ice hockey) for 30 years. For his work with the New York Guard, he received the New York State Governor's medal for Defense of Freedom.

Geraldine Tan-Ho, MSocSc, CT, is Senior Counselor and Research Associate of Psychology at the School of Social Sciences, Nanyang Technological University, Singapore. She holds a Master's of Social Science in Professional Counseling and is a Certified Thanatologist of the Association for Death Education and Counseling (ADEC) for her professional and educational achievements in the field of death, dying and bereavement. A passionate advocate for quality of life and quality of death, Geraldine has rich experience in community action and social change, as she was previously a medical social worker and counselor for low-income families, sick elderly people, terminally ill children, and caregivers. As a counselor in Singapore's biggest pediatric palliative home care team, she restructured and developed national standards of excellence in bereavement care for caregivers and families of children and young adults who died from various chronic life-limiting conditions. Currently, Geraldine focuses her efforts on pioneering a novel Family Dignity Intervention (FDI) for older, terminally ill patients and their families, as well as developing an innovative Narrative e-Writing Intervention (NeW-I) for advancing holistic pediatric palliative care and parental bereavement support services, with the ultimate goal to address the culture-specific psycho-socio-spiritual needs of Asian populations facing loss and mortality.

Denise Tanner works as a Senior Lecturer in social work at University of Birmingham, UK. She is a registered social worker and has worked with children and families, adults with mental health difficulties and older people in both the statutory and third sectors. She has held academic posts in three different universities in the UK. Her teaching and research interests include promoting the well-being of older people; service user involvement in education, research and practice; and social work skills. She has published articles and books on various aspects of social work with older people, including older people with dementia. Her current research projects include exploring ethical issues in older people's self-funded care and preventive initiatives in adult social care. Most of her research uses approaches which facilitate the direct involvement of service users and carers as co-researchers.

Andrew J. Vitale, CT, has over 25 years' experience working in the healthcare sector. He created, animated and directed a child and adolescent bereavement camp, "Friends: Christopher's Camp," while living in South Carolina. A bereavement specialist and certified in thanatology, he currently is bereavement coordinator-spiritual counselor for a non-profit hospice in northern Illinois. He is co-author of *Spiritual Growth and Healing* and *Children Surviving Traumatic Death*, and has been published in the international journal *Illness, Crisis & Loss*. Andrew is a past executive chef from Atlanta and enjoys cooking. He serves on the steering committee for the International Death, Grief and Bereavement Conference held annually at the University of Wisconsin–La Crosse. He was an invited guest for the 2018 gathering of the International Work Group on Death, Dying and Bereavement in London, Ontario. It was noted by an employer that Andrew "has the ability to bounce back after stressful situations," so empathy and resilience reside within him. He is currently a mindfulness practitioner and teaches mindfulness in his bereavement groups as a means to grow through grief and loss. He enjoys shepherding those who come, and go, from his flock.

Resilience

Suffering eases after years of living with death: threatened, expected & actual
All elements and rhythms of my life have been newly calibrated & adjusted
The world re-settles into a new normality that does not at all feel normal
While aching to hold on there is no going back, the direction is forward

Work invitations keep on coming, legal matters need to be attended
Old relationships require nurturing, are central to my recovery
Despite the time not being appropriate, decisions are made
The flow is forward, unstoppable, I am part of the stream

Giving up resistance, submitting to the strong current
Feels right, appropriate even, for wellbeing & sanity
And yet, there is a strong urge to give some steer
To influence the direction, intervene and guide

It seems central to find a good balance between
Submitting, floating, reflecting, acting, influencing
Not just for one's personal situation but also equally
For all environmental issues and associated resilience

Too easily is resilience tied to adjustment & acquiescence
Accommodation to the status quo is precisely not resilience
Needs to be resisted at all cost, differently defined & established
Past & future need to be embedded & encompassed on equal terms

To engage seriously with environmental problems and climate change
Needs resilience tied to flexibility, pliability and radical openness to change
Thinking the unthinkable and engaging with not yet existing invisible impacts
In the knowledge that we are responsible for the effects of present technologies

Barbara Adam

Part I
Understanding Resilience

Introduction to Part I

Part One consists of an extended essay that is intended to set the scene for the range of chapters that comprise Part Two. In this essay we seek to argue and illustrate the case for a much broader understanding of resilience than is currently captured by the existing literature. While individual, psychological factors are clearly at play and no doubt have a very significant role to play, we feel the need to emphasize the point that there are also sociological factors to take into account. Indeed, an understanding of resilience that limits itself to psychological factors without also exploring the role of the social context will be a partial and potentially misleading understanding.

Our focus in Part One is therefore very much on how sociological issues have a part to play in making sense of resilience and, therefore, in promoting greater levels of resilience where possible. However, that is not the only point we want to stress. As experienced and established scholars in the fields of thanatology and of loss and grief more broadly, we are well aware that there is a close association between the major challenges of grief and the role of resilience in rising to those challenges. We therefore see close linkages between resilience as part of a framework for coping with adversity and life challenges, and grief as so often, if not the source of such challenges, an important component of them. Consequently, a key part of the message we seek to put across is the need for a fuller recognition of the interrelationship between resilience and coping on the one hand and loss and grief as major challenges on the other.

What serves as an important linking thread between these two sets of issues is *vulnerability*. Grief is strongly characterized by a powerful sense of vulnerability and insecurity, while resilience can be understood as a way of coping with or managing that vulnerability by "bouncing back" to a position of greater security, confidence and coping. We regard vulnerability as an important existential concept that needs to be understood both psychologically and sociologically.

Papadatou's (2009) concept of being "vulnerable enough" is a useful notion in this regard. She argues:

> Vulnerability is not a trait that we possess or lack. It is a lived experience that unfolds in novel, stressful, or threatening situations and exists on a continuum. We experience ourselves as more or less vulnerable when we accompany people through loss, separation, and bereavement. . . . The factors that determine our vulnerability at a given time and its effects upon caregiving are many: personal, interpersonal, work related, and social.
>
> (p. 93)

Being "vulnerable enough" refers to finding a balance between being too vulnerable (and thus potentially disabled by vulnerability) and feeling "invulnerable" which means being unrealistic about the risk involved in the situations we are engaged with, and thereby neglecting self-care. Being "vulnerable enough" can therefore be understood as part of resilience, a core ingredient in a sense.

We are by no means offering a comprehensive review of the concept of resilience and related matters, but what we do hope we will have achieved in writing Part One is a foundation for further learning, a platform for broadening and deepening our understanding, a significant source of food for thought and a contribution to the major challenges human services professionals face in attempting to promote and capitalize upon resilience.

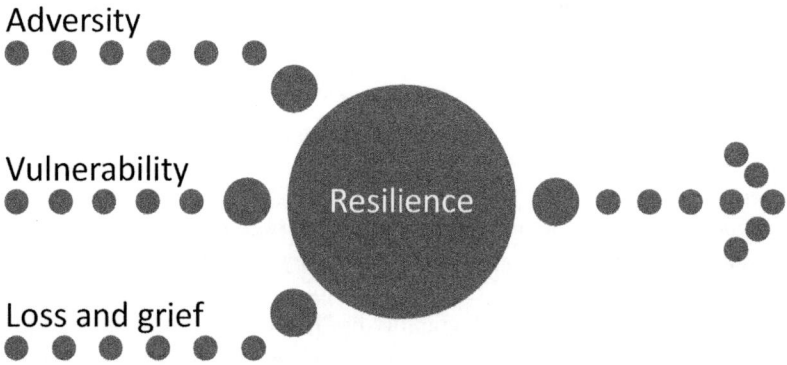

Figure 1.1 Resilience as a response to adversity, vulnerability, loss and grief

1 Making Sense of Resilience

Gerry R. Cox and Neil Thompson

Resilience is generally understood as a feature of our response to adversity, the ability to recover from the ups and downs that life presents and to be able to have increased hope, reduced stress, greater spirituality, plus more positivity in the face of the challenges of life. Resilience can be seen to arise in situations characterized by people being called upon to face financial crises, job loss, aging, losing their home in a fire or natural disaster, war and thousands of other such testing scenarios. Key to understanding resilience is vulnerability. Indeed, resilience can be understood as largely a question of how we manage our experiences of vulnerability. It is a part of the existential challenge of coping with what Sartre (2003) calls the "contingency of being," by which he means the relative lack of guarantees and the constant exposure to a range of risks as a core element of human experience.

Underpinning the notions of both resilience and vulnerability is loss, although its significance is not always appreciated. The existential challenges that we need resilience to help us deal with will generally include no small amount of loss and thus be a source of grief. The loss of a sense of security is just one aspect of how loss and grief feature in situations characterized by vulnerability and a need for resilience. Similarly, losing a sense of normality and the trust and reassurance associated with it is likely to feature. We shall return to both these points below.

Life involves a series of losses. Bereavement is just one such loss, but there will also be other significant losses (such as the ending of a relationship or indeed any major life change). Using loss and grief as a way of studying resilience can be found in such fields as psychology, theology and other important areas of study. To these the approach of sociology can add a different lens to the study of resilience. Sociology can help us to appreciate the value of a wider conception of resilience that goes beyond the personality characteristics of the individual.

The ability to become resilient in the face of grief and bereavement mirrors the ability to become resilient in the face of other losses and associated challenges that occur in our lives. Those who are able to withstand the loss of jobs, financial crises, danger, disasters and other such challenges are more likely to be resilient in the face of death and bereavement, and vice versa. This is one of the main reasons why an individualistic, traits-based approach to resilience is inadequate, as it fails to recognize that there will be significant variation in terms of (i) the social circumstances surrounding the experience of adversity; (ii) the differing loss issues involved; and (iii) the factors (psychological and sociological) that will play a part in shaping the individual's response to the grief challenges faced.

Resilience, then, can be understood as the basis for coping not only with adversity in general but also with loss and grief issues in particular, as these latter issues are never far away from matters involving distress and suffering. In turn, human vulnerability can be understood as serving as the linking thread between them. One of the points we want to emphasize here is that resilience, loss and grief, and vulnerability are all closely interrelated. To develop a fuller understanding of resilience, we therefore need to be alert to the role of loss, grief and vulnerability in shaping how resilience is used, developed and, at times, blocked. We begin by considering the significance of adversity.

Facing Adversity

Adversity is, of course, not a new phenomenon. There are many similarities between today and the past. For example, the 14th century was characterized by upheaval, change, insecurity, and fear concerning the future. While this was the beginning of the Renaissance, it was also the time in which much of the security of the Middle Ages was coming to an end. It was a time of many wars, natural disasters, famine, sickness (including the Black Plague), corruption, decadence, bribery, and fear for the future. Not only was there no answer to the Black Plague, but cities were filling with people with no jobs and few skills, and homelessness led to crime and destruction of property. While the people of today would view themselves as more enlightened than those of the 14th century, many of the anxieties, concerns, and fears that plagued those of the past still exist today. Poverty, oppression, homelessness, wars, hostilities between nations, ethnic cleansing, marginalization, political corruption, greed, materialism, economic domination and extreme nationalism still exist. Today, new problems of global warming, AIDS, drugs, potential nuclear annihilation, cyber threats and ecological destruction loom on the horizon. Polarization threatens the very structure of the political system and society. Yet, resilience, where it can be developed, enables people today, as in the 14th century, to manage to face the uncertain future with hope and effort to make the world a better place by promoting greater levels of safety, health and well-being.

Resilience enables people to develop self-knowledge. This is not simply introspection, nor is it merely a psychological self-understanding, but rather it is a knowledge of self gained by understanding our place in our family, community, society, nation, ethnic group, work organization and so forth—it therefore has a sociological as well as a psychological dimension. By understanding our place in the social world in terms of culture, social location and so on, we can come to appreciate our own dignity and reason for living. Resilience is generally characterized by people having a sense of purpose (for example, in knowing why they need to get up in the morning) and having an awareness of their obligations not only to themselves, but also to the wider realm of families, community and society, which again highlights the need for a sociological perspective to be brought to bear.

Responding to Disasters

Often social situations will create the social circumstances for resilience to emerge and be developed. For example, emergency workers, such as firefighters, police and other first responders, are called upon to make use of resilience in their daily work, constantly engaging in difficult, demanding and threatening situations. Disaster scenarios are particularly significant instances of such situations.

They are also examples of how making sense of resilience needs to involve considering loss and grief issues, as so many loss issues will arise in such circumstances. Firefighters who deal with disasters, both natural and human, are expected to respond effectively to floods, earthquakes, hurricanes, tornados and other "acts of God." Chemical spills, airplane crashes, nuclear contamination, terrorist attacks and so forth are human made, and, in such scenarios, firefighters are likely to face human losses of all types. Being able to adopt a resilient approach in such extreme conditions can serve as a model for many types of challenging situations across a range of contexts.

There is a tendency for people to be drawn to disasters, both at the time and later (as illustrated by the concept of "dark tourism," which refers to how scenes of tragedy can subsequently become a form of tourist attraction—Dermody, 2017). If there is a wreck or a fire, many will gather to observe and perhaps help. Many people will go to the scene of a chemical spill to see what is going on or to a fire or wreck or other such incident which may endanger themselves and others, thereby creating problems in many different ways. There is something intriguing about a disaster situation that brings to the fore human vulnerability and the contingency of which Sartre wrote.

Emergency workers are trained to cope with disasters of all sorts. What they are not necessarily trained to manage is the how to cope with the aftermath of disaster. This would include taking account of, and addressing, the vulnerability and insecurity generated by such situations. This is, of course, where resilience can be a significant feature.

Preventative efforts are limited in most cases, and so the main focus tends to be on what can be done after the fact. The disaster has an impact on both survivors and first responders. Some may be injured, missing, or may even have been killed. The people involved are likely to be in a state of shock, uncertain of what to do or where to go, not sure about the safety and well-being of loved ones, or even their own future. A profound sense of despair can emerge, an existential aloneness. What can be done to help? All of these scenarios involve a loss of security and normality—they introduce what sociologists call "anomie," an uncomfortable and disquieting sense of "normlessness" (Durkheim, 2002) in which our everyday sense of reality ("homeostasis," to use another technical term) breaks down and leaves us feeling very vulnerable.

Of course, emergency workers know that they must attend to immediate needs first: food, shelter, medical treatment, restoring community services. Emotional needs can easily be forgotten in the pressure of the moment. Ministering to the needs might include forming a missing persons group to help alleviate the anxieties of survivors worried about the safety and well-being of relatives and friends. Locating and caring for the dead is another form of ministry. While it may not make sense to dig up the dead and bury them again, it is critical for survivors to know and to have the appropriate rituals and ceremonies. Emergency workers are probably already doing these things. It is also important to know that what survivors may need most is compassion. Just as police officers want to get the facts of the crime and may neglect the emotions of victims, firefighters can easily neglect the emotional needs of victims in their zeal to "do their job." Of course, they know that it may take years to return to financial and emotional stability following a disaster, but what happens immediately can have a major impact on that journey.

Another side of the picture is that those who come to the aid of survivors have their own needs that are typically not met. Caring for the caregiver is often lost as well. A number of years ago, the Hyatt Regency Hotel in Kansas City had a walkway collapse, killing hundreds of people. Bodies were cut in half, decapitated and maimed. A chain saw was used to amputate a critically injured man's leg. The firefighters and police worked professionally and sensitively, saving many and helping many. Later many of these workers had severe emotional problems. A number resigned from their jobs. Even people with a high level of resilience can struggle to maintain their ability to face loss if the demands placed on them are intense and/or prolonged enough—there are limits to resilience.

When a fire or other disaster occurs, people can grieve twice. They have lost loved ones, but they may have lost their home, place of employment or other such important things as well. They may also grieve because they survived and a loved one did not. Why was it not me instead of them? Profound guilt, anguish and sorrow are common among both workers and survivors. Such mental anguish often leads to self-destructive behavior, such as drugs, drink or even suicide. In a sense, this reflects an absence of resilience, a continuing struggle to deal with the emotional challenges involved. Disaster situations are therefore significant sites of concern when it comes to promoting resilience.

Enter Sociology

The topic of resilience has become a fashionable buzzword in the study of human distress, including the field of loss and grief. For example, in recent years, the importance of resilience and resilient responses has been recognized in the study of responses to bereavement (Rubin, Malkinson, & Witztum, 2012). Because most of the research and writing on the topic has a psychological basis, the sociological approach has not come to the forefront. While there is a legitimate and valuable need for study of individuals' psychological reactions to adverse life experiences, such scholarship can be enhanced by the inclusion of a consideration of social factors and their influence upon reactions to adversity for individuals, groups and communities in general, and grief and its management in particular. The individual's psychological reaction is shaped to a large extent by a host of social influences and constraints, including structural factors (ethnicity, nationality, gender, region, religion, social status, income, occupation and education and so on), as well as a range of significant cultural issues. While individual factors are clearly important, we need to understand them in the context of wider cultural and structural factors if we are to develop a fuller picture of resilience and thus be in a better position to promote it wherever possible (Thompson, 2018a).

Human behavior can be studied from many different perspectives. Sociology offers a unique "lens" for viewing and understanding resilience. It allows individuals to have a better awareness and broader understanding of people by highlighting the significance of the wider social context—it emphasizes the importance of acknowledging that we do not exist in a social vacuum; everything we do in life, we do within a social context that will offer both opportunities ("life chances," as sociologists tend to call them) as well as constraints and obstacles at times (Thompson, 2018b). While both opportunities and obstacles will vary significantly from individual to individual in unique ways, there will also be important and influential social patterns—the "fault lines" of society, as it were—that have a powerful bearing on each person's circumstances and their experience of them.

The approach of sociology is not intended to be seen as superior to that of psychology, nursing, bioethics, literature, anthropology, history, philosophy or any other such approach, but it does offer a different lens to view people and their behaviors. All disciplines have added to the knowledge available to the study of human experience and its challenges. Sociology offers the opportunity to examine people's behavior in different cultures, cultural practices, roles and relationships, institutions, norms, values, attitudes and the impact of groups on the individual—all potentially important issues when it comes to making sense of resilience. Drawing on the insights of sociology increases our understanding of the workings of society. It provides a better understanding of the ways in which people work, pay taxes, invest, raise their children, face adversity and eventually die. Sociology assists in discovering how society is organized and how individuals fit into this seeming maze. Sociology fosters a more scholarly understanding of the social processes involved in facing adversity, including how we manage dying, death and grief in terms of both our own death and the deaths of others.

What is also distinctive about a sociological perspective is that it avoids the problem of an "essentialist" approach to resilience—that is, one which denies or minimizes the fluidity and social variability of identity and personhood. Much of the existing literature gives the impression that resilience is "within" the individual, part of their personality or "nature," as if it forms part of the essence of who they are. This is unhelpful for (at least) two reasons:

1. It lays a foundation for a judgmental approach in which individuals can be rated in terms of how resilient (or otherwise) they are, as if resilience were simply a personality trait, rather than a complex, multidimensional phenomenon. It makes it easy for individuals who struggle with resilience to be criticized, without taking account of the full picture of the circumstances.
2. Failing to take account of wider factors can distort the picture and thereby fail to address important elements of the situation. For example, in a culture where women are expected to be submissive, efforts to bounce back from adversity that require a degree of assertiveness may require that women concerned to go against their culture, a step that could in itself have adverse consequences.

What this means is that if we focus narrowly on individual factors and neglect wider sociological aspects of the situation, we run the risk of acting on the basis of a partial, distorted and misleading picture of what we are dealing with. This then has the potential to make a bad situation worse by potentially pathologizing and thus disempowering one or more of the individuals involved; failing to address other significant aspects of the situation (the abuse or misuse of power, for example); and/or failing to recognize potentially useful ways forward (community-based support, for example).

Resilience and Loss

The point was made above that the experience of adversity generally involves a significant element of loss and thus of grief. It is worth exploring these issues further, beginning with a consideration of death and then widening it out to other loss experiences. This is an important step to take as loss and grief issues also have important sociological elements that are often neglected in approaches that focus narrowly on the individual (Thompson, 2012a; Thompson & Cox, 2018).

Death is a part of human existence. Everyone dies. Grandparents die, children die, and everyone that we know will die. Despite major advances in medical science and public health, the mortality rate for humans remains at 100%. The deaths of pets, friends, teachers, other students, neighbors, celebrities, co-workers, plus natural disasters, wars and so many other causes of death are a part of the human experience. Social scientists have only relatively recently begun to conduct research in this area. When one of the present authors (Cox) first taught a course in the Sociology of Dying and Death, there was only a handful of books available. Now there are thousands of books and resources. Historically the work of theologians, poets, writers, philosophers and artists were the main sources used to interpret this universal experience of dying and death. The perspective of sociology has provided a more empirically grounded explanation of human behavior and one that pays fuller attention to the crucial role of cultural and structural factors.

Research on human behavior is difficult enough when studying normal, everyday human situations. It is even more difficult and troubling when studying extreme situations. The researcher's own thoughts and feelings will inevitably be compounded with the research process to a certain extent. While dying, death and grief are no longer taboo topics to study, it is still difficult to conduct meaningful research. As societies around the world have become increasingly secularized, the need seems to have arisen to have a more rational explanation for human behavior, as opposed to a religious one. Phenomena that previously were viewed as sacred (and therefore not open to study) are being examined, although at times with little regard for, or sensitivity to, cultural traditions or ethical concerns. As concern has also arisen in relation to ensuring cultural survival and maintaining traditions, many are now resisting the efforts to open up death management practices to study.

The entire death awareness movement has been popularized and, to some extent, has moved beyond the scientific community. Having said that, it is still important for social scientists to continue to study the death management practices of humans and to learn as much as possible to enhance our own such practices and those of future generations.

However, it is not only death-related losses that are significant in relation to resilience. We have used bereavement as an example because situations that call for (and play a part in nurturing) resilience will often involve death, especially in disaster situations, as discussed earlier. But, in addition to the losses arising from death, we need to acknowledge the role of other significant sources of grief. For example, experiences of being abused (child abuse, domestic abuse, abuse of vulnerable adults) also involve strong and significant elements of loss. Indeed, the list of losses that are not directly associated with death would be a very long one. We therefore need to ensure that, when we are talking about loss and grief, we are not restricting ourselves to death-related losses (Harris, 2020; Thompson, 2012a).

Grief is our reaction to a significant loss. Freud often used the term "cathexis" to refer to the emotional investment we make in a person or thing. The pain—and other reactions—felt when that "investment" is lost are what we experience when we are grieving.

What is learned from theory development and research can be of value to those who face their own dying and death and the dying and death of others. The following are some key questions to be answered: What should be achieved by sociological analysis and the study of cultures and societies? Why is what will happen to people who are grieving important? The answers may seem rather obvious, but raising these and other such questions is a way to point out the manner in which the subject of loss and grief reveals the social roots of human existence.

Dying, death and other major losses are disruptive. They are disruptive precisely because the very meaning of our life is based upon our interactions with others. As humans we are interdependent. Removing a member of the group reveals and emphasizes this interdependence, and requires adjustments to be made socially. This is the basis of grief, which can be understood in part as an expression of our fear of aloneness, our fear of disconnection. Aloneness is expressed when we talk about the loss of a loved one, the loss of support, sustenance, and care. Feelings of grief are directly related to our sense of dependence upon the person we have lost and/or the emotional investment in whomever or whatever we have lost. Resilience is in large part a reflection of how we respond to loss and to feelings of grief, particularly in relation to the vulnerability involved.

Part of the sting of grief is the revelation of our own personal vulnerability. There is a strong element of self-centeredness in our feelings of grief. Recognizing this phenomenon can aid the grieving process. This sting is accentuated by cultural prescriptions that can make us reluctant to admit that this is the case. Morgan (2002) suggests that, because humans are vulnerable, social support is needed to achieve anything in life, especially for the grieving who are rendered vulnerable by their very grief. This reflects the spiritual concept of "connectedness," the importance for our own well-being of feeling connected to others and to entities bigger than ourselves, whatever form that may take—faith community, political movement, profession, sporting affiliation and so on (Thompson, 2017a). The spiritual benefit of feeling part of a wider group or community can therefore be a significant source of resilience. This social emphasis is something that individualistic approaches can miss.

Similarly, in terms of spirituality, Rubin et al. (2012) argue, not only that human beings are resilient, but also that we can use that resilience to grow and change if we are able to maintain a relationship with the deceased, to self-repair, to respond to challenges, to actively respond to the traumas of life into a new narrative of their life story. This fits well with the idea of "transformational grief" (Schneider, 2012), which refers to how, regardless of how painful, frightening or exhausting grief may be, it offers the possibility of learning, growth, development and transformation.

This, in turn, fits with the theoretical basis of crisis intervention (Thompson, 2012b), in which the task for the professional helper is not to return the person in crisis to their previous level of functioning but to go beyond that level, to achieve the growth and transformation offered by the circumstances of the crisis (defined as a turning point in a person's life)—to come out stronger and better equipped to respond to future crises and challenges. This is clearly within the domain of what we would today call resilience—the ability to "bounce back" from adversity and, where possible, to achieve personal growth in the process. Achieving such growth and transformation will clearly depend to a large extent on the individual circumstances of the person(s) concerned, but it would be a mistake, and a significant one at that, to fail to appreciate how sociological factors are playing a part in such circumstances. It is to such factors that we now turn.

Social Factors Affecting Resilience

Space does not permit a full and detailed treatment of the role of social factors in shaping our response to crises and other life challenges (those scenarios where a degree of resilience is called for). However, it is worth highlighting at least some of the key issues involved, albeit briefly:

- *Social expectations* The media and other social institutions create powerful sets of expectations, often with significant sanctions (such as ridicule or marginalization) for anyone who goes against such expectations. In certain circumstances, such expectations can discourage resilience (for example, when other people's response to a person's adversity is one of pity).
- *Power dynamics* Foucault (1926–1984) was one of many sociologists to highlight the ever-present nature of power and its significant impact on individuals, groups, communities and their interactions. The operation of power dynamics can empower some while disempowering others— a process that can affect (positively or negatively) the development of resilience.
- *Discrimination and oppression* These issues reflect a double-edged sword. They can either discourage or stimulate resilience. For example, someone being discriminated against may be disheartened and undermined by the experience or motivated and determined by it.
- *Access to social capital* The extent and quality of support from key individuals, groups and/or organizations can make an immense difference in terms of how people respond to adversity.

Taking into account these and other sociological considerations can help us to appreciate that narrow, individualistic approaches to resilience and related matters tell only part of the story and leave out much of potential significance.

Returning to our theme of loss and grief and how we manage them and the associated vulnerability, we need to be aware of the complex interactions of both individual and social factors (along with biological and spiritual— Thompson, 2012a) and how these dynamics can contribute to the development of resilience.

Grief is not a problem to be fixed; it is a complex, multidimensional phenomenon. How we manage grief is decidedly social in its origins, in the sense that we have various rituals and social expectations that will play a part in shaping our responses. For example, historically, some societies would wear black for a year, avoid social commitments for an extended period of time, wait for a specified time to remarry, engage in public grief, or spend time fasting among other acts of socially supported grief practices. All societies have socially approved practices for those who grieve. Today, with modern communications, extended travel, many families no longer living in small, close-knit communities, individuals have more freedom to choose how to grieve but also less direction in how to grieve. For some people, having direction and help in how to grieve may be experienced as positive and supportive, and thus aid resilience, while those who prefer to feel that they are free to grieve as they wish, rather than as society expects them to grieve, may find the lack of constraints more helpful. Resilience will be different for different people, partly due to their differing social circumstances.

Today, bereaved individuals may receive fewer social invitations if they were part of a couple engaging with other couples; possibly loss of social status with the loss of the position of the spouse; possible economic loss if the deceased was the one who was the major earner in the family; the perception of no longer being a parent with the loss of a child; experiencing a social vacuum with the loss of a close friend; or loss of the anchor in one's life with the death of a parent, whether as a child or adult survivor. For example, when John F. Kennedy was assassinated, his wife was immediately no longer First Lady, needed to move from the White House, had to plan a massive funeral, endured 24 hours a day media intrusion and coverage, and had to manage not only her own grief, but that of her children.

Today's societies lack many of the standardized, predictable practices of the past for disposing of the body, distributing the possessions, carrying out rituals, determining who sits where, who presides and so forth. The decline of such rituals can be seen as the lessening of social support and solidarity at key times of personal challenge. Today, there are often quarrels over where, when, and how the body is disposed; who gets possessions, pictures, heirlooms and property; who pays for the funeral if there is no insurance; and who will make decisions. Social mobility means that families are often widely dispersed. Typically, after the older generation dies, there is less and less contact among the extended family. Many are often not told of the death of a relative, and this can lead to disputes among family members. Quarrels among members may lead to some not being told, even if others know their whereabouts. Traditional societies still exist, although many have dispersed and experience many of the problems of the larger societies in which they co-exist. Generally, traditional societies have community rituals, predictable funeral rites, set inheritance patterns, extended family to care for children and widows, and reorientation patterns for survivors.

The commonplace notion that grief is primarily, if not exclusively, an individual, psychological matter largely unconnected from wider society is therefore not a belief that can be maintained (Thompson & Cox, 2018). Grief is clearly a matter for sociological, as well as psychological study. Our point is that there is a direct parallel here with resilience. It is a *psychosocial* phenomenon, in the sense that it has both psychological and sociological roots and psychological and sociological consequences.

One of the implications of this is that expectations around both grief and resilience will change over time. As people change, so, too, do cultures and the societies of which they form part. The development of the funeral industry, hospice organizations, nursing homes and so forth has provided extensive social support for the bereaved. Support groups, internet websites, books, articles and therapies of all sorts are available to help with loss of pets, homes and people in our lives. This social support can also be a key factor in the development of resilience by giving people greater confidence and security in knowing that they are not alone in facing their challenges.

An important concept in this regard is "social capital" (Lin, 2002). This refers to the social resources each of us has available to us. Some people will have extensive social capital in the form of friendships, family support, community involvement, membership of various organizations and associations, and so on, while others will be quite impoverished by comparison. We can therefore recognize social capital as a key sociological contributory factor when it comes to resilience.

Community support and the associated social capital allow people to have more confidence in surviving major disruptions in their lives. Close family, extended families, friends, social groups and others will often give support to the person facing job searches, job loss, accidents, illnesses and other personal crises. Knowing that we have community support allows us to face future challenges and crises with more confidence. Knowing that we have support in the face of chaos and destruction in our lives allows us to react in a more positive fashion. Feeling prepared lessens panic and reduces the need to take flight or avoid facing the situation—for example, in the event of a bereavement, knowing that we have obligations that must be performed, such as notifying friends and family, making funeral arrangements, paying bills, cooking for survivors, or whatever provides a sense of purpose. A sense of purpose can be seen as a key element of resilience. Given that resilience is the ability to jump back from chaos and destruction, to reconstruct our lives, to help others and to continue to live our lives even though there is a huge hole in that life, it can help people to be better equipped to avoid becoming frozen into an emotional state. They can become better able to remember the happy times, while being able to mourn their loss at the same time. Having pets, children, a job, duties and so forth that require us to be required to help others or perform tasks contribute to resilience. While there is no formula to how to become resilient, those with a sense of purpose while facing loss are the most likely to exhibit it (Park & Slattery, 2014).

This illustrates that, in addition to the psychological and sociological aspects of resilience, there is a spiritual dimension. Indeed, resilience can be seen to relate to a number of spiritual issues: meaning, purpose and direction, connectedness, hope, wisdom and so on. Crisis situations and the loss and grief issues associated with them can disrupt our sense of who we are and how we fit into the world—thereby presenting us with major spiritual challenges (see Chapter 23 in this volume).

Factors Hindering Resilience

Traditional societies offer a framework for individuals to know how to behave when they are facing adversity. For example, in the case of a bereavement, it is typically the case that many people are involved in preparing the body, producing the container for the body, preparing clothing, preparing food, conducting rituals, notifying people of the death and offering support to the grievers. In traditional China, the funeral procession would be quite loud, with drums, horns, cymbals and wailing mourners, including some who are hired for the purpose (Cox, 2010). The Chinese might spend the entire fortune of the deceased, as the proper burial was viewed as the most important event of his or her life (Haberstein & Lamers, 1973). A few days after the funeral, mourners would return to where the body was placed to offer food and burn money. In traditional China, mourners knew what was expected of them, what roles they were to play, and what the future would bring to them (Chan & Chow, 2006). Like the traditional Chinese, the Potawatomi Indians had traditional mourning practices, but the coming of Europeans and Christianity made traditional practices difficult to follow. In 1838, the Potawatomi Indians, who had been Christianized, were forced to move from northern Indian Territory to Kansas, arriving in the winter, with little hope of finding proper shelter, food and safety after being forced to leave their homes and sacred burial grounds that they revered (Winger, 1939). Like the forced migrations of other tribes, many died along the way. The Potawatomi revered their dead and honored their graves, but they were forced to bury their dead along the way to Kansas. Not being able to perform traditional rituals and to maintain their graves left them unable to grieve their losses properly. Not knowing what is expected of us when mourning (what we referred to earlier as "anomie") makes a resilient response much more difficult. Not being able to visit the grave of a loved one to honor them and their loss left the Potawatomi struggling to know how to grieve their loss properly. Changes in China over time have made it more difficult for the modern Chinese to know how to grieve their losses properly. In view of this, having traditional community standards for behavior can be seen to facilitate resilience, while the absence of such norms can be understood as an obstacle to resilience.

Sociologically, the work of symbolic interactionists helps to explain this phenomenon. Erving Goffman in *Presentation of Self in Everyday Life* (1959) suggests that each individual puts forth an impression of who he or she is to others. The role of grieving person carries with it expectations of how the role is to be played. The concept of impression management implies insecurity, because it is not just a process of manipulations using scripts, roles, props and costumes to impress audiences, but also the consequence of being a griever, which may result in the person concerned not feeling able to play the role as expected. Those in more traditional societies tend to have greater understanding of the roles that they are expected to portray. If the person is expected to play the role of grieving widow but has been abused by her deceased spouse, she might not be able to perform that role as expected by others. Those who are grieving tend to play the roles that are expected of them by others. Many factors will hinder that performance, even in traditional societies: not only abuse, but financial problems, a cheating spouse, abusive in-laws, family secrets and many more issues.

The insecurity associated with anomie can be a major source of a sense of vulnerability. While there is always the danger that social expectations can be stifling and over-restrictive, and thus play a negative role, the sense of pattern, stability and reassurance that they offer at times of not only loss, but adversity more broadly, clearly plays a positive role in offering a degree of solace.

In view of this, a problem is likely to occur in non-traditional societies where roles are not so clearly developed and expectations are much more diffuse. Much of the United Kingdom and the United States, along with many other industrialized nations, has experienced a considerable loss of tradition. The indigenous populations have attempted to maintain their ways in the face of massive immigration, but that hold is tenuous. Between 1870 and 1915 around 25 million people entered the United States, ranging from the early groups of English, Welsh, Irish, Germans and Scandinavians to the later immigration of Italians, Greeks, Serbs and Poles. Still later many Jews fleeing persecution, along with many Chinese, Japanese, Filipino and other Asian groups, entered in large numbers. As the immigrants entered, large cities also grew even larger. The United States was no longer a rural nation. Immigrants brought with them many religions, languages, ways of life, and ways of thinking, and with them the benefits of social and cultural diversity. Those who came were forced by social pressure, economic survival and institutional pressure to make changes in the way that they lived, often including the language that they spoke, their dress, their way of making a living, their religion, the way their children were educated and so much more. In the United States, in the 19th century and early 20th century, people were required to work so many hours just to survive, that traditional patterns of grieving from China or Poland or wherever were simply not practical. If someone missed work, their family did not eat. Grief took a back seat to survival.

Simply moving to a different society can lead to loss of tradition. Many of the early immigrants to the United States would never see the family members who stayed in the old country ever again. Those who lacked the ability to read and write would probably never hear from them again. While the first generation of immigrants probably struggled with the loss of tradition, later generations assimilated and adopted the ways of those who lived in the United States. With the development of the funeral industry, those from many religions, cultures and ways of life used the same general practices for disposing of the deceased. The practice of grieving people being given three days off work meant that the patterns of grief also developed over time. The norm of "getting over" your loss emerged. Showing resilience came to be seen as being strong in the face of loss and basically not letting it stop you from working and fulfilling other responsibilities. In recent years, the norms have been changing to allow people permission to grieve and to recognize that we do not get over grief but, rather, that we learn to live with that grief.

A further way in which resilience can be hindered is by the seemingly uncontrollable chaos and loss of control that is often overwhelming to the person facing grief or other such forms of adversity. The situation takes our breath away. Feeling broken, abandoned, alone and without purpose, the individual is unable to rise to the challenge, becomes discouraged, loses control of the controllable and cannot understand why the world is still going on around them. Having a sense of control is an important part of mental well-being, and so being in a situation that overwhelms us can be highly detrimental and thereby present a real challenge to resilience.

Cultural Factors in Resilience

From a sociological point of view, it is also important to consider the significance of cultural factors. Consequently, in this section, we focus on the resilience demonstrated by cultures and communities threatened and oppressed by more powerful cultural groups.

At one level, cultures that manage to survive efforts to extinguish or marginalize them could be described as resilient. As with people, some cultures are more resilient than others. Certainly, the Lakota, Apache, Navajo, Hopi and Australian Aborigines have managed to survive (albeit at considerable cost), while the Harappan society of India, the Anasazi of North America, the Clovis people of North America, and many others did not survive.

Scholars, philosophers, historians and others have tried to explain why, when cultures meet, mingle and collide, some are able to survive, and others fail. Historically, the United States has been viewed as a melting pot, allowing broad patterns of social interaction, integration and sharing. Over time, the European dominance has led to the destruction of many of the indigenous cultures. Ethnocentrism, the tendency to see the world more or less exclusively through the lens of our own culture, with little appreciation of the value of other cultures, has been a part of the United States heritage since the Colonial Era. The newcomers from abroad always considered the Indians as outsiders and certainly not as equals, a pattern of dominance exhibited in other colonial situations across the globe.

Cultural resilience is typically characterized by belief in one's way of life, values, rituals, and customs, and by members of that culture viewing themselves as worthy. While the Europeans who arrived in the Americas, Australia, India and other places around the world were of different social classes, religions, languages, ethnic groups and so forth, they were united in their dislike and mistrust of the indigenous people, and their greed for the resources and labor that the indigenous people could provide, and their abhorrence toward the beliefs, values, customs and way of life of the indigenous people. The Europeans forced their language, way of life, religion, values and so forth upon the indigenous peoples around the world. As with individuals, losing one's belief structure, language, way of life, customs and values can create a need for resilience while also undermining it. The tribes, clans and societies that have been able to maintain their cultural compass have been resilient. The Europeans' greed and cunning were sharpened by centuries of feudal domination, rigid class structures, famine, plagues, and extreme wealth and poverty and thus inequality. Consequently, the Europeans did not bring a consistent cultural message to replace the strong cultural patterns that existed among the various indigenous groups around the world. As with resilient people, cultures that have strong culturally shared values, customs, ways of life, sharing, beliefs and social support are the cultures that have survived over time.

As indigenous people around the world had their land, their resources, way of life, language, religion, government and so forth taken from them, they also suffered from disease, war, and disrespect from their conquerors, and swindlers who tried to take everything from them. To justify their acts, Europeans developed the ideology of the vanishing Indian which forever consigned the American Indian to a marginal and historic position. While viewed as cultures from the past, American Indians continue to exist, as do indigenous cultures in other parts of the world. Like resilient individuals, resilient cultures are those that stand up to life's devastations, woes, and troubles and bounce back from the adversity involved. The imaginary Indian has come to represent ecology, community, spirituality and a harmonious relationship with nature that the modern world seems to have lost.

The conquerors seem not to notice that the Indian cultures still exist and have much to offer. Like resilient individuals, resilient cultures find their strength in helping others. Cultural sharing—language, way of life, values and so forth—continue to be taught by elders to the young. As resilient individuals find purpose for their lives by doing for others, so, too, do resilient cultural groups. The postmodernist would analyze modern US culture in terms of what has occurred post-colonially, while American Indians would argue that colonialism is still happening to them. The modern meltdown of European empires, the vast world migration, global economy, and constant media coverage around the world have made resilience more difficult for cultures that embrace these realities. For groups like the Hopi and other Pueblo peoples, the Lakota, Ojibwe, and others who have maintained their languages, way of life, customs, values, and homelands, cultural resilience has somehow survived the cultural onslaught that destroyed so many other groups. Like resilient cultures, resilient individuals need to maintain who they are in the face of the onslaught of daily life with its woes. Paul C. Rosenblatt (2016) suggests that cultural competence is the product of being an open and respectful learner (cited in Thompson, 2017b).

The role of culture in fundamental problem solving has implications for individuals' ability to be resilient in the face of adversity. Culture provides the individual with a mix of analytical, creative and practical abilities through the basic institutions of education, family religion, government, work. The view of what constitutes resilience is fostered by successful performances and adaptations or by failures and inability to adapt within the confines of one's own culture. Cultures provide models of how to respond to adversity, including bereavement, grieving processes and rituals, in addition to what constitutes recovery from such adversity. Institutionalized environments, such as hospitals, hospices, religious institutions, nursing homes, funeral homes and governmental entities that help with payments, make rules and thus require paperwork. These processes and entities can be instrumental in adapting successfully to loss, living out the rest of our lives, maintaining our sense of personal control and life satisfaction, maintaining our emotional and cognitive health, maintaining social competence, and constructing meanings of death, loss and adversity.

What should be clear, then, is that cultural factors are also part of what resilience is all about, once again taking us away from the common notion that it is simply a reflection of an individual's character or capabilities. The challenge of promoting resilience therefore needs to incorporate a fuller understanding of culture and its significance at various levels.

The Social Basis of Meaning Making as a Contribution to Resilience

When we encounter various forms of adversity, we experience the uncontrollable. Our world may be shattered. The losses involved can take our breath away. While there will be aspects that we have no control over ("facticity," to use the technical terms), we will always have choices about how we respond to any situation (what Thompson, 2016a, refers to as "transcendence," the ability to go beyond the elements that we cannot control). Resilience is in part a matter of how we deal with such situations and the transcendence we bring to them. If we focus narrowly upon the uncontrollable, it leads to helplessness, disorientations and brokenness. By responding to grief, we can gain a degree of control.

Social groups offer a level of support that allows people facing adversity to develop resilience through processes of meaning making (Neimeyer, 2001). While traditional societies offer greater social support and greater awareness of a person's place in society, modern societies also offer social support, though it may not be as obvious as in more traditional societies. In hunting and gathering societies, a person's place, daily work, and value to the society were evident. A person could look at another clan and observe how the loss of a hunter, leader or child affected the clan. In modern societies, the long lists of daily obituaries with people who are strangers do not demonstrate the value of their lives to the society, local community or families. The individual is no less important, but measuring his or her importance becomes more difficult. Thus, over the last century sociology and other disciplines have begun to develop and analyze the importance of meaning making as a concept. Thompson (2018b) suggests that social interaction rests upon meanings, and the meanings themselves arise from social sources. Meaning making can be applied conceptually to war, vocations, marriages, government service, sports, teaching and many more areas of society. Its application to grief, adversity and resilience is just one possibility.

Meaning making is a broad concept that draws upon multiple traditions in sociology, anthropology and other social sciences. Meaning making is essentially how people try to make sense of the world around them by developing and maintaining a coherent self-narrative. The basic element is how, as humans, we engage in attempting to explain or understand the world around us. By imposing meaning upon the world and its various parts, the individual can feel more comfortable with the world or become more concerned about what the world is or has become. This is an important source of ontological security and thus a means of managing the vulnerability that characterizes human existence.

The meanings applied to the world and its facets lead to moral understandings of what is right and wrong, why there are wars, why some people are rich and others poor, why my religion is superior or "true" compared to others, what is beauty and what is repulsive, our social identity or sense of who we are, and many more understandings. The meanings that are attached to our social world are not necessarily accurate, true or based upon reality, but they are powerful influences on us.

Meaning making can lead to a better understanding of our place in the world and an acceptance of the world as it is, or it can lead to great trauma and fear for the world as it is or as it seems to be becoming. The meanings attached to perceptions can lead to acceptance of self and our place in the world or fear of living in a disturbing, unsafe world (which takes us back to our theme of vulnerability). It can also motivate us to try and bring about positive change in the world and give us a sense of commitment to one or more important causes. Meaning making is therefore both a spiritual matter (addressing connectedness as well as meaning, purpose and direction) and a sociopolitical one, shaping in large part how or whether we engage with the wider world of power structures and social relations.

One further aspect of meaning making that sociologists would focus upon is how to explain the processes whereby the same facts lead to different interpretations. When someone smiles at us, is that because they are about to attack us or because they are trying to show that they like us? When a person is grieving, they can focus upon what has been lost, or they can focus upon the relationship that they had and its impact on their life now and in the future. Meaning making is the ability to make sense of our sense experiences, to use our mental processing to understand what we are experiencing through sight, sounds, touch and so forth. For sociologists, this would include an understanding of the collectivities that we are a part of that lead to interpretations, repertoires and rituals that have been established over time to allow us to process information in established categories of understanding. Those who have been subjected to great suffering, such as being in concentration camps or refugee camps, are likely to make interpretations rooted in suffering, inequality, stratification, exploitation, inevitability and so forth, while those who have lived in relative luxury are more likely to view the world from the perspective of entitlements, personal merit, good birth and so forth. Most societies have ready-made categories for individuals and small groups who make meanings outside of the dominant cultural set: seers, prophets, visionaries, those with mental health problems, religious leaders, elders and so forth.

Historically, the analysis of meaning making has been largely avoided in the sociological literature. Karl Marx, for example, talked of workers' alienation as a product of their relation to the means of production, and not as a result of the workers' processes of meaning making within a context of economic exploitation. That is, he explored the objective elements without considering the subjective element of meaning making, thereby omitting a key aspect of the situation (Sartre, 2004).

In addition, while meaning making would appear superficially to be a rational process, a more sophisticated analysis gives us a different picture. Those following the political situation in the world today, whether conservatives or liberal, would consider those of the "other" side to be irrational in their meaning making. How many people's lives have been demonized or glorified after death in spite of how ordinary their lives may have actually been? Goffman's concept of "framing" the cultural content and context of meaning-making messages can help explain the diversity of conclusions within the same social environments (Cox, 2017). Concepts often used in meaning making would include "collective identity" and "narrative." By drawing on research on social movements from over a century ago, we can see that the concept of collective identities can be applied to the study of meaning making in individuals who demonstrate a preference for having their meanings be consistent with the expectations and reactions of others in their social circles. Likewise, for the narrative to have social meaning it must be consistent with the narratives of others in our social world to a certain extent. Meaning making after a loss or other significant form of adversity is far more devastating than assessing the political situation, but both are extremely impactful on people's lives in their own way. This again illustrates the sociological basis of meaning making.

Indeed, we need to recognize that the foundations of meaning making about death, grief and adversity more broadly are socially constructed through forms of social discourse. Discourses are based upon creating and sharing the social world with others and having them respond, strengthen or disparage our meanings based upon those social interactions. Individuals gain experience by losing jobs, leaving school, going to school for the first time, moving away from home for a job or education, health and so forth, which helps prepare them for loss of life. As we develop the ability to make meaning out of losses in daily life, we can then develop an approach for managing any major loss or experience of adversity.

A basic part of the grieving process is making sense of the loss. Davis (2001) suggests that people appear to make sense of their loss by considering the event in terms of their existing worldviews to re-evaluate their purpose in life, their goals, and to craft new life goals and purpose. The "reframing" requires the individual to find the positive amid the pain of loss. How we respond to loss may be based upon demographic factors, mental health, physical health, type of loss, religiosity, social support (including differential levels of social capital), financial situation and so forth, which suggests that coping strategies for dealing with the loss involved in adversity (and the adversity involved in loss) are unique to the individual, offering no magical formula for a resilient response.

The ability to find meaning in adversity depends in large part on the individual actively attempting to change the situation by developing a problem-solving approach and reframing the problem. This can be described as "cognitive restructuring." The individual must engage, rather than disengage, as an explicit strategy. Expressing emotions and seeking social support is one strategy. Another would be releasing or expressing emotions and seeking emotional support. Others might disengage by avoiding facing the problem or engaging in wishful thinking by hoping things will get better. Others engage in self-criticism and social withdrawal, blame themselves for the situation, refuse to interact with others and avoid thinking about their situation—a form of escapism.

There is, therefore, a clear set of linkages between meaning making and resilience, but what we need to note in particular is that these linkages are rooted in the social context. Once again, it is not simply personal characteristics that we are talking about. And, once again, we are seeing how loss, adversity, vulnerability and resilience are intertwined.

Promoting Resilience

One framework that can be useful is the Three Rs proposed by Thompson (2016b):

- *Resourcefulness* This refers to the ability to be creative and draw in our personal resources as fully as possible. This is important for *preventing* situations characterized by adversity from arising by being as adept and skillful as we can in coping with the challenges we face.
- *Robustness* If our resourcefulness is not enough to prevent situations of adversity and loss, then how robust or hardy we are will play an important part in *withstanding* adversity.
- *Resilience* If our robustness is not enough to prevent adversity from knocking us down, our resilience should enable us to *bounce back* from that adversity and pick ourselves up.

Strengthening each of these areas can be important in promoting resilience, but, in keeping with our sociological emphasis, we should bear in mind that that this is not simply a matter of individual capabilities—much will depend on the wider social support. While there is no magical formula for promoting resilience, focusing upon cultural strengths is a useful approach to use to begin the process.

All cultures offer a basis for supporting and nurturing resilience that can lead to increased hope, reduced stress, greater self-awareness, compassion, meaning, openness and a positive approach. Whether through a wake, a celebration of life ceremony, a giveaway or a eulogy, all cultures offer ways to remember the dead that aid the living to achieve resilience. As a loved one was resilient in life, the bereaved can then be resilient in their grief.

However, one of the major challenges we face when it comes to promoting resilience is that death-related losses tend to have clear sets of rituals and expectations associated with them. The grief associated with other losses and experiences of adversity, however, will often be disenfranchised—that is, not recognized or socially sanctioned (Doka, 2001; Thompson & Doka, 2018). Consequently, one important step in the right direction needs to be a fuller recognition of loss and grief in situations of adversity where no death has occurred (Harris, 2020; Thompson, 2012a).

There will, of course, be very many ways of promoting resilience, and that is what Part Two of the book is all about, encompassing a broad range of relevant topics and considering how these can all play their part in not only taking our understanding forward but also highlighting practice implications.

Conclusion

As human beings we will face various aspects of vulnerability, and there will be times when our vulnerability is very much to the fore. Being able to cope with such challenges and the vulnerability involved is what resilience is all about, especially our ability to bounce back from such demanding experiences. As we have noted, the bulk of the literature on the subject focuses on individual factors and assigns a minor role to issues of loss and grief. What we have tried to do in this chapter is to highlight the need to add a sociological dimension and to think much more holistically about resilience and the situations that lead to a demand for it. We have also put forward a case for recognizing more fully the important interrelationships between loss and grief on the one hand and circumstances demanding resilience on the other, as we believe that this is also an important dimension of a more adequate, holistic understanding of resilience.

References

Chan, C. L. W. and Chow, A. Y. M. (2006). *Death, dying and bereavement: A Hong Kong Chinese experience*. Hong Kong: Hong Kong University Press.

Cox, G. R. (2010). *Death and the American Indian*. Omaha, NE: Grief Illustrated Press.

Cox, G. R. (2017). Erving Goffman. In N. Thompson and G. R. Cox (Eds.), *Handbook of the sociology of death, grief, and bereavement: A guide to theory and practice*. New York: Routledge, pp. 73–84.

Davis, C. G. (2001). The tormented and the transformed: Understanding responses to loss and trauma. In R. A. Neimeyer (Ed.), *Meaning reconstruction and the experience of loss*. Washington, DC: American Psychological Association, pp. 137–56.

Dermody, E. (2017). Dark tourism. In N. Thompson and G. R. Cox (Eds.), *Handbook of the sociology of death, grief, and bereavement: A guide to theory and practice*. New York: Routledge, pp. 194–209.

Doka, K. (Ed.) (2001). *Disenfranchised grief: New directions, challenges, and strategies for practice*. Champaign, IL: Research Press.

Durkheim, E. (2002). *Suicide: A study in sociology*. New York: Routledge.

Goffman, E. (1959). *Presentation of self in everyday life*. New York: Doubleday.

Habenstein, R. W. and Lamers, W. M. (1963). *Funeral customs the world over*. Milwaukee, WI: Bulfin.

Harris, D. L. (Ed.) (2020). *Non-death loss and grief: Context and clinical implications*. New York: Routledge.

Harris, D. L. and Bordere, T. C. (Eds.) (2016). *Handbook of social justice in loss and grief*. New York: Routledge.

Lin, N. (2002). *Social capital: A theory of social structure and action*. Cambridge, UK: Cambridge University Press.

Morgan, J. D. (Ed.) (2002). *Social support: A reflection of humanity*. Amityville, NY: Baywood.

Neimeyer, R. A. (Ed.) (2001). *Meaning reconstruction and the experience of loss*. Washington, DC: American Psychological Association.

Papadatou, D. (2009). *In the face of death: Professionals who care for the dying and the bereaved*. New York: Springer.

Park, C. L. and Slattery, J. M. (2014). Resilience interventions with a focus on meaning and values. In M. Kent, M. C. Davis and J. W. Reich (Eds.), *The resilience handbook: Approaches to stress and trauma*. New York: Routledge, pp. 270–82.

Rosenblatt, P. C. (2016). Cultural competence and humility. In D. L. Harris and T. C. Bordere (Eds.), *Handbook of social justice in loss and grief*. New York: Routledge, pp. 67–74.

Rubin, S. S., Malkinson, R. and Witztum, E. (2012). *Working with the bereaved: Multiple lenses on loss and mourning*. New York: Routledge.

Sartre, J-P. (2003). *Being and nothingness: An essay on phenomenological ontology*. New York: Routledge.

Sartre, J-P. (2004). *Critique of dialectical reason, Vol. 1*. London: Verso.

Schneider, J. (2012). *Finding my way: From trauma to transformation: The journey through loss and grief*. Traverse City, MI: Seasons Press.

Thompson, N. (2012a). *Grief and its challenges*. Basingstoke, UK: Palgrave Macmillan.

Thompson, N. (2012b). *Crisis intervention*. Lyme Regis, UK: Russell House Publishing.

Thompson, N. (2016a). *The authentic leader*. London: Palgrave.

Thompson, N. (2016b). *The professional social worker*. (2nd Edn.) London: Palgrave.

Thompson, N. (2017a). The role of religion and spirituality in grieving. In N. Thompson and G. R. Cox (Eds.), *Handbook of the sociology of death, grief, and bereavement: A guide to theory and practice*. New York: Routledge, pp. 337–50.

Thompson, N. (2017b). Culturally competent practice. In N. Thompson and G. R. Cox (Eds.), *Handbook of the sociology of death, grief, and bereavement: A guide to theory and practice*. New York: Routledge, pp. 237–50.

Thompson, N. (2018a). *Promoting equality: Working with diversity and difference*. (4th Edn.) London: Palgrave.

Thompson, N. (2018b). *Applied sociology*. New York: Routledge.

Thompson, N. and Cox, G. R. (Eds.). (2018). *Handbook of the sociology of death, grief, and bereavement: A guide to theory and practice*. New York: Routledge.

Thompson, N. and Doka, K. J. (2018). Disenfranchised grief. In N. Thompson and G. R. Cox (Eds.), *Handbook of the sociology of death, grief, and bereavement: A guide to theory and practice*. New York: Routledge, pp. 177–90.

Winger, O. (1939). *The Potawatomi Indians*. Elgin, IL: The Elgin Press.

Part II
Developing Resilience

2 Resilience in American Indian Communities

Gerry R. Cox

The very existence of American Indian communities is a testament to their resilience—an existence in the Americas for 30,000 to 60,000 years, while facing ever-increasing contacts with diverse civilizations, cultures, and religions; attempts to destroy their cultures, religions, languages and ways of life; and disease, war and poverty (Brown, 1982). Westward expansion came at the expense of Mexicans, Spaniards, and American Indians who were already there, with those American Indians who resisted, as well as those who were peaceful, being forced onto reservations. The Cherokee, who were farmers in the Carolinas and Georgia, and who had an alphabet, created a constitution, published a newspaper, and were peaceful, were forced into camps and taken on a 1200-mile trip to Oklahoma, which led to 4000 Cherokee deaths (Lockard, 2015). Many view American Indians as part of the past, but they have endured, and their cultures are still evolving.

American Indian resilience is based upon a way of life, rather than an organized religion. Its origins predate organized religion, with elements that have survived not only from oral traditions but also from experiential faith. While there are many diverse groups, clans, tribes, languages, religions and concepts of spirituality, the ideas that all is sacred and all is related would be generally accepted by all groups, sharing the concept that there is no place where the Great Spirit or Creator, or whatever name might be used, is not present. The resilience is a way of life, of living, of breathing, of existing. While there is no Bible or sacred writings where truths are taught, the truths (the harmony in nature, the interconnectedness of all things and the individual's place in the universe) are learned from elders, family and mentors.

Power

The concept of power is basic to resilience. It occurs in relationships with other beings, including rocks, animals, plants and so forth. While hunters may have power over the animal that is being hunted and ultimately killed for food, they are dependent upon the animal to give them the opportunity to dominate. In other words, it is power *with*, rather than *over*, other beings.

American Indians respect all peoples and all ways, and thus it is common for American Indians to integrate other religious practices into their spiritual practice without diminishing traditional ways of thinking. Each group would have individual customs, traditions, ceremonies, rituals and prayers which may or may not be incorporated into Christian practices. Depending upon the tribe, they may have participated in sweat or purification, giveaway, potlatch, Moon Lodge, Coming of Age, Blessing, healing ceremonies and many more. American Indian spirituality is not proselytizing, evangelical or open to the public. Organized religion focuses upon having a leader teach, guide and lead people to spiritual growth. For American Indians, there is no intermediary between the person and the spirits unless the person requests the aid of another on their spiritual journey. People are expected to follow the guidance of their heart. The guidance comes in the form of prayer, dreams, solitude, words and actions of elders, and from the power of others in the physical, natural and human world.

Power comes in many forms: from humans, non-humans, spirits, monsters, inanimate objects and so forth. Medicine bags, medicine bundles and other forms of sacred bundle are said to have power. The Blackfeet in Montana are known for their use of medicine bundles and the rituals associated with them. A person may learn in a dream what to include in the bundle, what songs to sing, what to paint on their body and what clothes to wear. It would not be unusual to bury the medicine bundle with the person who used it when they die. The bundle would be used to heal, to help in hunting or war, and in times of suffering. The Lakota have a sacred pipe bundle. The Crow often have shields in their bundles. Both the Crow and the Cheyenne also had arrow bundles. The Pawnee include corn. Villages, clans, tribes, and families develop their own bundles to give them power where additional help is needed. Grief is certainly one such situation. Opler uses oral history to describe how a Chiricahua Apache's father obtained power from the bear, the wolf and others while on a journey (Opler, 1969). For the Apache or Inde, power comes in one of two ways: either it finds you in the form of dreams, spirits, animals or whatever, or the person seeks power on their own by learning appropriate prayers, rituals and so forth, rather than having contact with animals or receiving offers of any kind for power (Basso, 1970a). Possessing power is a central concept in understanding American Indian resilience.

Death

For most American Indian groups, death is faced with little concern for deeds or failures. In living a life of integrity and giving dignity to others, they see no reason to fear death. Death is the natural end of life, merely a changing of worlds (Steiger, 1984). Each person has a place and purpose in the world. When our purpose has ended, so is our life! Death fulfills our destiny. It is not a defeat, but rather it was meant to be. We all face death; none of us can escape. It is not the result of an offense against God or other deity but rather everyone's fate. Death causes grief among our survivors. Each of us will, we hope, have others who care that we are no longer among the living, but each of us is alive as long as the living remember us. Death is meant to occur. Life cannot occur without death. We live, and then we live again. Time and space do not change our existence. Death is a painful separation for the living, but when we die, we can wait for our descendants to join us.

Spiritual Healing

As White people would go to a therapist for help in managing their grief, an American Indian would go to an elder. If the elder does not have the power to aid them, they might seek special ceremonies for assistance. They also might go to a shaman. Healing spiritual needs is just as important as healing physical needs. Medicine power allows the possessor of the spirit to make personal contact with the invisible world of the spirits (Steiger, 1984).

For the Navajo or Dine, the family mourns for four days, beginning with the night of the death, and they have many actions that ensure that the spirit of the deceased will go on its way to the other world and will not return to harm those who disturbed the spirit (Reichard, 1928). Underhill (1956) and Coolidge and Roberts (1930) describe the Navajo or Dine fear of the dead. Yet, many describe having a relationship with the spirits of the dead as positive. Similarly, the Apache or Inde are taught to obliterate all memory of the dead, and yet they are also described as having extended periods of mourning (Opler, 1941). Like the Dine, the Inde have many rituals of purification and healing after a death occurs. One explanation for why the body is avoided is that both the Dine and the Inde believe that the soul or spirit enters the body at birth and leaves the body at death, but with the caveat that the evil remains with the body and should be avoided (Perry, 1991). While early anthropologists saw the avoidance of the body as evidence of fear of the dead, it may have been simply fear of the dead body. Those who have contact with the dead body would be expected to go through purification rituals.

Rituals for Managing Grief

American Indians know that chanting and rituals have a miraculous effect on those who participate in them. A "sing" is good for a sad heart. Those who are grieving believe in the power of the ancients to come to help them manage their inner struggles by establishing a peaceful, serene, balanced, and harmonious world around them. Many different practices are used to help the grieving. The Navajo, Apache, Hopi, Arapaho, Cheyenne and some California tribes use sand-paintings. There are two types: those from the rhythm of the day and those from the rhythm of the night. The world is different at night, with different creatures, as too are the rituals different. Night chants would often begin at sunset and the painting be destroyed before sunrise. Similarly, a day sand-painting would begin at sunrise and be destroyed before sunset.

There are hundreds of designs, as many as 1200. The sand-painting draws upon the power of the Holy People, plants, animals, celestial bodies, the earth and other symbolic beings to help "heal" the person. Sand-paintings vary in size from a foot or so to 20 feet in diameter, with some being very complex and taking from 2 to 15 people and many hours over four days for a complete ceremony (Collier, 1949). Others are simpler and require fewer hours and people. Healing sand-paintings are different than those for public viewing. Healing sand-paintings are sacred, while public sand-paintings are for exhibition and possibly for profit. It takes years to learn the craft and the associated rituals. The healing power is in the belief of the person who is being healed.

The Sacred Pipe and the rituals with it are also used for healing the grieving. Like sand-paintings, the power of the pipe, tobacco and the rituals calls upon spirits to heal (Stolzman, 1989). The pipe itself is a sacred ceremonial object. Tobacco is a sacred plant. Even the way the pipe is smoked is sacred. The first puff is directed toward Mother Earth to thank her for gifts of food and so forth. The Four Directions are honored, starting with the east, ending with the west. Finally, Father Sky is honored.

Many American Indians find it difficult to use "White" grief management ways. Most White people are very verbal. Apache, for example, would view someone who is suffering from intense grief as being disturbed and unstable and prone to volatile outbursts (Basso, 1970b). While the wake and burial are often quite verbal and volatile, in the weeks after the close relatives are expected to resume normal activities and to "be with people who are sad," or suffering from intense grief, and to greet them with silence because talking is unnecessary, since everyone knows what happened (Collier, 1949). The Apache would also think that talking, offering sympathy or discussing what happened only reinforce the sadness and augment the emotional strain of dealing with death and personal loss, and lead to negative behavior (Basso, 1970a, 1970b). Like the Apache, the Navajo also believe in silence. Navajos speak very little when mourning a death, but they will mourn and cry together in pairs, men embracing and crying together, women holding each other's hands (Basso, 1970a, 1970b). The patterns of grief are culturally different than those of the dominant society.

Joy and laughter act like prayer as ways to relieve tension, balance the body and mind, and to learn to laugh at yourself and not take yourself too seriously. The American Indians are noted for their sense of humor, even in the face of tragedy. Carl Gorman, Navajo, Code Talker, artist and writer, was described by his son, R. C. Gorman, as maintaining an enormous sense of humor even in sad times (Gorman, 1996).

The use of ritual to aid grief also extends to the custom of gift-giving, described as "potlatch" for any ceremony involving feasting and formal gift-giving. The host is expected to offer gifts to the guests. Gifts are given at virtually every ceremony. It may be as simple as giving tobacco or as elaborate as thousands of dollars of gifts. At the same time, it is considered rude to visit an elder or spiritual leader without bringing a gift. Gifts are a sign of caring and respect. We all depend upon one another. The earth provides for people, and people care for the earth. The reciprocal nature of the world is extended to relationships. Giveaway ceremonies are not only spiritual acts but also social in nature. By giving and receiving gifts, social ties and obligations are developed, maintained and taught. Those giving gifts are people who have received spiritual wealth and powers. Gifts at potlatch are spiritual as well as material. Those receiving the gifts in turn give to others. While giveaways happen at many ceremonies and events, those at funerals, burials and memorials offer power to the bereaved. Traditionally, the family would give away nearly everything to honor the spirit of the deceased. American Indians are expected to be generous, sharing and caring members of their communities. Spiritual honors, such as naming, symbols, songs and dances, would also be a part of the giveaway. While there are many different practices, many tribes would hold the memorial service and giveaway a year after the death. For the grieving, the attendance of those in their community helps them know that their loved one was truly loved. The naming of children or others after their loved one, the thanking for the gifts, the sharing of food and song, and the many smiles and humor also help the grieving. The spiritual nature of the gathering and the power that is brought to it are of great assistance to the grieving. The American Indian way of grieving is a model that could work for other groups.

Conclusion

American Indian resilience in facing bereavement is based upon a worldview that all are related, that reciprocity is the basis of life, and that ritual and power are the keys to managing life's ills. The use of humor, the silence of words, and rituals are the major means of managing grief.

References

Basso, K. H. (1970a). *The Cibecue Apache.* New York: Holt, Rinehart, and Winston.

Basso, K. H. (1970b). To give up on words: Silence in Western Apache Culture. *Southwestern Journal of Anthropology,* 26(3), pp. 213–30.

Brown, J. E. (1982). *The spiritual legacy of the American Indian.* New York: Crossroads.

Collier, J. (1949). *Patterns and ceremonials of the Indians of the Southwest.* New York: Dutton.

Coolidge, D. and Roberts, M. (1930). *The Navajo Indians.* Boston, MA: Houghton Mifflin.

Gorman, C. (1996). *Power of a Navajo: Carl Gorman: The man and his life.* Santa Fe, NM: Clear Light Publishers.

Lockard, C. A. (2015). *Societies, networks, and transitions: A global history.* Stamford, CT: Cengage.

Opler, M. E. (1941). *An Apache life-way: The economic, social, and religious institutions of the Chiricahua Indians.* Chicago, IL: University of Chicago Press.

Opler, M. E. (1969). *Apache odyssey: A journey between two worlds.* New York: Holt, Rinehart, and Winston.

Perry, R. J. (1991). *Western Apache heritage: People of the mountain corridor.* Austin, TX: University of Texas Press.

Reichard, G. A. (1928). Social life of the Navajo Indians. In *Columbia University Contributions to Anthropology*, Vol. VII. New York: Columbia University Press.

Steiger, B. (1984). *Indian medicine power.* West Chester, PA: Whitfield Press.

Stolzman, W. (1989). *The pipe and Christ.* Chamberlain, SD: Tipi Press.

Underhill, R. M. (1956). *The Navajos.* Norman: University of Oklahoma Press.

3 "Yma o Hyd"

Language and Resilience

Neil Thompson

Introduction

Language is a central part of what holds society together. It forms much of the "glue" that allows social processes to occur and social interactions to take place. Despite, or perhaps because of, this key role, we tend to take language for granted; it tends to receive far less attention in theory and practice than its centrality merits. One of the key messages of this chapter, therefore, is that we need to make sure that language issues receive the attention they deserve. As Ballard (2016) explains,

> language is very much a social phenomenon. A study of language totally without reference to its social context inevitably leads to the omission of some of the more complex and interesting aspects of language and to the loss of opportunities for further theoretical progress. One of the main factors that has led to the growth of sociolinguistic research has been the recognition of the importance of the fact that language is a very variable phenomenon, and that this variability may have such as much to do with society as with language. (Trudgill, 1974, p. 32).
>
> (p. 90)

Neglecting the social nature of language risks omitting not only interesting and significant aspects of language as a phenomenon, but also interesting and significant aspects of social life, including resilience. Language therefore needs to be the concern of sociologists and other social scientists (and professionals whose knowledge base relies on the social sciences), and not just of linguists.

The other key message is that powerful dynamics operate in relation to language, and these can have significant implications in terms of resilience and the ability of minority language communities to thrive despite efforts to "homogenize" them into the dominant language.

A key theme, therefore, is power, and so it is with the relationship between language and power that I begin.

Language and Power

Language and power are two concepts that are closely linked. This is because there are (at least) two main interconnections between them. First, language is one of the primary ways in which power operates, and, second, complex power dynamics operate between languages in those circumstances where more than one language co-exist. It is worth exploring each of these in a little more detail.

Language as a Vehicle for Power

Language does not simply describe reality; it plays a central role in constructing that reality (Gergen, 2015) The philosopher Richard Rorty captures this well when he argues that "languages are not attempts to copy what is out there, but rather tools for dealing with what is out there" (1999, p. xxvi). In a very real sense, a language (and the cultural assumptions that accompany it) is a filter through which we perceive the world and, as such, is imbued with power. In particular, it is a major element of identity.

Bourdieu (1991) reinforces the significance of language in relation to power:

> One must not forget that the relations of communication *par excellence*—linguistic exchanges—are also relations of symbolic power in which the power relations between speakers or their respective groups are actualized.
>
> (p. 37)

The word "symbolic" in this passage is particularly significant, as it is through symbolism that language channels power relations. For example, consider how a police officer's badge not only represents the power of the law but actually embodies that power ("instantiates," to use the technical term)—that is, the badge enables its holder to exercise that power.

A language is, of course, a set of symbols, among other things. Those symbols operate in a systematic way to generate meanings, and meanings are, of course, also elements of power. For example, the ability of one person to impose their meaning, their definition of the situation, on another person is clearly an act of power.

Power can be exercised without a single word being spoken or written—through the use of force, for example. However, if we look more closely at the complex operations of power, we will quickly see that language is predominantly the vehicle of power. This can happen in the following ways:

- *Instructions* Whether oral or in writing, instructions are clearly an example of exercising power.
- *Documentation* Contracts, legal documents and so on are all examples of power being instantiated through language—that is, the power "flows through" language.

- *Shaping perceptions* The language we use in communicating with others will have a bearing on how they see the situation. Consider the difference between "Unusually heavy traffic meant that Sam was a few minutes late for the meeting" vs. "Sam failed to attend the meeting on time." The technical term for this is "implicature"—that is, where the basic meaning (denotation) has an often more powerful extra meaning (connotation).

- *Attaching value* The use of language is not neutral or value free. How we use language can assign positive or negative values to whatever we are commenting on. For example, consider the difference between "Sam is a mature, seasoned professional" and "Sam is a bit of a dinosaur." Stigma and status are both assigned through language.

What should be abundantly clear, then, is that, if we want to understand power, we need to understand language, and, if we want to understand language, we need to understand power. The two are interconnected in a number of ways.

Power Relations Between Languages

What is also significant in terms of the relationship between power and language is the power dynamics *between* languages. It is estimated that there are in the region of 6,000 languages spoken in the world. Although there are certain dominant, widely spoken languages, like English, Chinese and Spanish, bilingual or multilingual situations are the norm in a high proportion of cases. Where languages exist side by side, there is generally a hierarchy or set of power relations between them. For example, it will commonly be the case that one language will be associated with high-prestige situations, while another is seen as more informal and "homely," but less prestigious.

Diglossia is the technical term for when languages operate alongside one another. It is characterized by two significant phenomena:

- *Code switching* This refers to how speakers of two or more languages will tend to switch between the two with ease—sometimes even in the same sentence. This is a normal and unproblematic means of communication in such settings.

- *Linguistic domains* In situations involving diglossia, the two or more languages will often follow patterns in terms of the circumstances in which they are used. For example, children who are members of minority ethnic groups may use the dominant language of the country concerned while in school but the language of their family and ethnic group at home.

These two factors lead to a complex picture of language use, but a common theme is that of power. It is generally not the case that languages have equal status—there will normally be status (and thus power) differences. For example, in Wales, Welsh has full legal status alongside English. This means that, for example, Welsh speakers have the right for any court cases they are involved in to be conducted through the medium of Welsh. However, I have recently come across two examples, reported in the local press, of banks refusing to respond to a customer's letter that was written in Welsh. Despite the technical equal legal status, I cannot imagine a bank refusing to answer a letter written in English.

Avineri and colleagues (2019) make the point that

> over 40 years of scholarship in linguistic anthropology and sociolinguistics consistently demonstrates that language is neither a neutral communicative medium nor a passive way of referring to things in the world, but rather a crucial form of social action in itself.

(pp. 1–2)

Which language is spoken, when and by whom are therefore political issues; they are forms of "social action" and therefore reflect power relations. What this leads us to consider, in terms of power between languages, is the historic efforts of speakers of a dominant language to try and eradicate one or more minority languages (the attempts of slave owners to suppress the use of African languages is a prime example). Historic treatment of the Welsh language is a further example, and it is to this that we now turn.

The Welsh Not

Everett (2012) makes the point that "our thoughts rely on meaning and meaning in the human sense derives mainly from community and culture" (p. 43). In turn, a key factor in shaping community and culture will be language. Wales and the Welsh language are no exception to this. Welsh is a language spoken by approximately half a million people within Wales and a significant additional number of people outside Wales (for which statistics are not kept).

Holmes and Wilson (2017) argue that industrialization was a significant factor in the transition of the Welsh language from its one-time status as the main language of Wales to a secondary position. This was due to the rapid influx of English speakers into the newly industrialized areas that were previously rural and monoglot Welsh for the most part. In those circumstances it was not surprising that a diglossia situation arose.

Despite this, the Welsh language continues to hold its own. Today, there are Welsh books, magazines, newspapers, radio stations and a television channel, as well as plays, music and other artistic activities. There are festivals, events and educational programs conducted through the medium of Welsh, and so it is very much alive and well. It is as symbol of Welsh culture, identity and pride recognized internationally.

However, the historic picture is not so positive. At one time a system was devised to try and wipe out the Welsh language. This was based on the "Welsh Not." This is how I have explained it in a previous work:

> In the 18th, 19th and early 20th centuries, there were deliberate attempts to suppress and even eradicate the Welsh language. Children heard speaking Welsh were forced to wear a sign around their neck that said, "Welsh not." It could only be passed on to anyone else heard speaking Welsh. The person wearing the sign at the end of the school day would be punished. This was a very insidious way to not only deny Welsh speakers the right to speak their own language, but also to pit Welsh speakers against one another. This oppressive abuse of power by the dominant group to undermine and stigmatize the identity of the less powerful minority was effective in its day, but it ultimately failed, as the affirmation of Welsh language, culture and identity is very strong indeed today (Williams, 2011).
>
> (Thompson, 2020, Chapter 4)

This is where we encounter the significance of resilience, not as a personal characteristic, but as a collective endeavor by groups of people, whole communities, over centuries. That resilience involved swimming against the tide of powerful forces that threatened to fully replace Welsh with the global language of English.

Rights and Resilience

What has helped foster that resilience has been the notion of linguistic rights: "linguistic rights or the right of a people, community, or individual to have and use a particular language variety" (Avineri et al., 2019, p. 6). Given that language is a key part of individual and cultural identity, such rights have an important part to play—hence the significance of the Universal Declaration of Language Rights (UDLR). Milambiling (2019) explains:

> Linguistic rights (also known as language rights or linguistic human rights) are concerned with the rights of individuals and groups to preserve, use freely, and pass on their own languages and cultures to future generations. The stated purpose of the UDLR is to "encourage the creation of a political framework for linguistic diversity based upon respect, harmonious co-existence and mutual benefit" (UDLR, 1996, Preamble, para 4).
>
> (p. 208)

The situation pertaining to the Welsh language and its survival against the odds fits well with this picture of language rights. However, despite the important role of the Welsh Government in supporting the Welsh language, the main thrust has come from Welsh speakers themselves consistently and persistently making sure that the Welsh language is not allowed to fade away.

Conclusion

"Yma o Hyd" is the title of a song by Dafydd Iwan, a highly respected Welsh singer and songwriter. It means "still here" and is a political statement affirming the resilience of the Welsh language. "Er gwaetha pawb a phopeth" (despite everyone and everything), the lyric goes, we are still here. The phrase "yma o hyd" therefore strongly characterizes the impressive resilience shown by a language (and culture) the powers that be tried over an extended period of time to eradicate.

In an earlier work, I put it across in the following terms:

> As Crystal (2010) points out, in addition to the resurgence of Welsh in the UK, similar developments can be seen to be taking place in Hawaii, Ireland, New Zealand and Quebec. The continued survival of Welsh and other minority languages despite attempts to eradicate them is therefore testimony to the resilience, commitment and resourcefulness of the peoples concerned, but also to the power and significance of linguistic and ethnic identity.
>
> (Thompson, 2018, p. 63)

What this story of resilience in the face of intense and prolonged adversity nicely illustrates is the need to understand resilience holistically. If we are to develop a fuller understanding of this important concept, then we need to be able to move beyond the individual conceptions that have so far proliferated in the literature.

References

Avineri, N., Graham, L. R., Johnson, E. J. Conley Riner, R. and Rosa, J. (2019). Introduction. In N. Avineri, L. R. Graham, E. J. Johnson, R. Conley Riner and J. Rosa (Eds.), *Language and social justice in practice*. New York: Routledge.

Ballard, K. (2016). *The stories of linguistics*. London: Palgrave.

Bourdieu, P. (1991). *Language and symbolic power*. Cambridge, UK: Polity Press.

Crystal, D. (2010). *The Cambridge encyclopaedia of the English language*. (2nd Edn.) Cambridge, UK: Cambridge University Press.

Everett, D. (2012). *Language: The cultural tool*. London: Profile Books.

Gergen, K. J. (2015). *An invitation to social construction*. (3rd Edn.) London: Sage.

Holmes, J. and Wilson, N. (2017). *An introduction to sociolinguistics*. (5th Edn.) New York: Routledge.

Milambiling, J. (2019). The universal declaration of human rights. In N. Avineri, L. R. Graham, E. J. Johnson, R. Conley Riner and J. Rosa (Eds.), *Language and social justice in practice*. New York: Routledge.

Rorty, R. (1999). *Philosophy and social hope*. London: Penguin.

Thompson, N. (2018). *Effective communication: A guide for the people professions*. (3rd Edn.) London: Palgrave.

Thompson, N. (2020). Discrimination, oppression and loss. In D. Harris (Ed.), *Non-death related losses*. New York: Routledge.

Trudgill, P. (1974). *Sociolinguistics*. Harmondsworth, UK: Penguin.

Universal Declaration of Linguistic Rights (UDLR). (1996). https://culturalrights.net/en/documentos.php?c=18&p=184.

Williams, C. (2011). *Social policy for social welfare practice in a devolved Wales*. (2nd Edn.) Birmingham, UK: Venture Press.

4 Community Resilience

Reflections on a Community Response to Tragedy

Ros Scott

Introduction

It has been suggested that modern communities have become deskilled in caring for and supporting individuals facing loss, death and grief (Weigleitner, Heimerl, & Kellehear, 2016). This can result in such individuals becoming lonely and isolated. A response to this has been the emergence of Compassionate Communities in a number of countries throughout the world. Compassionate Communities use public health and community development approaches to reskill individuals, groups and communities, enabling them to reach out and support people facing life-limiting conditions, end of life or living through grief, and to develop capacity and resilience (Weigleitner et al., 2016).

What happens, however, when communities are faced by a sudden tragedy? What influences their response? How do they work through the enormity of the incident? Does their response help to develop community resilience? May it be that communities are not inherently deskilled, but that individual and community capacity may emerge through the need to deal with a major disruption to community life?

A sociological perspective is helpful in exploring some of these questions. Using this lens enables us to consider the reactions of individuals within the context of the community, in order to gain a broader insight into how wider societal need may influence their response to significant loss and grief. It may help us to understand more about how and why in the face of tragedy communities come together and what, if anything, helps to build resilience. This chapter aims to consider some of these factors through a reflection on the traumatic events of a school shooting in 1996 in Dunblane, Scotland. It is drawn solely from the few written accounts of events and the observations of a community member. It does not attempt to consider the perspectives of those whose children or loved ones died or were injured, for that is their story and theirs alone to tell.

Dunblane is a small town in Scotland with a current population of almost 9,000 people. On March 13, 1996 a lone gunman entered Dunblane Primary School, killing and injuring pupils and teachers in the school gymnasium, before taking his own life. Sixteen children, five to six years of age, died along with one teacher. A further 12 pupils and two teachers were injured. In common with a number of other school shootings there were circumstances that would suggest that this was a planned and premeditated act by a person with a grudge. That day Dunblane changed; the community left in a state of huge shock, disbelief, loss and grief as a result of such an unimaginable act of violence in their town (North, Ross, & Gilfillan, 2014).

In Part One, Cox and Thompson describe grief as being typified by a "powerful sense of vulnerability and insecurity," and resilience as a way of handling such vulnerability, enabling people to move towards a more secure, confident position with an improved ability to cope. Cox and Thompson also discuss the important influences of the social context on the individual response to loss and grief. This chapter is about a community, however. In reality, there are communities within communities—be they business, voluntary, religious or spiritual, sporting, educational, formal or informal. In Dunblane, each of these communities was affected differently by the events of March 13, 1996. Their responses to the events of that day were necessarily influenced by the needs and responses of individuals in any particular network and their connections within the larger local community.

This chapter explores these responses under four headings:

- Initial reactions;
- Coming together: trying to make sense of it all;
- Protection and practicalities; and
- Moving forward.

Initial Reactions

No two experiences of grief and loss are the same, and individuals in Dunblane were affected by the school tragedy in different ways. There is no doubt that there was a strong sense of vulnerability and insecurity within the community. No one had ever considered that this primary school and the town were other than safe places to be. Initially for parents, relatives and friends of children in the primary school there was significant fear for the safety of their child. For many of those whose children were safe there was no sense of relief. It was impossible to feel relieved when other parents faced such unimaginable loss.

The enormity of this event engendered feelings of helplessness and of being lost. These emotions were accompanied by complexity and doubt. It was difficult to know how to respond. What, if any, were the norms of this new situation? All these are good examples of "anomie," as described in Part One. The loss of normality made it difficult to know how to respond to normal everyday events. If a child's birthday was a few days after the tragedy and a celebration planned, what was the right thing to do? Should it have been cancelled out of respect for the bereaved? Should it have gone ahead to celebrate another year in the life of a child who survived? Suddenly, this was not an individual decision but was influenced by the wider sociological context and the feelings of others.

The influence of the sociological context of grief was also very evident in the questions asked by the wider community. Did they have the right to the intensity of emotions that many experienced? Did they have a right to grieve? Unsurprisingly, events had for some re-opened previous losses, some unresolved. Examples of the influence of social expectations and power dynamics, as outlined in Part One, could also be seen. Significant guilt was expressed by some who experienced distress from past losses, at a time when families had lost children.

Parental responses were also influenced by the reactions of their children. As survivors, even very young children tried to protect their parents from what had happened, often limiting the amount of information they were willing to share. It became clear that some of the older primary school pupils became a "closed group." "You weren't there—you can't understand" was a response from one ten-year-old. In this family, negotiating when, how and what was permissible to ask became the norm, respecting the new boundaries and responses, while dealing with anger and bravado.

Support was quickly mobilized, and a network of professional support was available to those whose children or loved ones were killed or injured, school staff and pupils. Voluntary sector groups provided support for the wider community. Even with this level of support, it was difficult to see how the community as a whole would be able to cope with such vulnerability and move forward towards a more secure, confident and positive future.

Coming Together: Trying to Make Sense of it All

Everyone had a personal story to tell about the events of that day, and there seemed to be a need amongst some to tell and re-tell the story. There were many conversations within immediate family, neighbors and friends about where people were on the day, how they found out what had happened and what they did. However, in the telling of the stories something else was also happening: the gathering of intelligence about what had happened in an attempt to gather the facts and make sense of it all. There was a hunger for information, a need to understand exactly what had happened. People also shared what they had read in the paper, seen on TV or learned from relatives of friends who had been there. Among the facts there were undoubtedly myths as well, but in the continual sharing, re-telling and cross-checking, the facts became clearer. On reflection, it is not clear how long this persisted, but eventually there was less need to rehearse the story. Perhaps this indicated an initial step in the process of gaining some sense of control, while managing vulnerability and reducing helplessness.

The community came together in other ways in an attempt to show respect and support for the bereaved and injured. Mass was held in the local Catholic church, huge numbers of people took part in a vigil at the Cathedral, and many funerals took place (North et al., 2014).

As a mark of remembrance and support for the families whose children and loved ones had been killed or injured, lit candles were displayed in houses. A memorial service was also held later in the year in October. These all allowed individuals to pay their respects, to come together for support and to reach out in some small way to those most deeply affected.

Protection and Practicalities

The community had to learn to cope with, and respond to, being in the media spotlight. There was a large and very intrusive international media presence. As highlighted in Part One, there were also "tragedy tourists," no doubt their intentions well motivated in coming to pay their respects. The community, however, considered such visitors as an unwelcome intrusion on the town's grief. In response, the community turned inwards as a means of protection. Few, if any, of the community spoke to the media, and few engaged with questions from visitors. This has, to some extent, been a lasting response.

It is interesting to note that common themes emerging from written accounts of that time were community activism, engagement and volunteering. It was clear that individuals and groups felt a strong need to act. Where this was most marked was in dealing with the practicalities arising from the tragedy.

Almost immediately flowers began to arrive; the world sent messages of love and support, cards, letters and gifts for children. Money poured in. There was a need to respond, to organize and to manage this outpouring of love and generosity. All of this required a response, enabling community members to become involved in a range of meaningful activities, countering helplessness.

There were many examples, including the establishment of a drop-in center. Staffed by volunteers, this provided a central point where people could find a listening ear and support.

Volunteers were also needed to respond to the huge numbers of letters, cards and gifts received from all over the world. Many people became involved, undertaking to read and respond to each letter and card individually. Groups of volunteers organized the distribution of toys and gifts to the children of the town. Individuals also volunteered as community representatives on committees and trusts developed to manage the significant financial donations and make decisions on how these would be used. These committees faced many challenges and conflicts as decisions were made and emotions ran high. In addition, a group of community activists started a petition against handguns, championed by the bereaved parents. This eventually changed the law in the UK.

These are examples of only a small number of the many responses that enabled the community to become involved in positive action, helping to mitigate "anomie." This also helped people to manage vulnerability and insecurity and was an important step in the community's journey to resilience.

Moving Forward

For the initial two weeks after the tragedy time seemed to stand still. The first steps in moving forward began when the primary school re-opened. Children returned to school and parents returned to work. Gradually in time, the normal routines of everyday life took over.

Much of what happened was guided by the wishes of the bereaved families. They did not want large anniversary events; they did not wish the community to be defined by the shooting. Anniversaries were marked very quietly, away from the public gaze as much as possible. Lit candles in the schools and in house windows on the anniversary continued for several years. It was perhaps the influence of attitude from those most directly affected that helped the wider community to find more positive responses and ultimately develop resilience.

As the years moved on, the makeup of the community evolved as people moved away and new people arrived. This altered the balance of the number of people who were part of the community on March 13, 1996. School children moved from primary to secondary school and ultimately on to work, college, university and relationships. However, the closed nature of the wider community, and particularly the school community, remained. Until a few years ago, some would say that they lived near Stirling, rather than mention Dunblane, in order to avoid the inevitable questions.

There were more milestones in moving forward. A new youth and community center, The Dunblane Centre, was built with the donations that had been received at the time of the tragedy. Opened in 2007, it was intended to be a place for future generations of young people in Dunblane and was a clear part of the journey of hope and looking to the future. Today it plays a large part in the life of the Dunblane community for children, young people and adults alike.

A new focus for Dunblane emerged in the guise of two very talented brothers: the international tennis players Andy and Jamie Murray. Once Dunblane was known only for the school tragedy in 1996, but today Dunblane is known for tennis. The community is immensely proud of the brothers' achievements and follows their lives and careers with great interest. There is no doubt that this also helped the community as a whole to move forward to a more positive future.

Implications for Practice

In thinking about the implications for practice from such a tragic event, there are parallels to the Compassionate Communities discussed in the introduction to this chapter. Undoubtedly, there will always be a need for skilled professionals to provide support to those most directly affected by such trag-edies. It is important, however, that the wider community is encouraged and empowered to play a role. The strength in community comes from individuals reaching out to support one another and in finding opportunities to make positive contributions in the aftermath. In the UK, for many years approaches to health and bereavement have often been about "doing to," rather than "doing with." However, people spend a much higher proportion of their time within their family and social networks than in the care of health, social care or bereavement professionals. What I hope this reflective essay demonstrates is that individuals and communities have enormous capacity to respond to traumatic events. To be enabled to respond is a vital step in addressing fear, helplessness and insecurity, which in turn helps the healing process and the emergence of resilience.

No one will ever forget the events of 1996 or those who died or were injured. But, the story of the Dunblane community is one of resilience and hope and of positivity about the future.

References

North, M., Ross, P. and Gilfillan, N. (2014). *The Dunblane Centre. The gift that keeps growing*. Dunblane, UK: Dunblane Youth and Sports Centre Trust.

Weigleitner, K., Heimerl, K. and Kellehear, A. (2016). *Compassionate communities. Case studies from Britain and Europe*. Oxford and London: Routledge.

5   Tragedy and Injustice

Michael Brennan

To talk in terms of tragedy almost always implies a sense of injustice. A serious accident, crime or natural catastrophe involving death or life-changing injuries invariably invokes feelings of unfairness among victims and survivors, not least because of the apparent randomness in which tragedy is visited upon them. Tragedy may also carry a sense of injustice because death or injury was in some way preventable, the result of negligence or incompetence on the part of authorities charged with ensuring public safety. A life cut unexpectedly short through terminal illness is also tragic, precisely when it affects those who—because they are in the prime of life—do not fit the category of those we expect to die. In such circumstances, and in the absence of an obvious candidate to blame, a terminal diagnosis may also routinely elicit feelings of anger at its apparent unfairness, embodied in the question "why me?" (Kübler-Ross, 1969).

How we endure in the face of adversity and loss of various kinds is routinely understood as owing much to one's own inner resourcefulness, psychological makeup, or "personal resiliency" (Harris Lord, 2000). Yet these prevailing assumptions neglect the primacy of other people, of social networks, society and what, in short, we might understand as the body social in helping to sustain resilience in circumstances of tragedy and injustice. Sociology has much to contribute here not just in revealing the social dimensions of tragedy and injustice but also in highlighting the social basis of resilience in response.

Personal Troubles as Public Issues

There are private as well as public dimensions of tragedy and injustice. The tragedy of suicide, of terminal illness affecting a young person or of an accident involving life-changing injuries are felt most keenly by the individuals and immediate family and friends of those involved. They are private, experienced at what sociologists would regard as the "micro" level of society, to the extent that the circumstances surrounding them may be known only to, and experienced predominantly by, the close personal family and friends of those affected. Such "personal troubles," as American sociologist C. Wright Mills (1959) has argued, are also "public issues" to the extent that they are experiences that may not only be shared by others but also have underlying structural causes and implications for society at large.

The devastating impact of suicide, for example, is a tragedy—the impact of which is felt most acutely by family and friends of the person who has chosen to end their own life. Such choices, however, are not made in a vacuum, and there may well be social factors that influence a person's predicament and subsequent decision making. A lack of social support born of a highly individualized society in which personal problems are internalized, inadequate mental health provision, or financial worries—resulting from unemployment, or the unregulated nature of lending and gambling leading to personal debt—are all *social* factors that may be implicated in the individual act of suicide. To understand suicide only as an individual act and in isolation of wider social or structural factors is do so "atomistically." Sociology and its adoption of a "holistic perspective," as Thompson et al. (2016, p. 176) suggest, are "very useful in this respect, because it enables us to see how small-scale micro interactions are linked to wider-scale macro processes, structures and institutions."

Half a century before Mills's observations linking "personal troubles" with "public issues," French sociologist Emile Durkheim had argued that suicide was not an individual act pure and simple but was, rather, socially patterned, affecting some groups more than others, in ways that revealed contributory social factors. Too little social integration *in* society or too little social regulation of the individual *by* society were, Durkheim argued, factors that may help explain suicide. Individuals without the stable, integrative and regulatory influences of marriage, the responsibilities of parenthood, or close-knit religious community were thus exposed to greater risk of suicide than those for whom these factors appeared to provide a buffer against the stresses of everyday life. The fallout from the financial crisis of 2008 may well be understood in such terms using Durkheim's concept of "anomie," which describes a sense of normlessness resulting from situations involving major social change that leave people feeling lost, and in which the social expectations governing behavior are unclear (Lukes, 2008; Thompson et al., 2016).

Many other personal tragedies occurring at the "micro" level of society can also be understood as public issues with structural implications relating to wider social processes and institutions. The tragedy of terminal illness, for example, while principally affecting the individual and family involved, highlights wider social issues about the provision, funding and delivery of palliative care in society, or indeed, about policy provision (if it exists at all) for assisted dying. At a wider social level, it may also highlight inequities in access to palliative care (or assisted dying) among certain groups, revealing inequalities in who has access to such services and who does not (Dixon, King, Matosevic, Clark, & Knapp, 2015; Cross Party Group on Hospices and Palliative Care, 2018).

When, where and how serious accidents resulting in tragedy occur may also reveal much about "macro" processes, structures and institutions, including the provision of health and safety in society, funding for public infrastructure, and the organization and support for emergency response teams. The very incidence of accidents among certain social groups may also illustrate the links between micro and macro levels of society, between personal tragedy and wider public issues. The landmark publication of The Black Report (1980) in the UK on health inequalities, for example, found that those lowest down the social scale were at greater risk of accidental death in ways that could be linked to poorer material conditions of housing, work and environment.

Aggravating Tragedy and Injustice

The grief people experience following bereavement may be hindered—or "complicated," to use the technical term—if the circumstances surrounding a person's death were violent or traumatic. Many personal tragedies fit this category, including deaths from terrorism, road traffic accidents or large-scale disasters, whether natural or human influenced. The failure to hold those responsible for such deaths to account or to adequately explain and make sense of the circumstances in which a person died may also intensify feelings of injustice in ways that aggravate the grieving process.

Many personal tragedies, whether personal or part of a much larger public disaster, do not just happen but are often the result of system failures or negligence on the part of individuals, institutions or authorities charged with ensuring public safety. Disasters such as the Hillsborough stadium disaster of 1989, Hurricane Katrina in 2005, and the Grenfell Tower fire in 2017 can all be understood as preventable tragedies that resulted from a failure of planning, preparedness and/or whose effects were exacerbated by a delayed or inadequate response on the part of public authorities. Worse still, in the case of Hillsborough, feelings of injustice were intensified by attempts on the part of the police to deny responsibility, conceal evidence and shift blame onto innocent fans killed in the disaster.

Such tragedies may also reflect, and be the result of, wider social inequalities in society, disproportionately affecting some of the poorest and most vulnerable sections. The failure to anticipate and evacuate the predominantly African American population of New Orleans following Hurricane Katrina, for example, served to give the impression that Black lives do not matter. When Michael Brown, director of FEMA (Federal Emergency Management Agency), insisted the emergency response "ignore the dead" and focus on the recovery of the living, he unwittingly ignored the funerary traditions of African Americans on the Gulf Coast—in which honoring the dead is a central part—and, in so doing, displayed an apparent lack of cultural sensitivity (Dass-Brailsford, 2010). In these circumstances, resilience and healing are hampered in the face of invalidation and social injustice (Boyd, Quevillon, & Engdahl, 2010).

Responding to Tragedy: The Social Bases of Resilience

The immediate response to public tragedy appears to be a desire to reconnect with others. Two recent tragedies serve as illustrations. The attack on a Pittsburgh synagogue in October 2018 which claimed the lives of 11 Jewish worshipers prompted a public vigil in which members of the community from across the city came together to support one another and, as one attendee put it, to be "together, not alone" in ways that would help heal the city (BBC News, 2018a). The helicopter crash in Leicester, UK, on the same day, in which the owner of Leicester City Football Club was killed, also prompted a social response, with eyewitnesses reporting staff of the club looking round, bewildered and crying, not knowing what to do and consoling each other (BBC News, 2018b). Death is thus a powerful motor of social solidarity (Walter, 2001). In the aftermath of tragedies of this sort, public ritual "offers reassurance and support, reaffirms community, shows solidarity, structures grief" (Doka, 2003, p. 186) and demonstrates to those affected that other people care.

Ritual displays of grief, allied to the anger generated by the injustice of preventable tragedy, can also be a spur to social and political activism. Such activism may involve lobbying politicians for legislative change to ensure that others do not have to suffer what victims, survivors and those bereaved by disaster have had to endure. A source of resilience may therefore be found in the "benefit finding" involving the search for something "redemptive" in tragedy by helping others. We see examples of this in lobbying by the bereaved for tighter gun controls following tragedies such as the Sandy Hook shooting; or in the Parents Circle Family Forum founded by Palestinian and Israeli families bereaved by the violence of the Israeli-Palestinian conflict, whose express aim is to foster reconciliation and prevent bereavement from becoming a vehicle for expanding enmity between the two peoples.

Such activism may also be driven by a desire for justice following a preventable tragedy. The desire for justice was what sustained families bereaved by the Hillsborough disaster over 27 long years, as they sought the truth behind how their loved ones died and to ensure those responsible for the deaths and cover-ups that followed were held to account. The overturning of the verdict of "accidental death" at the initial inquests by a verdict of "unlawful killing" at the new inquests in 2016 provided a significant milestone in the campaign for justice. Survivors and those bereaved by disaster may also find solace and have their resolve galvanized by the social support of others affected by similar tragedies, by their involvement in campaign or support groups whose existence is acknowledgment that more can be accomplished together than alone.

Re-engaging the Social

A sociological perspective thus emphasizes how resilience can be understood not simply as a gift of the individual (as a personal trait or characteristic) but has its locus in the social support provided by others, in the strength conferred upon us by the group. Such an approach can again be traced to the work of 19th-century sociologist Durkheim, who asserted that what we commonly perceive as resilience that comes from within is in fact bestowed upon us from *without,* from the friendships, social networks and communities of which we are a part.

This is a point reinforced powerfully by former UK Chief Rabbi Dr. Jonathan Sacks (2018), when he recalled how the support of another during a game of wheelchair doubles tennis in the Invictus Games helped "unfreeze" a teammate gripped by PTSD triggered by the sound of a helicopter overhead. Sacks goes on to remind us of a story from the Talmud in which a faith healer famed for healing others was himself taken ill. The Talmud, Sacks says, asks why he could not heal himself; the answer being that self-help is sometimes not enough and that we need the touch or word of another. That is why, Sacks suggests, community is so important:

> It's where we meet face-to-face to give each other strength. It's where people know who we are and miss us when we're not there. Community is society with a human face. It's the redemption of our solitude.
>
> (Sacks, 2018)

Recent research appears to confirm the benefits of social support in moderating the impact of stressful life events, including bereavement, providing a buffer that supports the maintenance of both physical and psychological well-being and guards against the potentially harmful effects of social isolation (Bottomley, Burke, & Neimeyer, 2017). Indeed, loneliness can itself be understood as a tragedy, albeit a personal tragedy affecting an estimated nine million people in the UK (British Red Cross & Co-Op, 2016); and research now indicates a firm link between loneliness and early death in ways suggesting it is as damaging to health as that of smoking and obesity (Holt-Lunstad, Smith, Baker, Harris, & Stephenson, 2015, cited in Department for Digital Media, Culture and Sport, 2018). Acknowledgment of the positive impact of social support can be found in both the Compassionate Communities approach (Kellehear, 2005; Aoun, Breen, White, Rumbold, & Kellehear, 2018)—in which "everyday assets" of family, friends, neighbors, school and workplace are mobilized as networks of support—and in social policy developments in the UK, especially the recognition of loneliness as a public health issue requiring the social prescription of services.

Conclusion

The implications of all of this for those in the caring professions whose work brings them into contact with survivors and those bereaved by tragedy, whether personal or public, are plain. Social support is key in facilitating recovery and sustaining resilience. It may be even more acute in circumstances in which our faith in everything we thought we knew about the world, including our faith in public authorities entrusted with keeping us safe, has betrayed us.

Providing support and promoting resilience should, then, be guided by sensitivity and, if tragedy is widespread, by involving the community in its own healing. Such support should also be reflexive; cognizant of cultural difference and diversity, recognizing and resisting attempts to force our own values on others, while at the same time listening to what those most in need of our help are telling us.

References

Aoun, S. M., Breen, L. J., White, I., Rumbold, B. and Kellehear, A. (2018). What sources of bereavement support are perceived helpful by bereaved people and why? Empirical evidence for the compassionate communities approach. *Palliative Medicine*, 32(8), pp. 1378–88.

BBC News (2018a). Pittsburgh shooting: Multiple casualties at Squirrel Hill synagogue. 28 October. Retrieved from www.bbc.co.uk/news/world-us-canada-46002549.

BBC News (2018b) Leicester City helicopter crash: "I have seen staff in tears— Eyewitness reports. 28 October. Retrieved from www.bbc.co.uk/sport/football/46006657.

Black Report (1980). *Inequalities in health.* London: DHSS.

Bottomley, J. S., Burke, L. A. and Neimeyer, R. A. (2017). Domains of social support that predict bereavement distress following homicide loss. *Omega*, 75(1), pp. 3–25.

Boyd, B., Quevillon, R. P. and Engdahl, R. M. (2010). Working with rural and diverse communities in disaster. In P. Dass-Bailsford (Ed.), *Crisis and disaster counseling: Lessons learned from Hurricane Katrina and other disasters.* Thousand Oaks, CA: Sage, pp. 149–64.

British Red Cross and Co-Op (2016). Trapped in a bubble: An investigation into triggers for loneliness in the UK. Kantar Public. Retrieved from https://assets.ctfassets.net/5ywmq66472jr/5tKumBSlO0suKwiWO6KmaM/230366b0171541781a0cd98fa80fdc6e/Coop_Trapped_in_a_bubble_report.pdf.

Cross Party Group on Hospices and Palliative Care (2018). *Inquiry: Inequalities in access to hospice and palliative care.* Cardiff, UK: Welsh Assembly. Retrieved from www.hospiceuk.org/docs/default-source/Policy-and-Campaigns/cpg-report_english_web.pdf?sfvrsn=4.

Dass-Brailsford, P. (2010). Ignore the dead: We want the living. In P. Dass-Bailsford (Ed.), *Crisis and disaster counseling: Lessons learned from Hurricane Katrina and other disasters.* Thousand Oaks, CA: Sage, pp. 33–48.

Department for Digital Media, Culture and Sport (2018). *A connected society: A strategy for tackling loneliness—Laying the foundations for change.* London: HM Government. Retrieved from https://assets.publishing.service.gov.uk/government/uploads/system/uploads/attachment_data/file/750909/6.4882_DCMS_Loneliness_Strategy_web_Update.pdf.

Dixon, J., King, D., Matosevic, T., Clark, M. and Knapp, M. (2015). *Equity in the provision of palliative care in the UK: Review of evidence. Personal Social Services Research Unit.* London: London School of Economics. Retrieved from www.pssru.ac.uk/pub/4962.pdf.

Doka, K. (2003). Memorialization, ritual and public tragedy. In M. Lattazni-Licht and K. J. Doka (Eds.), *Living with grief: Coping with public tragedy.* New York: Brunner-Routledge, pp. 179–90.

Durkheim, E. (1897/2002). *Suicide: A study in sociology.* (Trans. J. A. Spaulding and G. Simpson). Abingdon, UK: Routledge.

Harris Lord, J. (2000). *No time for goodbyes: Coping with sorrow, anger and injustice after a tragic death*. Burnsville, NC: Compassion Press.

Holt-Lunstad, J., Smith, T. B., Baker, M., Harris, T. and Stephenson, D. (2015). Loneliness and social isolation as risk factors for mortality: A meta-analytic review. *Perspectives on Psychological Science*, 10(2), pp. 227–37.

Kellehear, A. (2005). *Compassionate cities: Public health and end-of-life care*. London: Routledge.

Kübler-Ross, E. (1969). *On death and dying*. New York: Macmillan.

Lukes, S. (2008). Zero confidence. *New Humanist*, November/December, pp. 10–11. Retrieved from https://newhumanist.org.uk/articles/1889/zero-confidence.

Mills, C. W. (1959). *The sociological imagination*. New York: Oxford University Press.

Sacks, J. (2018). Sometimes, alongside medical treatment, we need the touch of another to heal our pain. *BBC Radio 4 Today Programme* (Thought for the Day), 26 October. Retrieved from http://rabbisacks.org/community-society-human-face-redemption-solitude-thought-day/.

Thompson, N., Allan, J., Carverhill, P., Cox, G., Davies, B., Doka, K., . . . Wittkowski, J. (2016). The case for a sociology of dying, death and bereavement. *Death Studies*, 40(3), pp. 172–81.

Walter, T. (2001). Sociology. In G. Howarth and O. Leoman (Eds.), *Encyclopedia of death and dying*. London and New York: Routledge, pp. 420–22.

6 Living With Terrorism

Andy Hau Yan Ho and Geraldine Tan-Ho

The threat of terrorism has embedded itself into our collective consciousness as wave after wave of terror attacks swarm the globe every year. The events of 9/11 in the United States marked a turning point in our human history where terrorism no longer can be assumed to be confined only to the annals of history or among politically troubled regions. Subsequent terror attacks that proliferated around the world reveal that terrorists indeed do not restrict themselves to a central point of operations but operate beyond borders. Instead of solely politicizing their objectives, terrorists now apply and integrate religious ideologies in their demands for radical social changes or upholding the status quo by disrupting structures, tarnishing peace and spreading fear in society, pulling at the heartstrings and belief systems of potential followers and expanding their support and recruitment. There is also a purposeful increase in arbitrary mass-casualty attacks and symbolic violence in efforts to produce a desired impact on society. Universally, 21st-century terrorism has evolved into a threat that is transnational, indiscriminate and ubiquitous in nature, with a rise in mass fatalities and intentional brutality (Männik, 2009).

Back home, this means that anyone setting out to do their daily grocery shopping in the neighborhood could end up on the tragic death toll from a sudden knife attack. College students on spring break vacation could find themselves in the middle of a bomb blast of a popular tourist attraction. A business traveler on a work trip could be taken hostage and his or her brutal murder streamed online in an attempt to horrify the masses and pressure governments. Such alarming possibilities, once seemingly far fetched, have become the new and frightening reality that all of us have to live with in the new age of terrorism.

What about the survivors of past terrorist attacks? When media attention has turned and the world has shifted its focus on newer events after an attack, survivors must continue to soldier on in the shadow of sudden violence, death and loss. They will have to live with the specter of terror, a heightened awareness of the possibility of sudden violent death or injury to them or their loved ones, and reminders of the trauma with each fresh terrorist attack that makes the headlines.

Terrorism has also shown to have unwanted and negative effects on groups of people who are perceived to be associated with terrorists due to similarities in their religion, nationality, language or culture. Strabac and Listhaug (2008) revealed that prejudices against Muslims are increasingly pervasive in western societies. This could be attributed to how the general media coverage of Muslims is often framed in a negative light (Ahmed & Matthes, 2016; Bowe, Fahmy, & Matthes, 2015; Powell, 2011), especially with the intensive media coverage on the Islamic State terrorist groups. Unsurprisingly, Muslims as a social group have suffered from being seen as potential terrorists and more religiously fanatical than those of other religions.

Terrorism robs communities and nations not just of life but of safety, security, connection and acceptance. People need to make sense of the grief, loss and disequilibrium that ensues right after an attack, as well as find an explanation for the tragic event. To this day the definition of terrorism is not universal; rather, it is determined by the various social, cultural and political roots of the community or country that has been impacted by the threat (Orr, 2015; Turk, 2004).

Schmid (2004, cited in Lucini, 2017) proposed 10 key characteristic elements of terrorism:

1. The demonstrative use of violence against human beings;
2. The (conditional) threat of (more) violence;
3. The deliberate production of terror/fear in a target group;
4. The targeting of civilians, non-combatants and innocents;
5. The purpose of intimidation, coercion and/or propaganda;
6. Its use as a method, tactic or strategy to cause conflict;
7. The importance of communicating the act(s) of violence to larger audiences;
8. The illegal, criminal and immoral nature of the act(s) of violence;
9. The predominantly political character of the act; and
10. Its use as a tool of psychological warfare to mobilize or immobilize sectors of the public.

While the definition of terrorism remains debatable, the characteristics of this destructive movement are intrinsically designed to create fear, mass panic, suspicion, anger and a slew of powerful reactions in order to evoke some kind of desired change, such as an insurrection, or to maintain a status quo.

Vulnerability or Strength?

The primary target of terrorism is rarely the individual but the community (Pfefferbaum, Reissman, Pfefferbaum, Klomp, & Gurwitch, 2008). Under the conditions of life-threatening danger, limited opportunity for escape and the presence of a crowd, people are theorized to succumb to their inherent tendencies for psychological frailty and maladaptive behavior, resulting in mass panic (Quarantelli, 2001). Mass panic is believed to pose critical public safety crises, as such human reactions to emergencies could result in even bigger problems than the original threat.

However, many studies have challenged this theory and concluded that orderliness and helping are far more common in mass disasters than panic (Sime, 1990; Barton, 1969). Case studies on one of the most well-researched mass disasters in history, the September 11, 2001, attacks on the World Trade Center, revealed that panic-related behavior was exhibited by only a minority (Connell, 2001). Similarly, research on the London Bombing in 2005 showed that survivors caught up in the attack predominantly demonstrated collective calmness, helping behaviors and even put themselves at risk to help strangers. Only a minority was reported to have displayed isolating behaviors like being focused on their mobile phones, ignoring others and walking past the injured. It seemed that the crowd that was directly impacted by the terror attack provided a psychological resource for each other and displayed a strong sense of collective resilience (Drury, Cocking, & Reicher, 2009).

Indeed, communities show an increase in group cohesiveness in the face of threats. We often see inspiring demonstrations of resilience, compassion and solidarity within domestic and global communities after a terror attack. This is because such critical events, though tragic, provide a unique opportunity for people to undergo a process of identification with their communities and countries, which in turn enables them to develop a stronger sense of social identity. Individuals now have a common enemy and thus would work together and support each other in the attempt to survive and eradicate the threat. An elevated sense of social identity is also helpful in facilitating individuals' chances of psychological recovery and the reorganization of the world around them (Drury et al., 2009).

Collective Victimhood

Sometimes, solidarity and unity may create more barriers instead of cohesion. Bar-Tal, Chernyak-Hai, Schori and Gundar (2009) explain that a major theme that has emerged amidst conflict in societies is the phenomenon of self-perceived collective victimhood among those affected by terrorism. This mindset can develop when a group collectively perceives that a great and unjust harm has been directed at them by another group. The collective group that has been harmed would express negative feelings and behaviors not just towards the perpetrator group but also to those who do not recognize their status as the victims, or those whom they associate with the perpetrator group.

The major consequences of such a system of victimhood include (Bar-Tal et al., 2009) the following:

1. The collective group affirms the world as a dangerous place and intensifies their sense of vulnerability and helplessness.
2. The collective group develops intense hostility, mistrust and hatred towards the perpetrator group and those they perceive to be associated to, or in favor of, the latter, leading to greater social distance.

3. The collective group becomes focused on their suffering and losses and finds it difficult to empathize with the suffering of other societies.
4. The collective group could justify negative in-group behavior towards other groups as punishment for the atrocities done to them.
5. The collective group could shift from the role of the victim to that of the victimizer through revenge-seeking behaviors.

In line with a sense of collective victimhood, people tend to focus on their collective group while displaying swiftness in excluding other groups. This process can create increased social and cultural distance, cultivate anti-immigrant perceptions and heighten support for coercive political decisions or parties. As such, communities are encouraged to form an inclusive national identity, rather than an exclusive social identity to face and rise above the losses and adverse impact of terrorism.

Arts, Resilience and National Identity

Bloom (1990) defined national identity as a result of a mass of people experiencing an identification process with its nation, as well as the global recognition and acknowledgment of its nation, so that they may act in one accordance in the face of a threat. National identity is usually made up of civic and ethnic characteristics (Poole, 1999; Brubaker, 1992, Smith, 1991 cited in Lödén, 2014). Civic characteristics are in line with certain laws or political values, such as democracy or liberalism, that citizens pledge to uphold. Ethnic characteristics, on the other hand, are those of shared common descent, mostly expressed by language, culture, religion and appearances. While intentionally unifying, such characteristics, as seen from studies on collective victimhood, can also be diversifying. This is because the emotions underlying such characteristics can either be compassionate and inclusive or antagonistic and exclusive.

Emotions serve as an active constituent in the formation and maintenance of social and national identity (Ahmed, 2004; Berzin, 2001, 2002; Fierke, 2004; Nash, 2003; Scheff, 1994 cited in Hutchison & Bleiker, 2008). In recognizing that emotions are often key to the outcomes of reconciliation or conflict, studies have looked at the arts as both educational and expressive forms of healing and inclusivity within communities and nations. The arts have shown to be effective in restoration of emotional well-being, facilitating meaning making in grief and reducing feelings of isolation through community building. Potash, Ho and Ho (2018) developed the Art, Compassion and Citizen Empowerment Model and posited that the arts can serve to nurture community building and acceptance of diversity and change, leading to a stronger sense of human citizenship. According to Figure 6.1, citizen empowerment can be achieved through the activation of four art elements:

1. *Narratives*: Narratives told through the process of art making would allow for creative framing and sharing of personal and traumatic experiences.

2. *Encounters*: Symbolic encounters between artists and public would facilitate dialogue that transcends social identities, leading to empathic understanding and balanced judgment.
3. *Reflection*: Reflection from the art making, narratives and encounters would clarify stereotyped cultures and value, widen perspectives and lead to deeper appreciation and compassion for the self and others.
4. *Community*: The art-based narratives, encounters and reflections can instill a sense of community and inclusivity, in which sociopolitical and cultural differences and isolations are transformed from an "I-it" relationship to an "I-Thou" relationship (Buber, 1937) that focuses on understanding, acceptance and compassion. Such a relationship involves a mutual, full experiencing of the self and the other, one that is indispensable for building a resilient and inclusive society for facing the real and constant threats of terrorism.

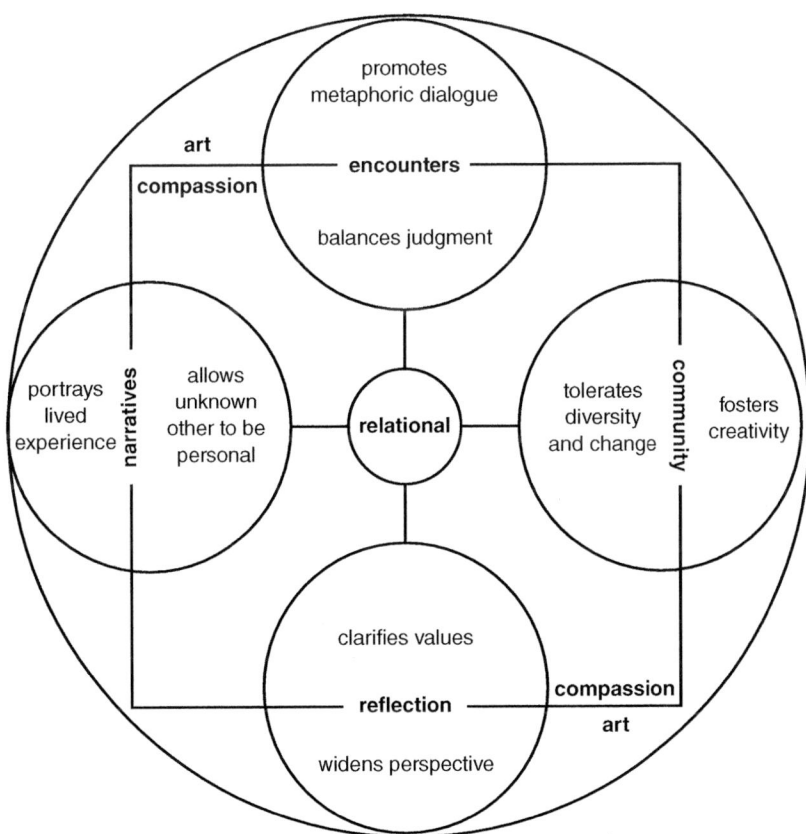

Figure 6.1 A citizen empowerment model with art and compassion

Culture-specific art spaces, such as The America's Islamic Heritage Museum and Cultural Center and the International Museum of Muslim Cultures in the United States serve as places to inform the general public on widely stereotyped groups, as well as provide opportunities for these groups to empower themselves by sharing their culture through arts and narratives. Art spaces and exhibitions can also serve as a conducive environment for survivors and all who are affected by terrorism to come together and build an inclusive and compassionate resilience as individuals and as communities.

From Vulnerability to Strength

As the new age of terrorism brings waves of trauma and attacks upon the world, people strive to channel their inner resilience to support communities in coping with the magnitude of grief, loss and uncertainty. In order to ensure that this collective resilience does not fall into collective vulnerability, individuals, communities and nations must safeguard and enhance inclusivity, cultural awareness and creative ways of promoting compassionate resilience. As Utøya survivor Helle Gannestad declared, "If one man can show so much hatred, imagine the amount of love we can show together" (cited in Anker & von der Lippe, 2018, p. 255).

References

Ahmed, S. and Matthes, J. (2016). Media representation of Muslims and Islam from 2000 to 2015: A meta-analysis. *International Communication Gazette*, 79(3), pp. 219–44. doi:10.1177/ 1748048516656305.

Anker, T. and von der Lippe, M. (2018). Coming to terms with terrorism? A case study on how schools are dealing with the terror attacks of 22 July 2011 in Oslo and Utøya. In J. Ipgrave, T. Knauth, A. Kors, D. Vieregge and M. von der Lippe (Eds.), *Religion and dialogue in the city: Case studies on interreligious encounter in urban community and education*. Munster, Germany: Waxmann, pp. 247–62.

Bar-Tal, D., Chernyak-Hai, L., Schori, N. and Gundar, A. (2009). A sense of self-perceived collective victimhood in intractable conflicts. *International Review of the Red Cross*, 91(874). doi:10.1017/S1816383109990221.

Barton, A. H. (1969). *Communities in disaster: A sociological analysis of collective stress situations*. New York: Doubleday.

Bloom, W. (1990). *Personal identity, national identity and international relations*. Cambridge, UK: Cambridge University Press.

Bowe, B. J., Fahmy, S. and Matthes, J. (2015). U.S. newspapers provide nuanced picture of Islam. *Newspaper Research Journal*, 36(1), pp. 42–57. doi:10.1177/07395329 1503600104.

Buber, M. (1937). *I and Thou*. (Trans. R. Smith). London: Continuum. (Original work published 1923).

Connell, R. (2001). Collective behavior in the September 11, 2001 evacuation of the World Trade Center. *Preliminary Papers*, 313, pp. 1–20. Retrieved from http://udspace.udel.edu/handle/19716/683.

Drury, J., Cocking, C. and Reicher, S. (2009). Everyone for themselves? A comparative study of crowd solidarity among emergency survivors. *British Journal of Social Psychology*, 48(3), pp. 487–506. doi:10.1348/014466608X357893.

Hutchison, E. and Bleiker, R. (2008). Emotional reconciliation: Reconstituting identity and community after trauma. *European Journal of Social Theory*, 11(3), pp. 385–403. doi:10.1177/1368431008092569.

Lödén, H. (2014). Peace, love, depoliticisation and the domestic alien: National identity in the memorial messages collected after the terror attacks in Norway 22 July 2011. *National Identities*, 16(2), pp. 157–76. doi:10.1080/14608944.2014.918 593.

Lucini, B. (2017). Terrorism, sociology and a resilience approach. In B. Lucini (Ed.), *The other side of resilience to terrorism*, pp. 5–18. doi:10.1007/978-3-319-56943-7_2.

Männik, E. (2009). Terrorism: Its past, present and future prospects. In A. Saumets and A. Kilp (Eds.), *Religion and politics in multicultural Europe: Perspectives and challenges*. Tartu: Tartu University Press, pp. 151–71.

Orr, A. (2015). A formula of terrorism? *Journal of Applied Security Research*, 10(1), pp. 97–120. doi:10.1080/19361610.2015.972285.

Pfefferbaum, B. J., Reissman, D. B., Pfefferbaum, R. L., Klomp, R. W. and Gurwitch, R. H. (2008). Building resilience to mass trauma events. In L. S. Doll, S. E. Bonzo, D. A. Sleet and J. A. Mercy (Eds.), *Handbook of injury and violence prevention*. Boston, MA: Springer. doi:/10.1007/978-0-387-29457-5_19.

Potash, J. S., Ho, R. T. H. and Ho, A. H. Y. (2018). Citizenship, compassion, the arts: People living with mental illness need a caring community. *Social Change*, 48(2), pp. 1–22. doi:10.1177/0049085718768911.

Powell, K. A. (2011). Framing Islam: An analysis of US media coverage of terrorism since 9/11. *Communication Studies*, 62(1), pp. 90–112. doi:10.1080/10510974.2011 .533599.

Quarantelli, E. L. (2001). The sociology of panic. In N. J. Smelser and P. B. Baltes (Eds.), *International encyclopedia of the social and behavioral sciences*. New York: Pergamon Press, pp. 11020–23.

Sime, J. D. (1990). The concept of panic. In D. Canter (Ed.), *Fires and human behavior* (2nd Edn.) London: David Fulton.

Strabac, Z. and Listhaug, O. (2008). Anti-Muslim prejudice in Europe: A multilevel analysis of survey data from 30 countries. *Social Science Research*, 37(1), pp. 268–86. doi:10.1016/j.ssresearch.2007.02.004.

Turk, A. T. (2004). Sociology of terrorism. *Annual Review of Sociology*, 30, pp. 271–86. doi:10.1146/annurev.soc.30.012703.110510.

7   Violent Crime and Resilience

Gerry R. Cox

All losses are difficult, but perhaps the most difficult losses arise from violent crime. The losses of being a victim or a loved one being a victim of violent crime are magnified by the fact that these events could potentially have been avoided. The pain and hurt can be intensified by the sense of injustice associated with the criminal nature of the loss. To cope with such tragedies requires skills that few are equipped to master.

The violent death of a loved one is a frightening prospect. It is forced upon us. It takes us away from our loved ones and way of life and introduces a strong sense of injustice. How can we face the fear that accompanies a violent death or other crime-related losses?

Coping Skills

Violent crime presents a unique challenge to our coping ability, shattering our hopes and dreams. Grief is personal and cannot be truly shared, just as we cannot eat for another or take away the pain in the finger of another caused by a hammer that missed the nail. Coping successfully requires that we focus upon reachable goals. Many seek to return to a "normal" life. The question is: how did you define "normal" before your loved one died? Grief brings pain, whether physical, emotional or spiritual, or acting out in unusual ways. Our sense of spirit is also wounded. We do not "get over" a death, but rather learn to live with the pain and loss and somehow continue to function. A reachable goal in terms of resilience would be to ask that we might learn to continue to live and be the person that we were before the loss, while at the same time keeping our loved one as part of our life.

In sociological terms, it is important to focus on relationships, including kinship systems. Relatives are part of our social circle and friendship groupings. We can look to others during grief, as ritual, family, community, spirituality and ceremony can all help.

Challenges continually occur in our lives, ranging from lost keys to problems at work, but over time we develop means to cope. Coping styles are generally learned from parents, teachers, significant others who may not have always had good skills themselves. We have learned to cope with graduations, changing jobs, moving to new communities, deaths of significant people in our lives, and yet violent death can be so much more difficult due to the strong sense of injustice involved. Our coping skills can seem to be quite inadequate. Yet, because we have survived other difficult times in our lives, we can learn that we can and will survive this loss too. While there is no "correct" way to cope, there is always the potential for improving how we cope.

Friends, family, caregivers, clergy, social workers, physicians and loved ones can sometimes compound efforts to cope by their own discomforts and attempts to be helpful. How does a vulnerable, fragile, suffering individual encountering a spiritual crisis and faced with existential meaninglessness bring meaning and hope back into their life? Those who have developed positive coping skills can be of great help in general terms but especially when a loved one dies from violent crime.

Coping skills are needed to help manage all kinds of life problems. Losses and challenges occur every day. With skill we can develop life's burdens into life's blessings. Coping skills enable us to manage divorce, widowhood, aging, death and other life challenges.

Rituals also help to promote resilience—for example, by having a wake or visitation, sitting Shiva with a body before it is buried in the Jewish tradition, having members of the Veterans of Foreign Wars or the American Legion provide burial rituals for fellow military personnel, or having the body "laid out" in the parlor as in the past. Long-term death rituals would include Memorial Day ceremonies, developing a memorial area in your home, making anniversary visits to the grave site, having Masses said for the deceased, planting a tree or other living memorial, or honoring their memory by working to prevent violent death. Such important social supports are even more significant when the loss has arisen from violent crime.

To cope, we need to recognize that there will be good days and bad days. Like the ocean, our ability to cope with grief ebbs and flows. Holidays, anniversaries, birthdays, and so forth can be faced with dread and a desire to avoid anything to do with them. Coping will require that we make our loved ones a part of these days. Their loss does not remove them from our lives. We can find many creative ways to continue to include them in our daily life. Time is not a healer. To cope, eventually, we must come to accept what life has given to us and go on. The pain of grief does not go away, but, rather, we become resilient by learning to live with the pain. One approach to managing traumatic death is spirituality. Spiritual beliefs, experiences and practices are a part of coping with high levels of distress and physical health symptoms (Richards, 2001). Spirituality is involvement with the sacred in thought, action, and social forms. It is part of a total system of symbols, such as music, dance, silence, rituals, meditation and ceremonies. Encounters with the sacred can lead to tremendous emotions and responses. Art, sculpture, drama, dance, music and more can inspire through spiritual experiences. Death seems to have great potential for transformation.

Bonding and Relationships

Each relationship with another person is unique. We choose to allow others to become a part of ourselves. Meaning arises through relationships. Others become part of who we are. Parents will acknowledge that, when their child was born, their life changed forever—with not only lack of sleep, changing social life and new expenses, but also new hopes and dreams. Friends become part of our hopes and dreams as well. Not only is the person lost but also the hopes and dreams as well. The greater the bond with another person, the greater the hurt will be. Likewise, the powerful impact of violent crime can intensify the hurt.

We have many bonds in our lives: with the server at a restaurant, the valet who parks our car, with people we greet while walking or jogging, with co-workers, with celebrities, with strangers who offer a smile, and with others who become part of our lives. People also choose to bond even more strongly with friends, partners, children, parents, siblings and others. While all deaths give hurt, violent deaths give more due to the element of terror involved.

As we bond with others, we also must know deeply in our heart that everyone that we love will eventually die. While knowing this may give anxiety, it may also allow an appreciation of relationships before they are lost. People marry, make friends, have children and become attached to strangers, all the while knowing that all relationships end. Is the choice to bond with another time bound? Would we say no to the relationship if we knew that it would end in 20 years? Five years? A month? A day? At what point would we decide that to bond and suffer the grief of loss is too great of a cost? If parents knew that their baby would only live a day or die at birth would they take the baby anyway? If the baby lived for 60 years would that be enough? What makes death by violent crime so challenging is that it brings life to an end prematurely—it is unnatural. However, how long relationships last is not the issue. The real issue is their quality.

Surviving Violent Crime

There are no magic ways to survive violent crime, no right or wrong ways, and not everyone is willing to help us on our journey. Many will refuse even to talk about their losses or yours. Sharing is helpful for many, but not all want to share or even allow you to. While we all experience the pain of loss, we all grieve differently. Memories can give us great pleasure; like viewing the many pictures in an art gallery, the memories can bring alive our loved one in many different portraits that fill us with joy. Those same memories can cause us pain because we are not able to make new memories with them. Part of our struggle is to understand why so many others do not want to help us or perhaps fail to help us because of their own grief or because of the horror associated with violent death. For many of us, remembering is the only way to survive.

People affected by such losses may not want to eat, go to work, make their bed, take out the trash or do other such tasks. It is important to realize that they are not obligated to do any of these things. Going back to work creates its own potential trauma. Because work is a central part of the lives of most people, it can create special problems (Thompson, 2009). An important element of resilience is to take time to rest, exercise, eat, bathe, and otherwise practice self-care to be better able to take care of others. When shopping, going to church, to work, or having a car repaired, trying to maintain a false front of strength is generally unhelpful. Others know about the hurt and the grief. Trying to "be strong" is not necessarily beneficial. Willingness to show emotions allows others to be freer to express their own. We need to avoid setting unrealistic goals, as grief is clearly a major event in our lives that cannot be minimized or denied.

William Isaac Thomas (1923) taught that the definition of the situation is real in its consequences. The process of definition is never ending. We can define our world as a dirty, miserable place or as a challenge to make better or as any other definition that we choose. The choice belongs to each of us. By learning to be fully conscious of our actions, we can take control of our life (Thompson, 2016).

The ability to manage traumatic loss competently and successfully is a key element of resilience. Sociologically, the social support and learning are key. Resilience is supported by empathy, modeling, internalization and reciprocity. Caring for others is basic to social survival. From the era of hunting and gathering cultures where people joined with others for basic survival to modern societies where others produce and distribute most of our goods, food and services, people have depended upon each other for survival.

Empathy, caring for others, sharing, and being social are the basis of society. As social beings, we cannot survive without each other. Sharing with the young, old, weak and most vulnerable people has made us more altruistic. Cooperation, caring, sharing and empathy are learned in our relationships in our families, schools and communities. Stable, safe and secure communities are best able to promote empathy in children who then become empathic adults. Those who are abused, neglected and mistreated may be less likely to develop empathy.

Modeling is also basic to developing values and behaviors. Parents and other significant adults who exhibit empathy, both within the family and beyond, are more likely to foster the empathy in children that is basic to becoming prosocial in values and behavior.

Internalization is the social process of developing empathy, values, mores and norms as part of our identity. Our ability to judge our own behavior, based upon community standards of behavior, is the result of internalization.

Reciprocity is also basic to empathy developing. As parents learn to respond to the clues, needs and emotions of their babies, children learn to accept the parents' way of responding to them. Social reciprocity is basic to all societies. All families socialize their children, as do schools. Peers socialize their peers.

Learning that we need others and that others need us is vital to developing resilience.

Our ability to cope is influenced by our empathy, and our need to help others also helps us. When we have experienced a traumatic loss to a criminal act, we are not alone in our loss. As we care for others, we are better able to understand our own loss. The nature of our social groups, our society, our culture and our religious and spiritual experiences will also impact our resilience. People in a society that has experienced warfare for generations will respond quite differently from those living in a peaceful, serene society. People in indigenous societies will respond differently from those living in crowded, urban areas. Social support is present in all communities, cultures and societies, but our response to the social support varies from individual to individual. Those with stronger empathy will have greater resilience when traumatic events occur. Our coping ability is strongly influenced by the nature of our social relationship with others.

Cultural Variations

Class, nationality, ethnicity, religion, education and occupation are all sociological variables that impact our ability to cope with loss. Societies where basic needs for food, shelter and housing are commonly not met will have more difficulty coping, unless they have a strong community with support. Those who are discriminated against, enslaved, mistreated and denied basic rights in societies will also struggle to cope, unless they, too, have strong communities to resist their treatment in the society. Most reservation and reserve tribal groups have strong, supportive communities. The largest reservation is the Navajo Nation, which is comprised of many clans and communities. Traditional Navajo include children in their daily activities. From the cradleboard to spending time with elders, Navajo children are attached to their families, both physically and socially. Navajo children who are separated have a more difficult time than White children, but Navajo children who are not separated tend to cope better than either of them. The separation of Navajo children has been part of the attempt to make them like those in the dominant culture. Reservation and reserve (the term used in Canada) schools were designed to make them "civilized," thus no longer Indian.

Conclusion

Surviving crime is difficult; surviving violent crime even more so. Each person needs to understand how choices impact their ability to cope and survive. By learning how to better make choices, perhaps we can better survive violent crime. Violent criminal acts occur in all societies. Our ability to survive them is enhanced by our resilience. This is tied to our ability to be empathic. In societies that foster empathy, we become better able to cope. Techniques for coping are also important in our ability to become resilient, as is social support.

References

Richards, T. A. (2001). The spiritual self and meaning. In R. A. Neimeyer (Ed.), *Meaning reconstruction & the experience of loss*. Washington, DC: American Psychological Association.

Thomas, W. I. (1923). *The unadjusted girl*. Boston, MA: Little, Brown and Company.

Thompson, N. (2009). *Loss, grief and trauma in the workplace*. New York: Routledge.

Thompson, N. (2016). *The authentic leader*. London: Palgrave.

8 Mental Health Problems

Getting to the HEART of Resilience

Neil Thompson

Introduction

The dominant approach to mental health problems for quite some time now has been a medical model, based on the assumption that the difficulties being encountered arise from chemical imbalances in the brain or other such biological misfirings. This approach remains dominant despite a wide range of criticisms that strongly question its validity (Cohen, 2018; Crossley, 2006; Hari, 2018; Maisel, 2018; Thompson, 2019). In this chapter I argue that we need to rethink our understandings of mental health problems and develop a more holistic approach, one in which resilience plays a key part. I therefore propose the use of the HEART framework put forward in my earlier work (Thompson, 2019).

Beyond the Medical Model

Hari (2018) tells the story of how, in his youth, he experienced problems relating to anxiety and depression. He was prescribed anti-depressants which made a positive difference to his well-being. However, over time, he realized that the medication no longer worked, and he came to the conclusion that there was more to what was happening to him than the "chemical imbalance" approach could explain. He subsequently developed a fuller understanding of his problems and the potential solutions by focusing on the range of losses (lost connections, as he calls them) and how they were affecting not only him but also people in general.

He is, of course, not the first to question the wisdom of conceptualizing mental health challenges as symptoms of an underlying illness, and he certainly won't be the last. His is one of the many voices that have spoken out against the injustices involved in labelling people as "mentally ill" and thereby oversimplifying a very complex picture. What is particularly helpful about Hari's contribution to the debate is his emphasis on loss. There is a growing literature that draws links between traumatic loss and mental health problems (Bentall, 2010; Thompson, Cox, & Stevenson, 2017), but Hari's work helps us to understand that the losses do not have to be traumatic to be harmful to our mental health and well-being.

Reducing the complex dynamics of mental health problems, with the subtle interweavings of biological, psychological, sociological and spiritual dimensions, to an illness fails to do justice to the multidimensional nature of human experience and, in so doing, dehumanizes the very people it seeks to help. This is why it is necessary to move away from this dominant medical approach in order to develop more sophisticated understandings that take account of the complex interplay of the different aspects involved. I developed the HEART framework precisely for that purpose.

The HEART Framework

This framework serves as a mnemonic for what I see as five separate, but nonetheless interconnected, elements of a more holistic appreciation of what leads to people experiencing mental health problems. HEART spells out:

- **H**olistic
- **E**motion focused
- **A**lienation aware
- **R**econsidering our assumptions
- **T**rauma informed

It is worth exploring each of these in a little more detail.

Holistic

The medical model prioritizes the biological dimension and thereby relegates the psychological, sociological and spiritual aspects to, at best, secondary considerations. A holistic approach, by contrast, seeks to draw on an understanding of human existence that takes account of all four dimensions and how they interact and influence each other. A holistic approach is therefore one that involves seeing the "big picture," with all the complexity it entails, while also appreciating that it is a moving picture—reflecting the dynamic interplay of the various elements.

Perhaps the most neglected element in terms of current biomedically based practice is the spiritual. While the need to incorporate a spiritual dimension has been emphasized in some quarters (Coyte, Gilbert, & Nicholls, 2008), it remains largely absent from the mainstream practice of mental health professionals.

In considering spirituality we should not limit our perspective to religion, as spirituality is, of course, not the exclusive property of members of faith communities. While the various religions of the world offer spiritual frameworks, the quest for meaning, purpose and direction is not restricted to adherents of any particular religion.

As Park and Slattery (2014) point out, finding a thread of meaning can be an important part of promoting resilience. At times of adversity—for example, following a major loss—we can feel disorientated, feel all at sea and be struggling to make sense of what is happening to us. Attempting to get back on an even keel and especially trying to learn and grow from the experience will involve establishing new frameworks of meaning or at least adjusting our existing frameworks (what Neimeyer & Anderson, 2002, call "meaning reconstruction"—see also Chapter 24 in this volume).

Mental health problems, ranging from anxiety and depression to psychosis, will also generally feature elements of finding or reshaping purpose and direction. I learned at a very early stage of my professional practice career that a common theme across the life experience of the people I was seeking to support was a sense of "drift," a lack of any sense of purpose, direction or focus in their life. I was left wondering to what extent the "numbing" effect of the medication was adding to this struggle to develop or sustain a coherent life plan.

The H of HEART is therefore intended to remind us of the need to look holistically at situations involving mental health problems.

Emotion Focused

Another thing that struck me quite early on in my career was that so much of the emphasis was on "mental" health, with a strong focus on *cognitive* aspects (the presumed "irrationality" of madness, for example), whereas what I was witnessing had much more to do with the *emotional* challenges of people's lives. On a more-or-less daily basis, I was encountering people experiencing:

- Anxiety and fear;
- Distress and panic;
- Emotional numbing and a sense of emptiness;
- A sense of disconnection;
- Feelings of rejection and abandonment;
- Intense mistrust; and
- Confusion and disorientation.

This emotional focus contrasted strongly with the accepted wisdom that what people were experiencing were "mental illnesses" rooted in cognitive dysfunction. My experience very clearly highlighted issues that had more to do, figuratively speaking, with heart than with head.

Even with people displaying psychotic behavior who were presumed to be "out of touch with reality," I found that emotional issues were generally at the heart of their difficulties and the challenges they faced. I was taught that psychosis is based on a failure of the "reality testing" that mentally healthy people do as a matter of routine. That failure, I was routinely told, is rooted in the brain's inability, due to the psychosis, to "think rationally"—again, a strong cognitive emphasis. While my experience taught me that reality testing was very much an issue in psychosis, it also taught me that this had more to do with feeling than thinking. I was working with people who were panicking and, in a very real sense, escaping an impossible reality (or trying to), rather than failing to "test" that reality.

Of course, it is a mistake to separate out thinking and feeling altogether. As Zautra (2014) points out: "Thinking and feeling are intertwined" (p. 191). However, my point is that the dominant thinking about mental health problems has a strong cognitive focus that tends to marginalize emotional issues, and it is in the emotional domain that resilience becomes a key issue. The E of HEART is therefore there to emphasize the importance of recognizing the central role of emotional issues.

Alienation Aware

To be regarded as "alien" means to be considered different, not belonging, "not like us." Interestingly, in the early days of psychiatry, its practitioners were referred to as "alienists." But what we need to recognize is that there are two sides to the relationship between mental health problems and alienation. First, there is the question of whether, or to what extent, being classified as "mentally ill" contributes to alienation and the associated detrimental consequences (difficulty in finding employment, for example). Second, there is the argument that alienation, in its various forms, is actually a contributor, possibly a major contributor, to mental health difficulties in the first place.

The significance of alienation awareness is that it helps us to lay a foundation for empowerment. While there are no simple and direct answers to the problem of alienation, there are steps that can be taken at both micro and macro levels that can at least play a part in addressing the causes and consequences of alienation. Standing against and, where possible, overcoming the effects of alienation can be seen to involve resilience.

Alienation can be linked to a sense of powerlessness, while resilience fits well with the concept of (self-)empowerment:

> People with mental health problems will face stigma, unhelpful stereotypes, exaggerated and distorted perceptions of the risks they pose to others, systematic discrimination, obstacles to employment, housing and other social and leisure services. Powerlessness can therefore be recognized as a significant feature of having mental health problems.
>
> (Thompson, 2019, p. 33)

A biomedical approach to mental health problems that takes no account of the significant sociological role of alienation and its contribution to powerlessness will therefore stand in the way of opportunities for resilience to develop by countering such alienation. This is why the HEART framework includes A for the need to be alienation aware.

Reconsidering Our Assumptions

The medical model of mental health problems, so it is claimed, is "scientific." This assumption and the associated presumption that psychiatry is a scientific process geared towards curing, or at least alleviating, mental "illnesses" are the foundations of the current dominant approach to the subject. However, there is a growing critique of the claims to scientific objectivity, an increasing number of voices of dissent (Bentall, 2010; Cromby, Harper, & Reavey, 2013; Davies, 2013; Kirk, Gomory, & Cohen, 2015; Tummey & Turner, 2008)— what Kirk et al. (2015) describe as a "firestorm of criticism."

A key part of what is concerning about the need to reconsider our assumptions is just how deeply ingrained and unquestioned those assumptions are. The degree of "taken-for-grantedness" underpinning the dominant approach is of major proportions and, despite the growing number and growing intensity of criticism of a narrow biomedical approach and its (unintentionally) harmful consequences, it continues to serve as the basic foundation of mental health services.

The significance of this is not just at the theoretical level. It is not simply a philosophical debate about how best to conceptualize such complex phenomena. There are also highly practical implications for people's lives to consider. We can think of the negative consequences in terms of additions and subtractions. Added are stigma, discrimination, medication side effects and so on, while what is taken away can include confidence and self-esteem; a sense of control; opportunities for empowerment; attention paid to loss and grief and other emotional distress challenges; and support in addressing spiritual challenges (Davies, 2012; Holloway & Moss, 2010). It is no coincidence that so many former psychiatric patients refer to themselves as "survivors." All of this, of course, calls for resilience, while remaining inimical to it. Continuing to take the medical model for granted therefore comes at quite a high price, hence the R of HEART focusing on the need to reconsider our assumptions.

Trauma Informed

I made the point earlier that the role of trauma, particularly childhood trauma, in the genesis of mental health problems is receiving increasing recognition. To experience a trauma is to face a major existential challenge, to have one's sense of normality and security shattered. Our frameworks of meaning are disturbed, if not actually dismantled to a certain extent.

Of course, it is commonplace for people to "recover" from traumatic experiences, but for many people they can be denied that opportunity (for example, because of the ongoing nature of the trauma—as in the sadly not uncommon case of a child being sexually abused on a regular basis by a person they should be able to trust and rely on for a sense of security).

The uncritical assumption that people affected by trauma will just "get over it" in time has led to a tendency in some quarters to miss the significance of the ongoing impact of trauma (Walsh & Thompson, 2019). By contrast, my own practice experience in the mental health field led me to recognize how loss issues in general and traumatic loss in particular were a fundamental part of the issues people with mental health challenges were wrestling with (echoing the conclusions of Hari, 2018). That experience also led me to note that such issues were often missed by professionals, hence the inclusion of T, representing the need to be trauma aware, in the HEART framework.

Conclusion

This short chapter has presented a five-part framework for addressing mental health problems, a framework that can help us to promote resilience by moving away from a medical model that, in so many ways, serves as an obstacle to empowerment and resilience. The complexity of the issues involved means that we still have a great deal of work to do to take our understanding forward, but it is to be hoped that this chapter has played at least a small part in that.

References

Bentall, R. (2010). *Doctoring the mind: Why psychiatric treatments fail.* London: Penguin.

Cohen, B. M. Z. (Ed.) (2018). *Routledge international handbook of critical mental health.* New York: Routledge.

Coyte, M. E., Gilbert, P. and Nicholls, V. (Eds.) (2008). *Spirituality, values and mental health: Jewels for the journey.* Brighton, UK: Pavilion.

Cromby, J., Harper, D. and Reavey, P. (2013). *Psychology, mental health and distress.* Basingstoke, UK: Palgrave Macmillan.

Crossley, M. (2006). *Contesting psychiatry: Social movements in mental health.* London: Routledge.

Davies, J. (2012). *The importance of suffering: The value and meaning of emotional discontent.* New York: Routledge.

Davies, J. (2013). *Cracked: Why psychiatry is doing more harm than good.* London: Icon.

Hari, J. (2018). *Lost connections: Uncovering the real causes of depression—and the unexpected solutions.* London: Bloomsbury Circus.

Holloway, M. and Moss, B. (2010). *Spirituality and social work.* Basingstoke, UK: Palgrave Macmillan.

Kirk, S. A., Gomory, T. and Cohen, D. (2015). *Mad science: Psychiatric coercion, diagnosis and drugs.* New Brunswick, NJ: Transaction Press.

Maisel, E. (2018). *Humane helping: Focusing less on disorders and more on life's challenges.* New York: Routledge.

Neimeyer, R. A. and Anderson, A. (2002). Meaning reconstruction. In N. Thompson (Ed.), *Loss and grief: A guide for human services practitioners.* Basingstoke, UK: Palgrave Macmillan, pp. 45–64.

Park, C. L. and Slattery, J. M. (2014). Resilience interventions with a focus on meaning and values. In M. Kent, M. C. Davis and J. W. Reich (Eds.), *The resilience handbook: Approaches to stress and trauma.* New York: Routledge, pp. 270–82.

Thompson, N. (2019). *Mental health and well-being: Alternatives to the medical model.* New York: Routledge.

Thompson, N., Cox, G. R. and Stevenson, R. (Eds.) (2017). *Handbook of traumatic loss: A guide to theory and practice.* New York: Routledge.

Tummey, R. and Turner, T. (2008). *Critical issues in mental health.* Basingstoke, UK: Palgrave Macmillan.

Walsh, M. and Thompson, N. (2019). *Childhood trauma and recovery.* Brighton, UK: Pavilion.

Zautra, A. J. (2014). Resilience is social, after all. In M. Kent, M. C. Davis and J. W. Reich (Eds.), *The resilience handbook: Approaches to stress and trauma.* New York: Routledge, pp. 185–96.

9 Alcohol and Drugs

Resilience in Use and Users

Wulf Livingston

Individuals who encounter sustained problematic experiences with alcohol and other drugs are among those in society who face high levels of adversity and vulnerability. Often their substance use is triggered by difficult events, including significant losses, and, in turn, becomes a means of coping with these experiences. While discourse around cause and consequence is often framed in the individual, behavioral and psychological, it is as important to see these experiences as sociological phenomena. Successful development of resilience and recovery are frequently grounded in the societal.

The complexity of these experiences frequently leads individuals to develop unhelpful long-term relationships with alcohol and other drugs. These in turn lead them to be involved in criminal justice, health and social care services. These experiences can be centered around excessive, harmful and dependent patterns of use, much of which results in an array of additional physical, psychological and social difficulties. These will include a significant amount of loss and grief. Losses might include death, employment, family, health, home, identity and self-confidence or worth. The involvements often attract social disapproval, invoke problematic circumstances or forbidden grief, and can thus be considered as disenfranchised grief (Standing, Dickie, & Templeton, 2019). In particular, drug use as an illicit activity is less likely to be acknowledged, and this in turn means that the loss and grief are potentially secretive or not recognized (Livingston, 2017). Some of these experiences may be individual or family tragedy, but many are of a broader economic, environmental, political or social nature, much of which plays out in the spheres of professional responses. As well as traditional psychological models of trauma response, sociological perspectives help us to understand that problematic substance use can be an answer to issues like environmental crisis, forced migration, mass redundancy, marginalization, poverty or social exclusion.

Whatever the potential explanation, emphasis has traditionally been placed upon personal (physical and psychological) interventions and treatment. This is often through combinations of medication and (cognitive) behavioral change. These processes invite a pathologizing of the individual, often as ill and in need of curing, adopting a very narrow, rather than broad, interpretation of well-being (Livingston, 2019). This is generally accompanied by an assumption that any stopping of the substance use will in itself be sufficient to resolve the problem. Such approaches often suggest the development of coping and resilience as internal to an individual's feeling and thinking as it impacts on behavioral choices. While such interventions are necessary to provide initial stability and begin changes, recovery needs to be meaningfully relevant to each individual. In this context, it becomes clear that neither the use, its complexities, problems or solutions exist in cultural or social vacuums, nor will they be resolved through mere changes in substance use alone, rather than requiring the maintenance of sustainable and rewarding lifestyles. This is what Lee-Coy (2010) refers to as "something better than drinking and, more importantly, something much better than the mundane robotic sobriety" (p. 34). This chapter now concentrates on a small number of examples of how adversity and the vulnerability that it leads to, and which is compounded by alcohol or drug use, can be understood and supported through social and cultural coping.

Resilient Individuals and Families

Humans are remarkably resilient to the negative effects of alcohol and drug use. Despite taking large volumes, perhaps over many years, of strong intoxicating and potentially poisonous chemical compounds, many of us have positive relationships with substances. Further, the majority either use problem free or make good recovery, avoiding permanent damage or death. In other words, most use by most people is without sustained long-term negative consequences. Robins's (1993) seminal study of returning US veterans from Vietnam highlights how, in one context, individuals can heavily use heroin, and yet the moment they are returned to a different social context, they do not continue to use what is perceived as a highly addictive drug. He shows an account of contextual use and post-use resilience grounded in a different positive social context. A similar, equally seminal study by Alexander (2010), known as the "Rat Park," also gave rise to the understanding that individual drug use or addiction is highly contextual and socially bound and dissipates with changes in external (environmental and social), rather than internal, considerations. These and other similar studies give rise to the notion that the chemicals in themselves are probably not addictive and that individuals choose to use in context, rather than due to having an addictive personality type, and thus can, in the right circumstances, determine not to use—that is, develop a resilience to the need to use.

This is not to deny the impact on the significant numbers of individuals and families that do experience harm and multiple losses, but just to make the more obvious statement that, given the endemic and intrinsic levels of use in cultures and societies (Gossop, 2013), it is surprising how much use is essentially problem free or quickly recovered from without any recourse to professional help. For example, drunken revelry does not automatically result in everyone being arrested or hospitalized. For most, the excesses of teenage and early adulthood are left behind through productive adulthood and parenting.

In many contexts, drug use (including alcohol and prescribed medication) is culturally endorsed and normalized, and the negative effects ameliorated in group monitoring. This promoting of healthy and positive understandings of substance use, as well as creating protective and supportive environments to defuse the negative consequences, occurs at the familial, cultural and societal levels (Valentine, Jayne, Gould, & Keenan, 2010). The resolve of users is thus often created through positive cultural and societal contexts.

Where drink and drug use take place in open, normalized and supportive environments, it appears to mitigate against some of the experiences of excess and isolation. For many, transgression from the normative or acceptable is often relatively transitory. Humans appear to be able to use drink and drugs in response to very specific matters, and then, where they have a sufficiency of social capital (Best, McKitterick, Beswick, & Savic, 2015), they are more able to sustain a return to everyday lives. This is the norm, and those who develop the long-term, serious problems related to use are a significant number but none the less very much the minority. Positive social network development, as opposed to circles of fellow users, along with engagement in formal (often peer-led) recovery support groups, improves individual resistance to use and supports lifestyle change (recovery—Best et al., 2015).

Families are a significant element of any individual's social network. Intervention therapies, such as social behavior network therapy, help develop resilience in both the induvial user and their families (Copello, Orford, Hogson, & Tober, 2009). It is often the family that has to deal with loss of a member to alcohol or drug use and manage the negative consequences of any use (Copello & Templeton, 2012). Often families are those that survive, have no choice but to cope and develop resilience as they pick up responsibility for debts, grandchildren and prison visits. It is also families that provide support at the critical moments of change. They can be the enablers, motivators, listeners and taxis to those who use. Increasing the capacity of families to cope, and in turn then to provide support to others, is thus a critical aspect of interventions that can support enhanced coping, leading to sustained change (Various, 2010).

Resilience in Numbers

Drink and drug users are a group of individuals who are frequently subject to some of the harshest discrimination, oppression and stigma that society casts on those different or less fortunate than others. To be referred to as an alcoholic or a junkie generally invites disrespect and prejudice, yet collective resilience, peer-led recovery communities and groups often openly acknowledge and adopt these labels into positive portraits of lives changed, the possibility of change and as nomenclature for support groups. In this sense, what becomes important is the quality of future lives lived and not the stigmatizing history of past experiences and labels. Resilience is achieved through not focusing on that which has been lost or the coping with adversity, but rather through the rebuilding of social or recovery capital.

There is increasing evidence to support the argument that recovery is best supported in peer environments. The characteristics and processes of recovery have become well recognized (and include constructions of unique, personal and non-linear journeys, often experienced within phases and without professional support (Moos, 2012; Timpson, Eckley, Sumnall, Pendlebury, & Hay, 2016)). There is a range of descriptions that are used, and it can be argued that the deliberations about exactly what is recovery are unresolved and still being contested (White, 2014). Within governmental policy aspirations the emphasis is often on maintaining abstinence and making a positive contribution to society. In wider interpretations, it is about the rebuilding, creation and maintenance of lifestyles, rather than a preoccupation with levels of consumption and economic contributions. Many of the accounts of recovery suggest processes that involve reframing identities, developing connectedness, building futures, meaningfulness (or usefulness) and empowerment.

Crisis and loss often lead to grief and illness where the first port of call is a treatment intervention. These are frequently necessary but are best understood as the processes by which individuals gain stability to begin to rebuild or reclaim healthier lives. Some of this treatment is supported by direct peer-led contributions—for example Intuitive Recovery (Intuitive Recovery, 2018) and SMART Recovery (UK SMART Recovery, 2018). While 12-step programs such as these can exist within treatment systems, the most common such program is Alcoholics Anonymous and, as such, is a peer-to-peer support network that exists outside of funding and professional referral systems. Peer-to-peer support, without government funding or as a part of formal systems, can thus be considered community resilience (Tracy & Wallace, 2016).

While changes in consumption behavior and lifestyle support can be an extension of formal interventions, the sustainability of reliance and recovery lies in the increased spread of networks of supported action beyond core service delivery, usually predominantly run by communities of peers (Best et al., 2015). This provision of distinct interventions by service users and carers to their peers often extends beyond supporting alcohol and other drug-use change and into helping to maintain much wider lifestyle changes (Livingston, Baker, Atkins, & Jobber, 2011). Such groups provide vital support for people away from the formal structures of professional help, often occurring outside of normal offices and operating hours, including creative, physical and social activities, such as art, climbing, dance, drama, dry bars, football, leisure outings, meals, music, photography and walking. Thus, what often starts out as seeking out others as a part of a means of coping can rapidly translate itself into the support of others into developing whole, resilient lifestyles.

Resilient Well-being

It becomes clear through these examples that alcohol and drug use, its causes, consequences, notable loss and resilient responses are complex and situated in the social as much as the individual. For practitioners, this perspective encourages new ways of understanding and new interventions. One of these ways is to adopt a framework that utilizes concepts of well-being and which understands alcohol and other drug use as an interruption in well-being and retorts to it as actively encouraging well-being (Livingston & Thompson, 2016). Increasingly, well-being is being expressed in policy terms—for example, the Welsh Government's Social Services and Well-being Act 2014, where it is often equated with quality of life. This is a critical consideration. Drug and alcohol use have a history of framing and treatment responses that are predominantly medical and psychiatric, with essentially ill individuals who need curing. In this context, well-being is often seen as the opposite of illness or poor health. However, a broader adoption of well-being recognizes the role of the environmental and social, including environmental (clean air/water); equality (access/income/rights); material (hunger); physical (longevity of life); satisfaction (existential); social (support) and spiritual (peace), in community, family individual and societal recovery (well-being). Drink and drug use can be responses to issues of environmental and social existence as they are to flawed psychological development. In considering resilience as response to loss across these domains invokes a sociological understanding consistent with such theorists as Bourdieu, Foucault, Habermas, Marx and Szasz.

This dialogue places an emphasis on the adoption of strength-based approaches and the capacity of individuals to achieve, rather than any incapacity. In this sense, achieving well-being is a far more useful consideration than treating illness. Rather than making individuals resilient in resisting alcohol and drug use or to the negative consequences of such use through behavioral interventions, perhaps practitioners should support them through enabling processes, focusing on developing more meaningful and sustainable lifestyles, concentrating on such things as activities, education, employment, families and social networks, to result in their being more resilient to life's challenges and less likely to seek coping through inappropriate self-medication of substances. Simply put, the supporting of well-being reduces the escapist use of substances.

Conclusion

Taking a sociological orientation to individuals' use of alcohol and drugs enables us to see that such activity is as much a response to difficult life experiences as it is a cause of them. This position then invites us to explore what it is it about collective and societal positioning that enables and supports people to make positive lifestyle changes. Resilience, just like alcohol and drug use, can thus be seen as being developed through, and supported by, cultural, familial, peer and social systems.

References

Alexander, B. (2010). *The globalisation of addiction: A study in poverty of the spirit.* Oxford: Oxford University Press.

Best, D., McKitterick, T., Beswick, T. and Savic, M. (2015). Recovery capital and social networks among people in treatment and among those in recovery in York, England. *Alcoholism Treatment Quarterly*, 33(3), pp. 270–82.

Copello, A., Orford, J., Hogson. R. and Tober, G. (2009). *Social behaviour and network therapy for alcohol problems.* London: Routledge.

Copello, A. and Templeton, L. (2012). *The forgotten carers: Support for adult family members affected by a relative's drug problems.* London: UKDPC.

Gossop, M. (2013). *Living with drugs.* (7th Edn.) Farnham, UK: Ashgate.

Intuitive Recovery (2018). Retrieved from www.intuitivethinkingskills.co.uk/intuitive-recovery

Lee-Coy, A. (2010). *From death do I part—How I freed myself from addiction.* Three in the Morning Press [ISBN-13: 978–0692009710]

Livingston, W. (2017). Death, grief and bereavement: Relationships with alcohol and other drug use. In N. Thompson and G. R. Cox (Eds.), *Handbook of the sociology of death, grief and bereavement: A guide to theory and practice.* New York: Routledge, pp. 224–36.

Livingston, W. (2019). Alcohol and drug use: From dual diagnosis to well-being. In A. W. Choeng Poen and R. Ow (Eds.), *Social work and mental health.* New York: Springer.

Livingston, W., Baker, M., Atkins, B. and Jobber, S. (2011). A tale of the spontaneous emergence of a recovery group and the characteristics that are making it thrive: Exploring the politics and knowledge of recovery. *Journal of Groups in Addiction and Recovery*, 6(1), pp. 176–96.

Livingston, W. and Thompson, N. (2016). Promoting well-being: Crisis, loss and alcohol. *Illness, Crisis & Loss.* Retrieved from https://doi.org/10.1177/1054137316668640.

Moos, R. (2012). Theory-based active ingredients of effective treatments for substance use disorders. *Drug and Alcohol Dependence*, 88, pp. 109–21.

Robins, L. N. (1993). Vietnam veterans' rapid recovery from heroin addiction; a fluke or a normal expectation? *Addiction*, 88, pp. 1041–54.

Standing, O., Dickie, J. and Templeton, L. (2019). Developing peer support for adults bereaved through substance use. *Illness, Crisis and Loss*, 27(1), pp. 36–50.

Timpson, H., Eckley, L., Sumnall, H., Pendlebury, M. and Hay, G. (2016). Once you've been there, you're always recovering: Exploring experiences, outcomes, and benefits of substance misuse recovery. *Drugs and Alcohol Today*, 16(1), pp. 29–38.

Tracy, K. and Wallace, S. P. (2016). Benefits of peer support groups in the treatment of addiction. *Substance Abuse and Rehabilitation*, 7, pp. 143–54.

UK SMART Recovery (2018). Retrieved from www.smartrecovery.org.uk/.

Valentine, G., Jayne, M., Gould, M. and Keenan, J. (2010). *Family life, alcohol and consumption: A study of the transmission of drinking practices.* York, UK: Joseph Rowntree Foundation.

Various (2010) in A special supplement of *Drugs: Education, Prevention and Policy*, 17, Supplement 1 (on the work of the UK Alcohol, Drugs and the Family (ADF) collaborative research group).

White, W. L. (2014). *The boundaries of recovery.* Retrieved from www.williamwhitepapers.com/blog/2014/11/the-boundaries-of-recovery.html

10 The Spirit of Resilience Through the Prism of Homelessness
Avoiding Stigma and Labelization

Gerry Skelton

Introduction

I have been personally and professionally involved in the field of homelessness for over 50 years. When younger, I witnessed homelessness and encountered the "explanations" proffered by "well-meaning" people, predominantly focused on the "*person*"! These included highlighting an assumed lack of self-control (addiction, violence, budgetary skills, inability/capacity, irresponsibility) or "*choosing*" to be homeless. Disappointingly, I lacked the ability to see the pervasive pathological approach—namely, blaming the person for being homeless.

A cursory examination of the literature on homelessness would reveal a plethora of medical, psychiatric and psychological factors that apparently account for homelessness and which have their place in the lexicon of explanations. Nevertheless, I passionately believe this provides a myopic perspective, so I will focus on other factors that can account for homelessness and contribute to addressing it more holistically.

Reflective Exercise 1

Please place your personal keys in front of you and consider which of these is the *most important* to you—and *why*.

Homelessness

Homelessness is not a homogenous experience, with a single causal factor, but results from a complex interplay between the personal and the social, with the latter often relegated in favor of a more pathological perspective. Various complicating social factors (including affordability, depleted resources, impoverishment) all contribute to barriers people face in securing accommodation and averting homelessness.

Homelessness can happen to anyone and is a growing world problem (Roche, 2015; Skelton, 2017; Fry, Langley, & Shelton, 2017). History is festooned with narratives of homelessness caused by racism, sexism, greed, terrorism, slavery, famine, holocaust (American Indians, Aborigines, Arabs, Jews, Africans, Irish!). Nonetheless, while homelessness can "knock" unexpectedly, many consider themselves invulnerable (due to relative affluence, arrogance, security and so on) to its insidious threat and consequences.

For example, returning to Reflective Exercise 1, was *your* house key highly prized or taken for granted? Yet, homelessness is no respecter of social stratification systems (class, gender, age, color, belief, ethnicity).

Friends' Home-Lessness

Recently, a friend confided about his relationship breakup and prospect of homelessness, despite his good job and comfortable lifestyle. It was something of an abrupt realization for him, and, weeks later, he shared that, despite supporting my homelessness campaigns, its reality and consequences had never impacted at more than a cerebral level.

Conversely, another friend with a history of homelessness (which many attributed to her personality and life choices) faces homelessness, as the landlord abruptly sold the house. The fact that one is relatively "well off" and the other a "welfare recipient" obviously draws attendant, unfair judgments. Critics know little of the child abuse this friend suffered, while the former experienced a loving and more fortunate upbringing.

These personalized examples encapsulate how homelessness can simply erupt into someone's life, without warning or choice. It is also illustrative of several social factors that can give rise to homelessness, that have to be endured during it and that can help one out of it.

While readily conceding that personal choices can contribute to avoidable homelessness, I recognize the importance of giving weight to both the wider social contextual realities that can lead to unanticipated homelessness and, once in that situation, the accompanying factors that can lead to bettering or worsening the person's circumstances.

People are often quite scathing of those who are homeless, habitually describing them in pejorative terms, such as "the homeless," "homeless man/ woman." This is indicative of what Skelton (2017) calls "labelization," namely the social process whereby people and their plight are distanced.

Having facilitated a plethora of events addressing homelessness, I have encountered ample evidence of the various stereotypes, stigma and associated taboo that results. Indeed, both friends were sensitive to the potential censorious reactions of family, friends and colleagues, should news of their situation emerge. But, the former had more than adequate resources to meet this challenge and was soon living in a new, comfortable place of choice. My other friend is awaiting the vagaries of public sector allocation and remains distraught.

Reflective Exercise 2

How would *you* find a way out of being homeless?

1. *Where* would you turn to?
2. *Who* would you turn to?
3. *Who* would turn towards / away from you?

I distinguish between coping and managing: the former is the immediate, often instinctive reaction we will inevitably have. The factors that will help or hinder are closely related. How we address our vulnerability to face adversity and galvanize personal and collective resilience is central to well-being.

Loss is a recurring theme in this book, and *home-lessness* brings its share of it, for instance, the loss of one's home (leaving care, bereavement, illness, disability, aging, inability to manage, family breakup, adverse childhood experiences); loss of community (intimidation, sectarianism, racism); or the necessity to flee one's country (seeking asylum). These loss experiences traumatically challenge the very core of our being, identity, belief system, and our faith in self and humanity.

We need to practically and conceptually reconsider how we understand resilience and its social application, in an effort to blame less and empower more. The widely accepted deficit model within resilience theory is counterproductive and simply reinforces much of the associated labelization (Skelton, 2017) and marginalization (Thomas, Gray, & McGinty, 2012) visited upon those who become homeless. This is readily apparent in much of the lazy and sensationalist journalistic headlines, in contrast to sensitive and dignified reporting.

Adopting a sociological prism helps to see homelessness, vulnerability, adversity, loss—and resilience—as being dependent upon personal and social foundations that are often framed as mutually exclusive. Having acknowledged personal failings can lead some towards "the spectre of homelessness" (Skelton, 2017), I wish to draw more obvious attention to social factors that play a significant contributory role.

Unquestionably, having a home is a basic human need and right (FEANTSA, 2013) and is enshrined in most countries' legislative and aspirational exhortations (for example, United Nations' and European Union's declarations of human rights). Yet, a major social reality is the presence and pressure of poverty (FEANTSA, 2013; Fry et al., 2017: Van Breda, 2018) and associated structural disadvantages (Freire, 1970; Bramley & Fitzpatrick, 2017).

Therefore, I contend that the scale and persistent (often co-occurring) social problems (including poverty, inequality, injustice) are not simply accounted for by personal failings but are indicative of the social structures and state they exist within (Freire, 1970; Roche, 2015). Homelessness can result from any of these, leaving people at the mercy of political, social and economic policies that impact the impoverished in terms of freedom. For example, many are priced out of the rental/housing market, due to the Marxian "vampire-like" excesses and volatility of capitalism. This is compounded by often insecure/low employment ("zero-hours" contracts!), job losses; limited tenant rights, increasingly expensive rents/property, low security of tenure, poor quality/unsafe accommodation, shorter rental periods, and an implicit threat that those on benefits need not apply for private rented accommodation! This is then further complicated by political upheaval, including dysfunctional governments.

Additionally, within an *apparently* post-austerity climate, it is obvious that a rapid rise in many countries' inflation, interest rates (coupled with a slow-down in public investment or government support for social housing/homeless provision), welfare reform and cuts to benefits (Fitzpatrick, Pawson, Bramley, Wilcox, & Watts, 2016; Crisis, 2018) will result in a tsunami of homelessness. It is a universal truism that many cannot afford to rent/purchase good housing, especially welfare recipients.

Paradoxically, the state is (albeit imperfectly) cognizant of the rising political, social, economic costs and impact of unaddressed homelessness. This is despite previous governments' policy encouraging home ownership that inevitably led to a 20th-century housing "boom and bust" in many countries, with effects still currently being felt. These include "negative equity" and a shortage of social housing further pressurizing the public purse.

It is important to remember people can struggle to cope or manage alone, and need support. Increasingly loneliness is recognized as a concern for many, culminating in the UK Government appointing the first Minister for Loneliness (2018), because it is a potential public health epidemic (Royal College of General Practitioners, 2018). Needing to feel connected and belonging is not a psychological failing but often an individual and community need; and many of us know the tremendous value of help that prevented escalation. Arguably, the 21st century western world is characterized by an existential search for meaning and purpose in "an age of endemic uncertainty" (Bauman, 2006). This can be exacerbated by homelessness, potentially decreasing people's confidence and opportunities and increasing fear, distress, loneliness, isolation.

Thus, understanding resilience as a personal quality is restrictive. Rather, it is a capacity and resource (Benard, 2004; Van Breda, 2018) built up within the person through successfully negotiating life challenges and fostered within a supportive community: and it can be learned. This is not to deny that many found courage to build their resilience from impoverished resources, having been let down by an uncaring or abusive family, community, country. Nevertheless, it is incumbent upon decent societies to value their citizenry sufficiently by providing a more compassionate infrastructure and, in terms of rights to protection, housing, education, employment and so on.

I also wish to highlight the socializing narratives many are exposed to about homelessness. There are structural, cultural and institutional factors that readily contribute to, or result in, homelessness. For example, there is an underlying social exclusion narrative apparent in citizens and communities, families and friends, practitioners, educators and researchers, government and services.

Social exclusion is obviously inimical to well-being and undoubtedly feeds an internalizing inferiority and dysfunctional narrative. For many, their upbringing may well have been "challenging" (through no fault of theirs), which weakened the usual family and community ties that help anchor our sense of self, undermining our aspirations for our anticipated pathways.

Another socializing narrative is labelization (Skelton, 2017), predicated upon a pathological approach that serves to blame people for presumed irresponsibility and being homeless (Thomas et al., 2012; Roche, 2015). Moreover, homelessness can result from famine, wars, drought, natural disasters, displacement, increased national debt, market crashes—all of which are rarely the responsibility of the citizen.

This serves to legitimize and sustain the given social order, with clear lines of demarcation between the powerful and those they wish to discourage, distance and disenfranchise as pariahs for fear of social contamination. In turn, this is facilitated through the application of familiar stereotyping and stigmatizing processes, further reinforcing social exclusion and feelings of diminished identity, self-confidence, worth and belonging.

Regrettably, an internalized oppressive subculture can emerge, with those *labelled* readily accepting it and developing (arguably false) pride and resulting identity, camaraderie, belonging and "survivor identity" (Thomas et al., 2012; Roche, 2015). Indeed, some may apparently "choose" to become and remain homeless, however ill informed that choice may be.

While I would not wish homelessness on anyone, I appreciate many in, or emerging from, it who have demonstrated resilience (Wolin & Wolin, 1993; Fry et al., 2017) and developed it accordingly. This includes strengths (survival, self-reliance, resourcefulness, courage) that many commentators and researchers appear to overlook or underestimate in addressing homelessness. Furthermore, I am indebted to those currently or previously homeless who help my campaigning in an effort to make wider society more aware of people's plight and the need for understanding.

Finally, I wish to challenge a prevailing stereotypical orthodoxy that "street homelessness" is the dominant manifestation of homelessness. It is not. In reality, the vast majority of homelessness is "invisible," including those in care, shelters or "sofa surfing." Those on the streets generally represent a smaller, yet public, expression of homelessness (albeit some countries are worse than others).

Suggested Practice Implications and Recommendations

1. Establishing a *legal* requirement on all government apparatus to take homelessness seriously;
2. Addressing wider social systems, structures and processes that contribute to homelessness or fail to respond appropriately;
3. Inculcating a "duty *to* care" for eradicating blame-inducing, social-excluding and individualistic narratives/explanations and the associated implied criminalization;

4.   Increasing appropriately costed social and private rented housing, coupled with greater tenant protection;
5.   Addressing "hidden homelessness" groups (including care leavers; LGBTQ people);
6.   Practitioners adopting a more enabling strengths-based approach;
7.   Engaging those with homelessness experience in informing policy and practice;
8.   Committing to social justice rather than a "just us" basis for living and flourishing;
9.   Ensuring homelessness is not a personal/professional blind spot; and
10.   *Never* placing a label before a person.

Conclusion

People possess a sense of invincibility, but adversity can (re)visit anyone; and the experience of significant loss(es) reduces resilience. Therefore, insisting on an individualistic understanding discredits both the person and society, as people may be home-less but not hope-less. Truthfully, timely concern and intervention can meaningfully address homelessness.

Optimistically, what about imbuing current neoliberal policies and reinforcing blaming rhetoric for social inequalities and disadvantage, with a reminder of our shared humanity and need for kindness? Let's challenge the power of capitalism's resilience and unjust pillars by advocating "resilient architecture," providing an infrastructure (health, housing, education, employment, resources, well-funded services, social supports, speedy intervention for those on the margins) that enables people to live well, feel connected and flourish (RCGP, 2018; Van Breda, 2018). These preventative measures could be complemented by encouraging a view of resilience as something everyone can learn and draw upon.

Whatever approach we adopt, it has to be holistic and based on helping, not hindering, people, while appreciating that resilience is a protective factor in which personal and underlying social issues overlap. It's also a tremendous resource to access and deploy as a bulwark against or response to adversity, including homelessness.

None of my observations are intended to eradicate individual responsibility, self-agency and a spirit of resilience, coupled with collective responsibility for citizens to contribute meaningfully to society. Rather, they are to encourage these. And I am mindful that, with the help of the state and community, many of us facing adversity do not end up homeless; and that is in itself a significant resilient outcome.

References

Bauman, Z. (2006). *Liquid times: Living in an age of uncertainty.* Cambridge, UK: Polity Press.
Benard, B. (2004). *Resilience: What have we learned?* San Francisco, CA: WestEd.

Bramley, G. and Fitzpatrick, S. (2017). Homelessness in the UK: Who is most at risk? *Housing Studies*, 33(1), pp. 96–116.

Crisis (2018). *Homelessness and the impact of Brexit: Tackling the challenges and grasping the opportunities*. London: Crisis.

FEANTSA (The European Federation of National Organizations working with the homeless) (2013). *Homelessness in Europe: Better than cure? The role of homelessness prevention*. Brussels: FEANTSA.

Fitzpatrick, S., Pawson, H., Bramley, G., Wilcox, S. and Watts, B. (2016). *The Homelessness Monitor: Northern Ireland 2016*. London: Crisis.

Freire, P. (1970). *Pedagogy of the oppressed*. New York: Continuum.

Fry, C., Langley, K. and Shelton, K. (2017). A systematic review of cognitive functioning among young people who have experienced homelessness, foster care or poverty. *Journal of Child Neuropsychology*, 23(8), pp. 907–34.

Roche, S. (2015). The salvaging of identities of homeless men: Reflections for social work. *Journal of Australian Social Work*, 68(2), pp. 228–43.

Royal College of General Practitioners (2018). *Tackling loneliness: A community action plan*. London: Royal College of General Practitioners.

Skelton, G. (2017). *Giving homelessness a home in social work education, training and practice*. Belfast: Simon Community.

Thomas, Y., Gray, M. and McGinty, S. (2012). An exploration of subjective wellbeing among people experiencing homelessness: A strengths-based approach. *Social Work in Health Care*, 51(9), pp. 780–97.

Van Breda, A. (2018). A critical review of resilience theory and its relevance for social work. *Social work (Stellenbosch. Online)*, 54, pp. 1–18.

Wolin, S. and Wolin, S. (1993). *The resilient self: How survivors of troubled families rise above adversity*. New York: Villard.

11 Resilience and Poverty

Signe Dobelniece

Poverty has been a widespread phenomenon at all times; however, its manifestations and dimensions are different. Also, in the comparatively developed and prosperous European Union countries, more than 112 million or about one in four people are at risk of poverty or social exclusion (EUROSTAT, 2018). According to the definition accepted in the EU, "a person or a household is considered to be poor when their income and resources are worse than what is thought to be adequate or socially acceptable in the society in which they live" (Council of Europe, 2017). Poor people's basic rights are restricted or denied; these people cannot fully participate in their society's economic, social and cultural activities. Living in poverty means isolation, lack of information, restricted access to services, residence in an unsafe neighborhood, inability to afford essential things, exclusion and powerlessness. Reducing poverty and social exclusion is one of the priority objectives of both the EU strategy, *Europe 2020*, and the national development plans. Still, as stated by the Social Protection Committee: "Partly due to the effects of the crisis, the EU continues to be far off-track in reaching the Europe 2020 poverty and social exclusion target, even when the most recent and more encouraging data is taken into account" (Social Protection Committee, 2017, p. 26)—that is, the recent crisis has led to an increase in poverty and still affects the fight against it.

Economic Crisis

In order to understand resilience in relation to poverty, fundamental prerequisites are (i) a change in external conditions that have led to an undesirable situation, and exit from it; and (ii) a recognition that resilience is the ability to recover quickly from change (Kripke, 2012). The 2009–2011 economic crisis affecting several EU countries, especially Latvia, is an example of this.

Resilience can be interpreted in different ways: it can be a situational adaptation, adjusting to conditions and surviving in the current circumstances with limited resources, using different coping strategies, or it can also be a change of situation, a way out of poverty. This approach is brought up by Hall and Lamont (2013), framing resilience "as the achievement of well-being

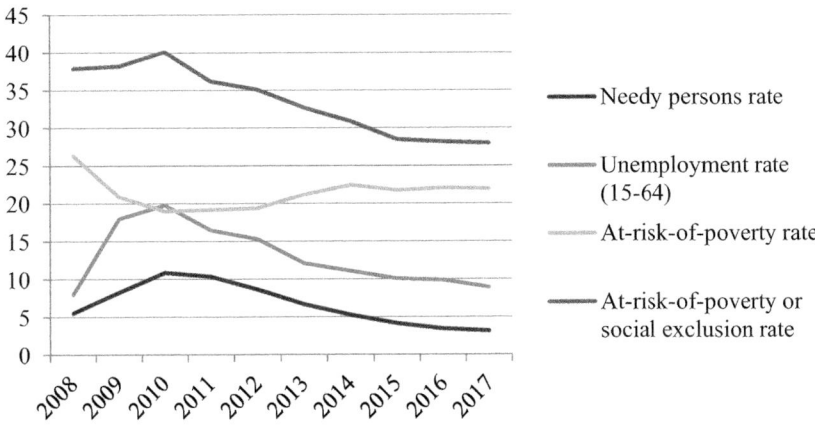

Figure 11.1 The rate of needy persons,[1] unemployment, at-risk-of-poverty and at-risk-of-poverty or social exclusion in Latvia 2008–2017 (%)

Source: LM Sociālās politikas rādītāji. http://lm.gov.lv/lv/publikacijas-petijumi-un-statistika/statistika

even when that entails significant modifications to behavior or to the social frameworks that structure and give meaning to behavior" (p. 25). Positive results can be achieved both in new, changed circumstances, as well as by deploying new resources and means not previously used.

The crisis had a significant impact on the economic situation of the population: the unemployment rate increased, income level decreased, the number of needy people doubled, the number of people at risk of poverty and social exclusion increased, but the at-risk-of-poverty rate decreased (Figure 11.1). The latter is, however, related to the methodology of calculation, not to an improvement in the material situation of the population. According to the survey, 80% of respondents admit that the crisis has affected their lives (Kruks, 2016). People were not prepared for such significant changes, and many of them ended up in poverty.

Both micro-level (individual and family) and macro-level (government) issues were brought up on how to reduce the unwanted effects of the crisis and survive in the current situation, with many people facing poverty or being at risk of it.

Coping Strategies/Methods

Many researchers have focused on the strategies and methods used by people to respond to poverty (for an overview, see Gojová & Lindowská, 2014) and have discovered a great variety of them; they differ in the level, mode and type (active/passive, formal/informal and so on) of implementation.

Resilience at the macro level can take the form of preventing and reducing the risks (macro-economic stabilization, crisis prevention, and so on); limiting damage potential when risks occur (activating and information measures); providing direct help and compensation when damage occurs (social insurance and social assistance) (Sattelberger, 2016).

When overcoming the effects of the crisis and addressing the problem of poverty at the macro level in Latvia, the Government took borrowings from international lenders—the IMF, the European Community and the World Bank; an austerity strategy, being rather unpopular among the population, was implemented—fiscal consolidation, structural reform and support for the financial system. Budget consolidation came together with employment reduction by 22% in budget institutions, 25% cuts in public sector wages, tax rises and new taxes, and an increase in retirement age. Although there was growing necessity for social support, social benefits and allowances were revised and reduced; "ceilings" for many of them were introduced. These measures worsened the micro-level situation (Dobelniece & Lace, 2012). In addition, as support for the most deprived persons the Social Security Strategy 2009–2011 was implemented; it included the state co-financing of guaranteed minimum income benefit and housing benefit (regularly paid by municipalities); work practice in local municipalities to support long-term unemployed persons; several activities in healthcare; and transportation services in the education system. However, for a number of reasons, the support was insufficient; it neither improved the welfare of the population nor significantly affected the level of poverty. Although these government-level solutions have improved the macroeconomic situation in the long run, and the government has described them as a success story for Latvia, other opinions exist. According to the data of the research company SKDS, more than a half of Latvia's population believes that the strategy for overcoming the crisis has been wrong and very devastating. The implemented measures reduced the material welfare and social protection of the population, particularly affecting risk groups, including poor people. "The financial woes have been successfully resolved, but economic, social and political challenges remain. The negative results of the crisis are continuing to affect the fabric of social and political life in Latvia" (Austers, 2014, p. 23). However, it must be admitted that, although painfully achieved, there are positive trends in the long term. The number of municipality social assistance recipients dropped by almost half (more than 300,000 recipients in 2008–2011, about 146,000 in 2017); also, the resources spent for this purpose have fallen by almost half; the needy persons rate is three times less than in 2010–2011; and the at-risk-of-poverty or social exclusion rate decreased from about 40% in 2010 to 28% in 2016 (LM Gada dati, 2018; LM Sociālās politikas rādītāji, 2018).

At the micro level, the activities carried out by the government led to mistrust of politicians, government and the social security system, increasing the gap between the ruling elite and the population. If you cannot rely on the system, you have to rely on yourself, your family, informal ties, as well as use your individual coping strategies.

Micro-level resilience and individual coping strategies have been the focus of many studies. Czech researchers Gojová and Lindowská, analyzing the works of several authors, have detected 31 possible ways of coping with poverty and grouped them within three basic umbrella categories, with 11 subcategories:(i) distinction (avoidance, discrediting of others, "the deserving poor"); (ii) adaptation (passive, positive and situation instrumentalization); (iii) defense (escape from reality, complete submission, intentional exclusion, "let's do something about it," release) (Gojová, Lindowská, 2014). Differences in strategies stem from the differences in the behavior of individuals, which are determined by acceptance or denial of their status, as well as by the time spent in poverty, the depth and severity of poverty, the environment, the availability and possibilities of using resources, as well as by individual characteristics. Some researchers distinguish between active coping (searching for supplementary means of existence), the opposite of active—not loudly expressed, "passive" coping (including debts, informal redistribution and so on)—and social assistance (Gassmann & de Neubourg, 2000). Others focus more on formal and informal strategies (Trapenciere, Rungule, Pranka, Lāce, & Dudwick, 2000). However, most frequently the emphasis is put on what coping strategies are generally used by people, as well as on their descriptive analysis.

World Bank researchers Lokshin and Yemtsov (2001), in their study of coping with poverty in Russia, mention 16 possible activities, focusing mostly on changes in consumption patterns and decreased expenditures on food, help from relatives and friends, cohabitation as a response to economic hardship, and government help. The latter is the least popular, as used by less than five percent of respondents.

Research shows that poor people are creative. To secure themselves, they use a variety of methods—legal, semi-legal or illegal. In addition to those mentioned above, most common strategies are casual work, additional work, work in the zone of the "gray economy" and not paying taxes, smaller or larger theft, rendering sexual services, sale or pledge of property, debts and postponing of obligatory payments, savings, abstention from purchases, a subsistence economy, use of social networks and informal support, mutual assistance and so on. People also apply for formal social assistance (Trapenciere, et al., 2000; Gassmann & de Neubourg, 2000; Lokshin & Yemtsov, 2001; Grushetsky & Kharchenko, 2009).

The main coping strategies at the individual level during the crisis were related to the decrease in consumption, the "shadow economy" and emigration (Dobelniece & Lace, 2012; Austers, 2014; Kruks, 2016). Formal support systems—social insurance and social assistance—also played an important role. However, these do not exclude the use of other above-mentioned strategies.

Influencing Factors

The economic crisis directly or indirectly affected all members of society, but its impact was not the same for everyone. There were differences even among those who were severely affected and were facing poverty at that time—some were more successful and were able to escape, but not everybody could do it. In this context, the question arises: what determines which individuals or groups have resilience, and what factors influence it?

Generally speaking, resilience is influenced by social (structural) and individual factors. Structural factors (the economic and political situation, the social environment) can be considered as background factors, but individual factors could be the direct determinants of resilience.

The level of resilience differs among individuals. As stated by Promberger (2017), resilience is generally a rare phenomenon, especially in households living at low income and risk of poverty. The author considers that these are in principle non-resilient situations, and just a few might escape by their own means. Therefore, support is necessary to promote and develop resilience, and the author relates it to the social policy in the following ways: (i) keeping up the welfare state in the narrow sense of transfer incomes and job-uptake support, (ii) taking care of common goods, (iii) supporting practical knowledge and culture, (iv) supporting network and community building.

Resilience is influenced also by "positive personality traits and dispositions; family protective and recovery factors; and community strengths" (Seccombe, 2002, p. 384). An important role is played by the culture that affects the choice of coping strategies that an individual utilizes in any given situation and provides different institutional mechanisms by which an individual can cope (Aldwin, 2004). This is evidenced by the different responses of the Latvian and Greek people to the austerity measures introduced. In Latvia, though reluctantly, people were comparatively submissive, "tightened their belts," started looking for solutions to everyday problems; basically, they went on hoping for a better future. When the Greek people faced similar demands from the international lenders for budget consolidation and reforms that would inevitably lower their standards of living, loud protests, strikes and demonstrations followed.

Resilience can also differ between those who have experienced poverty for a long time and those who have not had such an experience before. For instance, as described by the author of the culture of poverty theory, Lewis (1962), those who embody the culture of poverty can perceive life in poverty as a norm; in the process of socialization, they have adapted to the situation and learned how to survive with few resources. They do not express resilience. However, individuals who suddenly face poverty can look for different ways to get out of it. The longer the contact with an undesirable situation, the lower the probability of resilience.

The research also shows that some demographic groups have greater ability to overcome difficulties. These are the working-age population, not exceeding or just about to exceed the threshold of 30, with the highest level of education and comparatively higher income (Kruks, 2016). Also, human capital plays a significant role in resilience: the higher its level, the more likely individuals choose active coping methods (Lokshin & Yemtsov, 2001), thus facilitating escape from poverty.

Conclusion

Poverty is a complex, multidimensional phenomenon that has a negative impact on many spheres of life. Dealing with it is complicated and requires a complex approach.

Resilience in the context of poverty can manifest itself differently: adaptation to the situation of poverty or escaping it; change in individuals or social conditions and environment. Resilience is related to micro- and macro-level activities—the readiness of individuals and groups to change, the coping strategies used; and measures taken by the government for prevention of risks, response to and elimination of harmful conditions and direct support to those who are exposed to suffering.

Resilience to poverty is influenced by culture, social policy, social capital and support systems, human capital and also such individual factors as social-demographic characteristics, economic status and others.

Note

1. According to *Cabinet Regulation No. 299* (Adopted March 30, 2010) the family (person) shall be recognized as needy if its average monthly income during the last three months per each member of the family does not exceed EUR 128.06 and if it does not own savings of monetary funds or property.

References

Aldwin, C. M. (2004). Culture, coping and resilience to stress. Retrieved from www. researchgate.net/publication/241639325_Culture_Coping_and_Resilience_to_ Stress.

Austers, A. (2014). How great is Latvia's success story? The economic, social and political consequences of the recent financial crisis in Latvia. Friedrich-Ebert-Stiftung. Retrieved from www.fes-baltic.lv.

Council of Europe (2017). *Poverty*. Retrieved from www.coe.int/en/web/compass/ poverty.

Dobelniece, S. and Lace, T. (2012). Global economic crisis in Latvia: Social policy and individuals' responses. *Filosofija. Sociologija*, 23(2), pp. 111–18.

EUROSTAT (2018). People at risk of poverty or social exclusion. Retrieved from https://ec.europa.eu/eurostat/tgm/refreshTableAction.do?tab=table&plugin=1&pco de=t2020_50&language=en.

Gassmann, F. and de Neubourg, C. (2000). *Coping with little means in Latvia*. Riga: Ministry of Welfare of the Republic of Latvia and United Nations Development Programme, p. 90.

Gojová, A. and Lindowská, E. (2014). Coping with poverty and the risk of poverty. In A. Gojová, V. Gojová and M. Špiláčková (Eds.), *On the ways of coping with poverty from the perspective of families—Incentives for social work*. Ostrava, Czech Republic: University of Ostrava, pp. 31–41.

Grushetsky, A. and Kharchenko, N. (2009). Poverty, gender and coping strategies in Ukraine. In S. Mannila and S. Vesikansa (Eds.), *Social problems and policies in Central and Eastern European countries*. Helsinki: National Institute for Health and Welfare, Report 42, pp. 64–77. Retrieved from www.kiis.com.ua/materials/articles/ Poverty,%20Gender%20and%20coping%20strategies%20in%20Ukraine.pdf.

Hall, P. A. and Lamont, M. (2013). *Social resilience in the Neo-Liberal era*. New York: Cambridge University Press. Retrieved from https://scholar.harvard.edu/hall/ publications/introduction-social-resilience-neoliberal-era.

Kripke, G. (2012). *Resilience: What it means and what it doesn't*. Retrieved from https://politicsofpoverty.oxfamamerica.org/2012/06/resilience-what-it-means-and-what-it-doesnt/.

Kruks, S. (Ed.) (2016). *Ekonomiskākrīze Latvijā: veiksmesstāstapēcgarša*. Riga: Riga Stradins University.

Lewis, O. (1962). *Five families: Mexican case studies in the culture of poverty*. New York: Science Editions.

LM Gada dati (2018). Retrieved from www.lm.gov.lv/lv/publikacijas-petijumi-un-statistika/statistika/valsts-statistika-socialo-pakalpojumu-un-socialas-palidzibas-joma/gada-dati.

LM Sociālās politikas rādītāji (2018). Retrieved from http://lm.gov.lv/lv/publikacijas-petijumi-un-statistika/statistika.

Lokshin, M. M. and Yemtsov, R. (2001). Household strategies for coping with poverty and social exclusion in post-crisis Russia. *Policy Research Working Paper Series 2556*, The World Bank.

Promberger, M. (2017). *Resilience among vulnerable households in Europe. Questions, concept, findings and implications*. Institute for Employment Research (IAB). Retrieved from http://doku.iab.de/discussionpapers/2017/dp1217.pdf.

Sattelberger, J. (2016). What links poverty, vulnerability and resilience? KfW Development Research, No 27.

Seccombe, K. (2002). "Beating the odds" versus "changing the odds": Poverty, resilience, and family policy. *Journal of Marriage and Family*, 64(2), pp. 384–94.

Social Protection Committee (2017). *Annual report 2017. Review of the social protection performance monitor and developments in social protection policies*. Retrieved from http://lm.gov.lv/upload/sociala_ieklausana/a/spc_annual_report2017.pdf.

Trapenciere, I., Rungule, R., Pranka, M., Lāce, T. and Dudwick, N. (2000). *Listening to the poor—Social assessment of poverty in Latvia*. Riga: Ministry of Welfare of the Republic of Latvia and United Nations Development Programme, p. 146.

12 Resilience in the Alice Springs Town Camps

Shirleen Campbell, Maree Corbo and Ronnie Egan

The Northern Territory has the highest rate of domestic violence in Australia. Aboriginal women are particularly vulnerable to domestic violence and are in fact 45 times more likely to experience domestic violence than non-Aboriginal women. Aboriginal women are 35 times more likely to be hospitalized due to family violence than non-Aboriginal women.

Territory Families, 2019

These figures are shocking and, however one wishes to interpret them, one cannot ignore the widespread grief and ongoing communal vulnerability left in their wake. This chapter's authors want to highlight something that may escape immediate attention in these same figures—the emergence and growth of a determination within these communities to draw a line in the sand, to say "enough." This chapter examines the experience of the Tangentyere Women's Family Safety Group as an example of both individual and community resilience. It highlights the history, outcomes and implications for practice. The chapter identifies the links between the development of resilience through experiences of loss and grief and how this community has transcended vulnerability to create social change. It analyzes the importance of going beyond individual psychological understandings to include social and cultural perspectives to enhance our understanding of what resilience means in practice. The chapter draws on the definitions of resilience throughout the book but pays particular attention to these cultural dimensions.

In response to the loss and grief experienced from specific domestic murders on the Alice Springs Town Camps (Inquest, 2016), the female Indigenous Alice Springs Town Camp residents began to demand a voice on family and domestic violence prevention and early intervention issues. This led to the development of the Tangentyere Women's Family Safety Group (TWFSG), and from this a development of activities and services. The TWFSG are leaders of the Town Camps communities. Their knowledge of, and experiences in, relationships, connections, language and culture make them the experts on Town Camp issues. Struggling to overcome communal and personal vulnerability, drawing upon personal and cultural strengths, the women channeled their grief to develop a sense of purpose guided by an awareness of their obligation not only to themselves but also to the wider Town Camp community. Much has been written regarding the multiple sources of grief for Australia's Aboriginal and Torres Strait Islander peoples in terms of loss of land, kinship ties, way of life and the profound impact this has on social and emotional well-being (Swan & Raphael, 1995; Merritt, 2007; Commonwealth of Australia, 2008; McGrath, Fox-Young, & Phillips, 2008; Purdie, Dudgeon, & Walker, 2010). However, programs developed by Aboriginal people for Aboriginal people are likely to be most effective (Raphael & Delaney, 2011). This is evident in the experience of the TWFSG. Growth and transformation offered by the circumstances of the Family Violence crisis transformed how family violence is now understood in the Town Camps. While there is no unified view about resilience in Indigenous communities, there seems to be a common link between Aboriginal identity, land, history and resilience (http://akneahr.ciet.org/publications/resilience).

As mentioned above, the core members of the TWFSG Governance Group are the experts of Town Camp history and of the relationships within and between them. Critically, no group of individuals is in a better position to make judgments between the best and worst of practice provided to, or imposed upon, the Town Camp communities as these relate to family safety. Their lived experience of family violence has forged a determination to find long-term, systemic solutions to this problem. They are committed to the program because of their commitment to their families and communities (www.tangfamilyviolenceprevention.com.au). The TWSFG has both older and younger women members, and this has been a deliberate strategy to encourage the mentorship of younger women by their older women colleagues to ensure sustainability of the group.

The TWSFG is auspiced by Tangentyere Council, which began operating in the early 1970s and was established to assist Aboriginal people to gain some form of legal tenure of the land they were living on in order to obtain essential services and housing. The resistance evident in the political history and struggle of Tangentyere Council speaks resilience and determination. Through a long-term fight with local, Territory and national governments there are now 16 Town Camps on special purpose leases, offering security of tenure. There are approximately 1600–2000 Town Camp residents, plus many visitors from remote communities (Tangentyere Research Hub, 2005). The overall population increases during football tournaments and other special events. Each Town Camp comprises a largely distinct Aboriginal community based on language and kinship groups. Other Town Camps have residents belonging to other language groups, whose traditional lands are further out of Alice Springs but who have moved to Alice Springs over a period of time for various reasons. Town Camps residents often have strong links with remote communities, and there is substantial mobility between bush and town (www.tangentyere.org.au/about/). It is the history and cultural trust developed between the Council and the Town Campers that has enabled the development of the TWFSG. There is a cultural safety, not evident in mainstream services, that has facilitated the communities to take into their own hands the challenge and meaning of family violence in the Town Camps and create change.

Thompson (2018) makes the existential point that social interactions rest upon meaning and that meaning arises from social sources. We see this with TWFSG and family violence, of how the women make sense of the tragedy by picking up the gauntlet and fighting to transcend the constraints of their personal and communal vulnerability. Thompson (2018) suggests that the meanings applied to the world lead to moral understandings of right and wrong, and this is evidenced in how TWFSG have powerfully influenced a better understanding and conversation about family violence in the Town Camps. The hurt and pain experienced by the women that have been caused by family violence could not be ignored. Their experience told them that withdrawal and self-blame were self-defeating. Rather, they became pivotal in opening up conversations about family and domestic violence, which in the past has been challenging or shameful to discuss within communities. Previously the Northern Territory (NT) Government approach to family violence (Territory Families, 2019) was a government-led one. At that time the women wanted a grass roots response and culturally safe conversations that enabled them to take control. At the time of the coronial inquest outcome and recommendations, the value of social support among the TWFSG women was evident in bolstering the women's confidence and security that they were not alone and that other Camp women had a similar purpose, sense of direction, connectedness and hope. Individuals could easily have been overwhelmed by the situation, but coming together as a group generated a determination that strengthened their communal resistance. Their response to the oft uncontrollable chaos and loss of control, a situation that could easily have undermined communal resilience, has strengthened it.

Thompson's (2016) discussion of transcendence resonates with the work of the Town Camp women. They have responded to situations of devastating communal and familial loss through domestic murders and assaults, have risen above them in order to change their community's response to family violence. As if acknowledging Neimeyer (2001), the TWFSG have developed resilience through processes of "meaning making." Their sense of community and cultural safety brought them together in new ways. TWFSG is realistic that family violence has not stopped in the Town Camps and that bad things continue to happen. However, they now have a mechanism to mobilize when bad things occur. In response to the brutal stabbing of a Town Camp woman in 2017, TWFSG undertook the first women's Action March against Family and Domestic Violence, with over 300 people turning up in support. The protest, the first of its kind in Alice Springs, gained local, national and international media coverage. Their actions represent examples of hope and a determination, which comes directly from the women, to confront the issue. The following section details the TWFSG's actions of hope that represent the implications for practice.

We began this chapter referencing the high incidence of assaults, murders and hospital admissions suffered by aboriginal women through family violence. The factors leading to this are complex and include social, political and structural issues that arise from the impact of dispossession, discrimination and oppression and the social and cultural dislocation accompanying this. In relation to the TWFSG this impact has stimulated communal resilience. It has stirred the women to use their local knowledge and experience, a key element of which is their understanding of the cultural strengths of their communities, to lead and use a "ground-up" approach, thereby getting key messages out to their communities around the impact of family and domestic violence on women and children. Examples such as the development of the TWFSG highlight the cultural resilience standing up to adversity and finding strength in helping others resist the onslaught that has devastated so many others. As Cox and Thompson suggest in Chapter 1 of this volume, a fuller understanding of culture and its significance at various levels needs to be incorporated into our consideration of resilience and responses to adversity. It is in the strategies used by the TWFSG that the implications for practice are translated and the centrality of culture is evident.

This "daring to do" TWFSG response to family violence demonstrates resilience in action, and it is their emphasis on "ground-up" strategies that has implications for practice. Their approach to prevention and early intervention has been multilayered and their response has been publicly acknowledged in the various awards they have received, the most recent being the Northern Territory Government Human Rights Award for Northern Territory Fitzgerald Human Right Award for Social Change. This has also been accompanied by social action strategies, including in early 2018 the TWFSG leaders took their bipartisan message to Canberra to ask governments to "listen to us, support us and stand with us" when it comes to family and domestic violence prevention in Town Camp communities.

Training is another concrete example of this ground-up approach. Since 2014, sixteen women leaders and seven male leaders participated in six weeks of family and domestic violence training as well as participating in the Secretariat of National Aboriginal & Islander Child Care's "Through Young Black Eyes" program. The leaders receive ongoing family violence primary prevention training through our project, "Mums Can, Dads Can," and participated in eight weeks of training through the Australian Childhood Foundation in relation to the impact of violence and neglect on children. From May 2016, the Tangentyere Family Violence Prevention Training has been run on the Town Camps by the TWFSG and has now trained over 200 women in family violence prevention training. Demand has been increasing from Aboriginal women following each training that is delivered.

Resource development provides another example of the strategies that have been, and continue to be, developed by the TWFSG. With close consultation and participation by the community we have seen the production and merchandising of an animation film (*Stand Up*, 2016, Tangentyere Family Violence Prevention Program) that highlighted the impacts of family violence on women and their children and calling on men to "stand up" and end family violence. *Stand Up* and another mini-documentary film about the TWFSG Action March in 2016, called *Stories of Hope and Healing*, were part of the action research support for the "Building Safer Communities for Women" project. Other resources include the development of signs that are located at the entrance of each of the 16 Town Camps Communities which say, "The Town Camp Women of Alice Springs Say No To Violence"; the creation of posters, help cards, T-shirts and hats which have been distributed throughout the community of Alice Springs; and the development of a website, online training and social media presence for the Tangentyere Family Violence Prevention Program (www.tangfamilyviolenceprevention.com.au).

As indicated above, consultation and engagement have covered a variety of ongoing and one-off work. These include regular monthly meetings with Alice Springs Police (and previously with the NT Assistant Police Commissioner); regular meetings, consultations and engagement with NT and federal politicians and government officials; partnerships and good working relationships with other NGOs, such as Alice Springs Women's Shelter, Ngaanyatjarra Pitjantatjara Yankunytjatjara Women's Council, Central Australian Women's Legal Service; the attendance at the Round Table Forums on Family and Domestic Violence; and presentations to the Judicial Council of Australia, Australian of the Year, United Nations Special Rapporteur on Violence Against Women and Australian Human Rights Ambassadors for the United Nations.

The TWFSG provides an example of communal resilience in action, how it unfolds, how it links to their ability to resist and to develop. The group understands, more than most, the complexity of family violence, its capacity to overwhelm individuals and the impact of the loss of hope on community. However, it is the cultural connection with access to strong familial links, ceremony, language and the Tangentyere Council's history of resistance that provide protective factors where the group has a shared commitment and aim. The implications for practice are clear and support the proposition that our role is to assist the community in doing it for themselves and to resist the temptation to do it on their behalf.

References

Anisnabe Kekedndazazone Network Environment for Aboriginal Health Research (2019). *Building resilience in Aboriginal communities*. Retrieved from http://akneahr. ciet.org/publications/resilience/.

Commonwealth of Australia (2008). *Closing the gap on indigenous disadvantage: The challenge for Australia.* Retrieved from www.facs.gov.au/sa/indigenous/pubs/general/Documents/closing_the_gap/default.htm.

Inquest into the deaths of Wendy Murphy and Natalie McCormack (2016). NTLC 024: A0056/2014 and A0017/2015 (Coroners Court, Alice Springs September 21, 2016).

McGrath, P., Fox-Young, S. and Phillips, E. (2008). Insights on Aboriginal grief practices from the Northern Territory, Australia. *Australian Journal of Primary Health*, 14, pp. 48–57.

Merritt, S. (2007). An Aboriginal perspective on resilience: Resilience needs to be defined from an indigenous context. *Aboriginal and Islander Health Worker Journal*, 31, pp. 10–12.

Neimeyer, R. A. (Ed.) (2001). *Meaning reconstruction and the experience of loss.* Washington, DC: American Psychological Association.

Purdie, N., Dudgeon, P. and Walker, R. (Eds.) (2010). *Working together: Aboriginal and Torres Strait Islander mental health and wellbeing principles and practice.* Canberra: Office of Aboriginal and Torres Strait Islander Health, Department of Ageing.

Raphael, B. and Delaney, P. (2011). Loss and grief: "Closing the gap" for Aboriginal people. *Grief Matters: The Australian Journal of Grief and Bereavement*, 14(3, Summer), pp. 67–69.

Swan, P. and Raphael, B. (1995). *Ways forward: National consultancy report on aboriginal and torres strait islander mental health.* Canberra: Australian Government Publishing Service.

Tangentyere Council (2008). History of Tangentyere Council. Retrieved from www.tangentyere.org.au/about/

Tangentyere Family Violence Prevention Program (2019). Retrieved from www.tangfamilyviolenceprevention.com.au/

Tangentyere Research Hub (2005). *Populations and mobility study.* Alice Springs: Tangentyere Council.

Tangentyere Women's Family Safety Group (2017). *Women's Family Safety Group program plan 2017–2018.* Alice Springs: Tangentyere Council.

Territory Families (2019). *Domestic, family and sexual violence reduction strategy: Domestic, family and sexual violence reduction framework 2018–2028.* Darwin: Northern Territory Government. Retrieved from http://asws.org.au/info-andsupport/who-does-domestic-violenceaffect/ and https://territoryfamilies.nt.gov.au/domestic-violence/domestic-and-family-violence-reduction-strategy.

Thompson, N. (2016). *The authentic leader.* London: Palgrave.

Thompson, N. (2018). *Applied sociology.* New York: Routledge.

13 "It Takes a Lot of Energy"

Surviving Sexism

Tashel C. Bordere, Elizabeth A. Sharp and Celeste Medina

Sexism is a major source of cultural trauma and loss. Although boys and men experience sexism, cisgender women are overwhelmingly the targets of overt sexism and are faced with cumulative losses that accompany this form of oppression across their lifespan. Approximately 85% of women report experiencing their first harassment before age 17 and 11.6% of women report their first harassment before age 11 (Livingston, Grillo, & Paluch, 2015). An astounding 43.6% of all women will experience some form of contact with sexual violence in their lifetime (Basilel, Breiding, & Smith, 2016, p. 2).

Women live in a world characterized as uninviting, hostile and physically and psychologically unsafe (Pain, 1991). As one indicator of the breadth of sexism and associated losses in our current socio-historical context, social movements such as #MeToo and Time's Up have recently helped bring into public awareness the decades-old and insidious problem of sexual violence and sexual harassment. #MeToo posts—encouraging women to share their stories of sexual harassment and violence—were shared more than *12 million* times within the first 24 hours (Mendes, Ringrose, & Keller, 2018).

In this chapter, we address women's experiences with sexism, loss and survival as they navigate male-centered spaces and patriarchal contexts throughout development. Research and illustrations are utilized to delineate ways in which mental, physical, emotional and social resources are taxed both in everyday encounters with microaggressions and in efforts aimed at maximizing opportunities (for example, contacting legislators) and reducing losses (for example, cognitive resources).

Sexism in Context

Coined in 1965, sexism refers to prejudice, stereotyping or discrimination on the basis of sex (Shapiro, 1965). Sexual harassment and sexual violence are manifestations of sexism, and they exist on a continuum, with sexual violence, including sex trafficking, being at the most severe and traumatic end of the continuum and sexist language being at the other end. Sexism is built into the fabric of our culture (Johnson, 2005). It includes, but is not limited to, the following:

- sexist language ("mankind," "chairman," "freshman"; Kleinman, 2002);
- unequal pay;
- objectification of women in advertising and the media;
- sexist jokes;
- unfair distribution of household labor;
- unequal distribution of childcare;
- gender disparity in status and positions in the workplace;
- inequity in sports, including the amount of time and money focused on male-only sports;
- inequity in leadership at all levels and nearly all occupations;
- mansplaining;
- unequal hiring practices;
- sexual violence, gender and sexual harassment;
- unequal legal protection;
- men taking up more physical space than women; and
- protection of male sexual perpetrators in various institutions (religious institutions—Catholic Church and male clergy sexual assault perpetration).

Sexism goes beyond hurt feelings. Negative prejudiced beliefs about female youth and adults transcend into discriminatory behaviors that reduce opportunity structures and produce disparities and losses across the lifecourse (Bordere, 2017). This is particularly the case for underrepresented women with intersecting marginalized identities. Transwomen, especially transwomen of color, are highly likely to be targets of severe forms of sexism, including sexual violence and murder (Cantor et al., 2015). Transwomen of color disproportionately die by homicide by the time they reach middle adulthood or age 35 as a function of hate and discrimination. In 2018, 82% of transgender individuals who died due to violence were transwomen of color (Human Rights Campaign, 2018). An astounding 64% of those deceased by hate and violence were younger than 35 years of age.

Additionally, cisgender women of color, women with disabilities, undocumented women, and women in low-wage jobs are also at a greater risk of being subjected to extreme forms of sexism. For example, an estimated 39% of women raped in the 12 months preceding the survey had a disability at the time of the rape. Disability status was associated with an increased risk of sexual coercion and noncontact, unwanted sexual experiences (Basilel et al., 2016).

As a part of the cultural and structural landscape, sexism is pervasive, powerful and incredibly harmful. Sexism exists across institutions, including but not limited to families, government, legal system, church, education, employment, media, medicine, academia, business, the military, sports and Hollywood. The seamless thread of sexism across institutions creates conditions whereby women are subjected to the possibility of hostility, harassment and/or violence in nearly every domain of their lives.

Relationships: Dating, Family, and Workplace

In exploring familial relationships, sexist practices and expectations exist among families across all racial-ethnic groups. Latino families, however, may be especially likely to endorse sexist notions, with strong links to familism and the stark cultural divide of masculinity and femininity (Bermúdez, Sharp, & Taniguchi, 2013). Moreover, ideas of contemporary heterosexual romance are firmly embedded in hetero-patriarchal sexist notions, with men as active and "the pursuers" and women as passive and objects of male desire (see Sharp & Keyton, 2016; Tolman, 2000). Traditionally masculine domains—for example the military and sports—tend to have heightened and hyper-concentrated climates of sexism. According to the Annual Report on Sexual Assault in the Military (2017), in 2016, 14,900 military members experienced unwanted sexual contact, of which 43% were female. Recently, the National Academies of Medicine, Engineering and Sciences released a two-year consensus study documenting that sexism in academia is second only to the military (Smith et al., 2018).

Academia

The effects of sexism are multidimensional, entailing cognitive, emotional, social and physical losses and adjustments for girls and women. Sharp and Lewis (2014) studied the experiences of women participating in a two-day "feminist women-only" gathering in the UK. In contrasting feminist, women-only space with her everyday experiences in a male-centered space, one participant expressed: "I was thinking about that kind of energy that takes women all the time to deal with that low-level and high-level shit that we get—and it could be just a look. . . . It could be a stare, it could be worse. . . ."

Only when in a "safe space" was the participant, a White, cisgender, woman professor in her 40s, able to relax and think free of the distraction and energy expended in oppressive contexts. The contrast of this world was the relief and relaxation she felt in a feminist, women-only space (Lewis, Sharp, Remnant, & Redpath, 2015). She highlighted: "[there was] something about being in an environment that is physically and psychologically safe, I can just relax and . . . my head can work—I am not having to look over my shoulder. . . . We all accommodate various levels of hostility at various times in this society as women."

Reinforcing the notion that sexism impacts women across their lifespan, in the same study, similar sentiment was expressed by younger women in their 20s. One college student woman explained:

> I felt . . . more clever . . . or more creative and . . . better at a lot of things, because often I spend so much time . . . justifying that I even

get to be those things in the first place, and starting from that point and I didn't have to expend any energy as to like why it's important I share this idea, . . . just expended all my energy on what I was gonna say, and how I was gonna [say it]. I think there was a lot of things that I didn't even know I felt, and it was only being in that *environment* [feminist, women-only] . . . that I said things aloud and I surprised myself. I didn't know I thought them until I said them. . . . and I think just having that part of my brain freed up, I genuinely thought . . . I know it might sound silly, but I did feel more clever.

(Sharp & Lewis, 2014)

Resisting Sexism

In response to the cultural trauma women experience by living in a sexist world dominated by male-centered spaces, women engage in multiple and creative ways to cope with losses and disenfranchisement associated with sexism. Women forge resilience through solidarity, social movements, narrative storytelling, adoption of / adherence to feminist ideology, and connection with alliances.

One of the most common survival strategies is solidarity with other women. In many contexts, women nurture, affirm and take care of each other as a form of resistance and forward movement. For example, recognizing the larger hostile and male-centered space of the academy (Sharp & Messuri, 2017), some US universities have implemented Women Faculty Writing Programs to carve out spaces for women to do their research in environments that minimize losses of time and energy that occurs in male-centered spaces. Such programs can be highly productive—as a case in point, in one semester, 10 women faculty wrote 20 grants, totaling more than $32 million in federal and foundation grant submissions (Sharp & Messuri, 2019). When asked about Women Faculty Writing Programs, many women participants indicated that being connected to, and supported by, other women is the most valuable aspect of the program.

Women's abilities to identify and name experiences with stereotyping, discrimination and losses and to be heard and acknowledged is enfranchising and promotes healing (Bordere, 2016, 2017; Boss, 2010). As the #MeToo movement poignantly illustrates, for many women, being able to name and share their experiences with sexual violence, loss, and injustice is an important aspect of their healing processes. For decades, women have shared their stories of violence in public forums (for example, Reclaim the Night, Take Back the Night marches). Sharing stories, whether in person or online, helps cultivate solidarity and support (Mendes et al., 2018) necessary for coping with losses associated with sexism, particularly in cases of unacknowledged non-death losses (Doka, 1989) and grief that is suffocated or penalized (Bordere, 2014, 2016) in systems of oppression (see Bordere, 2017). Similarly, the #ThriveOver35 hashtag was developed by an African transwoman as a social media campaign for transwomen and allies to promote the existence and persistence of transwomen who are overwhelmingly vulnerable to violent death by age 35 (see Hale, 2018).

Allies are also central to survival for women coping with cultural trauma and loss as a function of everyday social injustices encountered in oppressive spaces (Bordere, 2016, 2017). According to Ayvazian (2007), allies are individuals who are able to recognize their privileged status(es) (for example, White, athletic, able-bodied) and use their accompanying unearned advantages (for example, economic power) in ways that benefit marginalized populations. Thus, allies are powerful collaborators in women's efforts to disrupt and dismantle systems of social, economic and political oppression. One example of the power of alliances is illustrated in fundraising efforts designed to shift power structures and exploitation of women in workplaces. More than $20 million has been donated by more than 20,000 donors from 80 countries to the Time's Up Legal Defense Fund to end sexual harassment in the workplace (Gose, 2018).

Conclusion

Women experience losses related to sexism across their lifespan and demonstrate resilience through creative coping and survival behaviors in contexts of male-centered spaces and political environments. Trauma and losses may be exacerbated for women with intersecting marginalized identities, such as African-American female youth and adults who are confronted with the combined forces of racism and sexism.

References

Ayvazian, A. (2007). Interrupting the cycle of oppression: The role of allies as agents of change. In P. S. Rothenberg (Ed.), *Race, class, and gender in the United States.* (7th Edn.) New York: Worth, pp. 724–29.

Basilel, K. C., Breiding, M. J. and Smith, S. G. (2016). Disability and risk of recent sexual violence in the United States. *American Journal of Public Health*, 106(5), pp. 928–33. doi:10.2105/AJPH.2015.303004.

Bermúdez, J. M., Sharp, E. A. and Taniguchi, N. (2013). Tapping into the complexity: Ambivalent sexism, dating, and familial beliefs of young Hispanics. *Journal of Family Issues*, 36(10), pp. 1274–95. doi:10.1177/0192513x13506706.

Bordere, T. C. (2014). Adolescents and homicide. In K. Doka and A. Tucci (Eds.), *Helping adolescents cope with loss.* Washington, DC: Hospice Foundation of America.

Bordere, T. C. (2016). Social justice conceptualizations in grief and loss. In D. Harris and T. C. Bordere (Eds.), *Handbook of social justice in loss and grief: Exploring diversity, equity, and inclusion.* Amityville, NY: Routledge, pp. 9–20.

Bordere, T. C. (2017). Disenfranchisement and ambiguity in the face of loss: The suffocated grief of sexual assault survivors. *Family Relations*, 66(1), pp. 29–45.

Boss, P. (2010). The trauma and complicated grief of ambiguous loss. *Pastoral Psychology*, 59(2), pp. 137–45. doi:10.1007/s11089-009-0264-0.

Cantor, D., Fisher, B., Chibnall, S., Bruce, C., Townsend, R., Thomas, G. and Lee, H. (2015). *Report on the AAU Campus climate survey on sexual assault and sexual misconduct* Rep, PA: University of Pennsylvania, pp. 1–251. Retrieved from https://ias.virginia.edu/sites/ias.virginia.edu/files/University%20of%20Virginia_2015_climate_final_report.pdf.

Doka, K. J. (1989). *Disenfranchised grief: Recognizing hidden sorrow.* Lexington, MA: Lexington Books.

Glick, P. and Fiske, S. T. (2011). Ambivalent sexism revisited. *Psychology of Women Quarterly*, 35(3), pp. 530–5. doi:10.1177/0361684311414832.

Gose, B. (2018, April). Time's up takes off as Hollywood allies with worker advocates. *The Chronicle of Philanthropy.* Retrieved from https://www.philanthropy.com/article/Time-s-Up-Fund-to-Fight/242722

Hale, J. L. (2018, June). *The "thrive over 35" hastag by Ashlee Marie Preston draws attention to a devastating statistic about black trans women and life expectancy*, Bustle. Retrieved from www.bustle.com/p/the-thrive-over-35-hashtag-by-ashlee-marie-preston-draws-attention-to-a-devastating-statistic-about-black-trans-women-life-expectancy-9563755.

Human Rights Campaign (2018). *A national epidemic: Fatal anti-transgender violence in America in 2018.* Retrieved from https://assets2.hrc.org/files/assets/resources/AntiTransViolence-2018Report-Final.pdf?_ga=2.237405699.2022707758.1551392785-297148328.1551392785.

Johnson, A. G. (2005). *The gender knot: Unraveling our patriarchal legacy.* Philadelphia: Temple University Press.

Kleinman, S. (2002). Why sexist language matters. *Qualitative Sociology*, 25, pp. 299–304.

Lewis, R., Sharp, E., Remnant, J. and Redpath, R. (2015). "Safe spaces": Experiences of feminist women-only space. *Sociological Research Online.* Retrieved from www.socresonline.org.uk/20/4/9.html

Livingston, B., Grillo, M. and Paluch, R. (2015, May). *Cornell International Survey on Street Harassment.* Retrieved February, 2019, from www.ihollaback.org/cornell-international-survey-on-street-harassment/#us

Mendes, K., Ringrose, J. and Keller, J. (2018). #MeToo and the promise and pitfalls of challenging rape culture through digital feminist activism. *European Journal of Women's Studies*, 25(2), pp. 236–46.

Pain, R. (1991). Space, sexual violence and social control: Integrating geographical and feminist analyses of women's fear of crime. *Progress in Human Geography*, 15(4), pp. 415–31.

Shapiro, F. R. (1965). Historical notes on the vocabulary of the women's movement. *American Speech*, 60(1), pp. 3–16. Durham, NC: Duke University Press. doi:10.2307/454643.

Sharp, E. A. and Keyton, K. (2016). Caught in a bad romance? The effect of normative dating and marital ideologies on women's bodies. *Sex Roles*, 75(1–2), pp. 15–27.

Sharp, E. A. and Lewis, R. (2014, April). *Safe from misogyny and safe to be fully human: Dimensions of safety in women's only space.* Paper presented at the 30th Annual Women's Studies Annual Conference. Texas Tech University, Lubbock, TX.

Sharp, E. A. and Messuri, K. (2017, December). *Women-only writing space: Disrupting and enhancing the academy.* Northampton, MA: Smith College.

Sharp, E. A. and Messuri, K. (2019). *Women Faculty Writing Program.* Annual report to the President at Texas Tech University.

Smith, S. G., Zhang, X., Basile, K. C., Merrick, M. T., Wang, J., Kresnow, M. and Chen, J. (2018). The national intimate partner and sexual violence survey (NISVS): 2015 Data Brief—Updated Release. Atlanta, GA: National Center for Injury Prevention and Control, Centers for Disease Control and Prevention.

Tolman, D. (2000). Object lessons: Romance, violation, and female adolescent desire. *Journal of Sex Education and Therapy*, 25(1), pp. 70–9. doi:/10.1080/01614576.2000. 11074331.

14 Family Resilience in Dealing With Grief and Loss

A Sociological Perspective

Paul C. Rosenblatt

"Resilience" was not a term initially applied to families. The first psychological writings about "resilience" in humans were about "resilience" in individuals, particularly children and youth. In about 1985, when families began to come into the discussion of resilience, the writings were not about family resilience but about what families could do to help individual children and youth be resilient. This origin for the concept of resilience suggests that we need to be cautious in addressing family resilience. We might, if we are not careful, find ourselves actually addressing resilience of individual family members and not of whole families.

Families are interacting entities in which much of what there is to understand and observe is what goes on between and among members who inevitably differ from one another in what they think, do, feel, remember, know, need and understand. That means understanding, assessment, evaluation and professional help focused on family resilience has to be sensitive to differences among family members and to the complexities of what goes on between and among them. It is possible to use the term "resilience" in ways that attend to and respect family member differences and what goes on between and among family members. But a great risk in applying the term "resilience" to families is that we may do it in a way that personifies families, imputing to them properties of individuals—as though, for example, the family has feelings, thinks certain things and has specific psychological needs. With personification we would pretend or persuade ourselves that the diverse members of a family, with their many differences, do not have differences. Worse yet, personification takes family member interaction with one another out of the discussion, so we tune out what is crucial in understanding and helping a family.

Cultural Limitations of the Family Resilience Concept

Cultures differ in what is considered good family functioning. So, whose culture is to say what family resilience is and whether it is desirable? Consider, for example, intercultural couples in which one partner draws on a strong cultural upbringing to believe that it is proper to grieve intensely and for a long time, and the other partner draws on a different strong cultural upbringing to believe that when grieving it is proper to suppress emotions and focus on work life and chores. Which partner's view of resilience would be the proper one for members of their family? Similarly, partners from different cultures might have different standards for family grieving. One might feel that it is best for every family member to be free to grieve in whatever ways they are inclined to grieve, and the other might feel that every family member should grieve in the same way. Who is to say which approach is best? This question is an important one, since in a sense all couples are intercultural couples, and hence all families are intercultural and must deal with clashing standards from different families of origin.

The clinical and academic literature on grief arguably implies that one culture's standards for individual and family grieving are healthiest, the culture represented in the most influential and frequent writings about grief. But one can question the cultural bias that underlies the preference. Do we do grieving people of diverse cultural backgrounds a service if we hold them to one particular culture's standards for grieving? The concept of "resilience" is culturally loaded. In fact, the term does not translate precisely from English to many other languages, which is a warning that applying the term "resilience" to families of diverse cultures could be a mistake. In English, "resilience" commonly means being able to bounce back, to return to the state that existed before something adverse happened. But in Indonesian, to take one example, the best translation of "resilience" is, according to Google Translate, *ketahanan*, which back translates to English as endurance and tenacity. That is not the same thing as the English meaning of "resilience." The difference between the two languages is worrisome. If diverse languages lead to diverse understandings, how does an intercultural family come to terms with the different ideas of ways to deal resiliently with grief and loss? And there is the question of whether "resilience" or *ketahanan* or whatever the term might be is actually good for a family. Is it necessarily good to bounce back to where the family was before a loss, or does the loss call for new social arrangements, new division of labor, and new emotional engagement with one another? Similarly, is it good to endure persistently in the face of great pain? Or is it better to do something about the pain rather than endure it?

Where in Society Might the Valuing of Family Resilience Come From?

In a sociological perspective the valuing of family resilience comes from a particular social system at a particular time. I believe that the valuing of family resilience comes from an economic and social system in which those with power and great wealth benefit from others dealing with grief and loss "resiliently." Those with great power and wealth might want to minimize the taxes they pay by seeing to it that governments spend little on families and individuals who are hurting. Also, the valuing of family resilience comes from a system in which those with great power and wealth do not want to be held responsible for the grief they have caused through their decisions about fighting wars, closing places of employment, causing deaths (through pollution, faulty products and dangerous products), paying wages that are too low and blocking access of many to good healthcare. Thus, many with great power and wealth may value resilience in everybody else to the extent that resilience means nobody will sue or complain about family deaths that arguably were caused by those with great power or wealth. In fact, the valuing of family resilience may be a way of blaming families that are hurting as a result of the actions and neglect of those with great power and wealth, making family grief seem a result of family failure to be resilient.

As another implication of a sociological perspective that sees the valuing of family resilience as something that works for those with great power and wealth, think of employers who want workers to return to work immediately after a death. For those employers, family resilience may refer to a family that gets its members back to work immediately after a loss. And that improves the bottom line of businesses.

As still another implication of the idea that valuing family resilience benefits those with great power, consider families targeted by racism. Arguably, racist standards for the resilience of Black and other minority families might often include that those families be resilient in the face of losses caused by racism. Consider a family with a member whose death was caused by medical or environmental racism. Asserting that the family should be resilient in their grief in the sense of bouncing back rather than suing, denouncing or fighting to end medical or environmental racism could be seen as helping to maintain racist oppression that benefits those who gain advantage from racism.

Elements of Family Resilience in Dealing with Grief and Loss

What might be family resilience when dealing with grief and loss? The following list (which draws on Walsh, 2014, 2019) is a view of how to achieve resilience at the family level while being sensitive to individual and cultural differences. This does not mean the list escapes culture. Authors cannot escape their own culture. But I try, with this list, to give room for standards from diverse cultures to be valued.

1. Family relationships include emotional sharing, mutual support and shared meaning making. That does not mean that things always go well for everyone, that there is no family conflict or hurt feelings, that all family members are equally articulate, grounded and courageous, or that family members will think, feel or communicate in the same way. It means that in general in the family there is a capacity to share and interact. And that implies that family resilience in dealing with a death or other loss begins long before the death or other loss.
2. If individual family members or the family as a whole needs help, there are resources for help from within the family or resources that the family can access outside the family.

3. The family does not block members from finding new and diverse invest-
    ments of emotional and social energy and new ways to do things following
    a death.
4. Family members at times talk with each other about the loss, share memo-
    ries and feelings, and even feel free to talk about negative things about a
    family member who died. This does not mean that everyone in the family
    has to agree or that everyone in the family will participate to the same
    extent. It means that in general family members will at times share and
    get to know what one another has to say. In the process, relationships may
    be strengthened and wounds from the past may be acknowledged.
5. Families find ways to acknowledge a deceased person, at least on certain
    occasions, rather than collectively acting like the person never existed.
6. They move forward with reorganization of the family system, given who
    the survivors are, what their situation is and whatever individual and fam-
    ily needs might be.
7. Family members have room to grieve as it fits each of them at the moment.
8. One or more family members sees to it that crucial needs of people in the
    family are met (for example, seeing to it that children are taken care of).
    But then maybe it is not a sign of family resilience if some family member
    is grossly overloaded because other family members do not help in meet-
    ing some crucial need.
9. Family members work toward shared realities related to the loss. That
    does not preclude having unshared and differing private realities (Nadeau,
    1998), but it means there are areas of shared reality. With a death, shared
    realities often include a sense of what the deceased person was like, what
    the cause of death was, who if anyone was responsible for the death, what
    the family was like before the death and what the family is and will be
    now that the death has occurred.

Practical Implications

For practitioners trying to help grieving families, this chapter makes clear that
proper therapeutic goals for helping a family dealing with grief and loss would
focus a great deal on relational goals and would respect the diversity of needs
and processes among family members (Hooghe & Neimeyer, 2013; Shapiro,
2008). As part of that it would have to focus at least to some extent on the
processes of coming to shared family meanings about the loss (Hooghe &
Neimeyer, 2013; Nadeau, 1998). At the same time, therapeutic work with
a family struggling with grief and loss could well benefit from the resilience
already present in the family.

Can individual therapy connected to grief and loss benefit a family? It might,
because a family member who gains traction in dealing with a loss may act in
ways that are good for the whole family. But we must be skeptical about the
impact on a family of therapy with a single family member. That person's views
of her or his family, the loss and everything else are just one family member's

views. Other family members may have very different realities, and so what addresses the realities of the one family member receiving therapy may miss or be contrary to the realities of other family members. Further, therapy with one family member may make that person different in ways that disengage the person from her or his family, make trouble in the family or turn the person from processing things with family members to processing things with the therapist or counselor. None of that may be good for the family. By and large therapeutic help for a family dealing with loss must involve facilitation of family interaction and family members working together.

For practitioners trying to help families dealing with grief and loss and for those of us who are not professionals but try to help families dealing with grief and loss, listening can be good. Family members who are hurting may need to say whatever they have to say, and our listening may help them to know themselves, to define issues, to feel what they feel about what has been lost and to find their path ahead. Creating a situation in which family members hear one another speaking about grief and loss may advance the family in dealing with a loss and in coming to constructive post-loss relationships. It is not our responsibility to define where a family might go, and doing anything intended to help a family to be resilient (in the sense of returning to where it was, in the sense of enduring the pain or in any other way) may do a family a great disservice.

This chapter argues that there are powerful players in society profiting from families being pushed to work on their own at being resilient. This chapter further argues that in the view of these powerful actors it is not the responsibility of governments or employers to foster family resilience or to take responsibility for the losses that families experience. But contrary to what powerful actors want, a strong case can be made that family resilience is largely a matter of family policy at the level of government and other powerful societal entities, that families are more resilient when governments, employers and other societal players see to it that families and family members are safe and live decently and that premature deaths are rare. From that perspective, those of us who want to help people should work hard for humane policies in governments, corporations and other social entities. Resilience is very much about the quality of the sociocultural environment (Ungar, 2013).

References

Hooghe, A. and Neimeyer, R. A. (2013). Family resilience in the wake of loss: A meaning-oriented contribution. In D. S. Becvar (Ed.), *Handbook of family resilience*. New York: Springer Science, pp. 269–84.

Nadeau, J. W. (1998). *Families making sense of death*. Thousand Oaks, CA: Sage.

Shapiro, E. R. (2008). Whose recovery of what? Relationships and environments promoting grief and growth. *Death Studies*, 32, pp. 40–58.

Ungar, M. (2013). Resilience, trauma, context, and culture. *Trauma, Violence, and Abuse*, 14, pp. 255–66.

Walsh, F. (2014). Conceptual framework for family bereavement care: Strengthening resilience. In D. W. Kissane and F. Parnes (Eds.), *Bereavement care for families*. New York: Routledge, pp. 17–29.

Walsh, F. (2019). Loss and bereavement in families: A systemic framework for recovery and resilience. In B. H. Fiese, M. Celano, K. Deater-Deckard, E. N. Jouriles and M. A. Whisman (Eds.), *APA handbook of contemporary family psychology: Foundations, methods, and contemporary issues across the lifespan*, Vol. 1. Washington, DC: American Psychological Association, pp. 649–63.

15 Building a Narrative of Resilience for Refugees

Christopher Cox

Immigrants of all types adapt not only as individuals but also as families and communities. The receiving community, irrespective of whether or not the newcomers adapt with ease, adapts as well and does not remain unchanged. The reflections shared in this chapter are the fruit of almost 20 years of serving immigrant Catholic communities in the US and abroad. The perspective that follows is one that aims to see the community dimension within the resilience of refugees and the strength that comes from effectively martialing the resources of the refugee community's heritage to obtain greater satisfaction in a new land. Communities immersed in their own loss, both the refugee community and the receiving community, may have a difficult time also seeing their separate and joint potential. Resilience, for both communities, requires a certain shift in vision. Leadership plays a critical role in casting an honest vision of that potential for both communities.

Daily, conflict and persecution drive more than 44,000 people to flee their homes. The United Nations High Commissioner for Refugees (UNHCR) cites a figure of 68.5 million people forcibly displaced worldwide: one person out of every 100 on the planet. This includes 40 million who are internally displaced, 25.4 million legally classified as refugees and another 3.1 million asylum seekers. Of those refugees, about half came from three countries: Afghanistan, Syria and South Sudan. Nearly 9 out of 10 refugees are hosted in developing countries. Since 2005, when the UNHCR counted just under 12.9 million refugees, the number has surged (UNHCR, 2018). Sadly, the numbers are not expected to decline in the foreseeable future.

When referring to those born in another land, definitions and distinctions abound, be they legal definitions, social science terminology or one's self-description. The political and legal framework continues to evolve. Attempts to reform US immigration processes have occasioned increasingly sharp political conflict over the past 20 years. Some politicians capitalize on polarization. Domestically, racial tension and anti-immigrant sentiment have grown. Internationally, the member states of the UN finalized a Global Compact on Refugees in 2018, augmenting the 1951 Refugee Convention. Nonetheless, legal vacuums exist. The international standards do not provide for "climate refugees." While the July 2018 Global Compact for Safe, Orderly and Regular Migration recognized climate change as a growing factor, the December 2018 Global Compact on Refugees eschewed the subject, using the term "climate" only twice and, in one instance, in the context of a "business climate" (United Nations, 2018). The World Bank estimates there will be as many as 143 million climate refugees, with a minimum of 92 million, by 2050 (Rigaud et al., 2018). It is a growing crisis for which the world remains woefully unprepared.

Losses

Refugees may have many flight motivations. Many suffer traumatic experiences of severe and repeated exposure to violence in their countries of origin as well as over the course of their journey to resettlement. Most have lost relatives, some have lost almost their whole family, and many have suffered severe personal or religious persecution. Those traumatic experiences affect men, women and children differently. In some instances, the brunt of the violence is borne directly by men; in other instances, armies use rape and sexual enslavement as instruments of war. Refugees also have left behind persons unwilling or unable to leave. Refugees have lost homeland, job, home, possessions, social status, freedom and security.

A refugee's status may resolve itself in one of three possible outcomes: remaining in the camp, repatriation, or resettlement. In each, refugees face anew their losses. First, the time in the camp may last years, even generations, as Palestinians in the Dheisheh Camp (founded in 1949) near Bethlehem have learned. Rawlence (2016) dubbed camp life a "strange limbo" in his compelling portrait of the Dadaab Camp in Kenya. While the largest camp in 2016, with more than 235,000 refugees, it had fallen to the third largest by 2018. In the liminal space of a refugee camp, communal practices and rituals, especially death practices, may not be able to be observed as in the homeland. Second, the international norms around refugees prohibit their forced return, but, with the growing numbers of global refugees, the pressure for repatriation increases as resettlement grows more remote and the camp limbo becomes increasingly untenable. Repatriation means a return to homeland, but, in the return, everything is different. The preceding flight means the relationship with home has been violently ruptured and demands reconciliation. Provision for reconciliation and a just return is essential. Third, in addition to previous losses, refugees in resettlement will experience grief, perhaps from isolation, unemployment, poverty, discrimination or the loss of social networks.

Not only does the refugee community grieve its losses, but the receiving community must face its own losses as well. Manufacturing jobs may have disappeared because of automation and globalization; familiar business closed; and old storefronts fallen into disrepair. The smaller the receiving community, the more intensely it may experience loss as new languages, new foods, new customs and new faces appear. What follows examines the implications of resettlement on both communities.

Competing Narratives

Stories and metaphor are significant structures that humans use to make sense of people and their behavior. There are multiple ways of telling the story of immigrants and refugees. To grossly overstate it, one might tell a story of refugees that can be characterized as "danger, disease and terror." Alternatively, one might tell another very different story of "beauty, gifts and goodness."

A culture organizes itself around a worldview, presented and passed on in stories. A worldview offers a comprehensive and generally coherent account for a set of beliefs about the nature of the universe, how it operates and one's place within it. A wise community leader has the potential to draw the stories of a group into a worldview that enlivens their hope and to envision and articulate new possibilities in the life of a particular community. Such a narrative sees a deeper reality in both communities, a reality enriched with veiled beauty, hidden gifts and unseen goodness, and then brings that vision to reality. The narrative within both communities is significant. Humans depend on their created language to make sense of the world. The words of a president, a mayor or a school principal to describe the refugee community matter.

While a service provider may meet with an individual refugee or a family of refugees, it is crucial to see them in a larger context. Hein (2006) studied refugees from the Hmong people of Laos and Vietnam as well as the Khmer people from Cambodia. He assessed their adaptation in two small towns and two big cities. Hein found that, in both quantitative and qualitative data, racial and ethnic adaptation is primarily shaped by ethnic origin. Secondarily, the adaptation is shaped by the urban environment. Ethnic backgrounds are found to be more important in shaping adaptation patterns than the place where the refugees settle. Finally, the adaptation is shaped by the interaction of past and place.

Based on Hein's understanding of a tri-part influence over adaptation, it is particularly in this third element where community leaders and service providers can act. That is, the refugee community's adaptation depends on their narrative, imbued with their values, and respecting their traditions. In this sense, narratives are mediations of the past. While memories of home may be idealized and nostalgic, they are oriented to the present and the future, forging continuities between time and place.

Faith Community

World religions are steeped in the language of exile, abounding in migration stories. For example, Deuteronomy outlined the treatment of migrants in several places, with a reminder of their time as migrants: "You too must befriend the stranger, for you were strangers in the land of Egypt" (Deut. 10:19). The Quran also addresses a number of migrations, including some of those from the

Hebrew Scriptures. The most evocative is the journey of the Prophet from the city of Mecca to the city of Medina. Clearly, global faith traditions have deep narratives concerning migrations. Without denying the refugees' losses, these texts allow for the imaginative construction of an alternative story of beauty, gifts and goodness.

Ritual, an essential medium for those stories, can be subversive. Ritual can mediate the religious imagination, showing that another world is possible. In my experience, the spiritual devotions of a people can be powerful in strengthening a community that experiences loss. For example, for a Mexican Catholic community, there is power in connecting Our Lady of Guadalupe, who cared for and accompanied not the bishop but the marginal Juan Diego to their experience as an immigrant community that can feel bereft. Ritual can be used to cast a new vision for those who have been marginalized.

Not only do faith leaders have a role within their faith community, but they have a critical role to play in the broader community. In the US, faith community leaders have an unparalleled capacity to convoke diverse sectors of a community that often remains, sadly, untapped. While the faith community need not direct or lead the conversations, faith leaders can bring the parties to the table (Nelson, 2017). When a local community navigates its course with a refugee community, many elements of the community—education, employment, healthcare, housing, law enforcement, economic development, local government, to name but a few—are challenged in new ways. As the refugees adapt to their new locale, the local community engages in a mutual adaptation. One side does not simply bend to fit the other; both will change. It is not that the refugees simply assimilate, but the move is reciprocal. Faith leaders have a unique opportunity to bring those parties together to imagine new ways of guiding and resourcing the community.

Collaboration

Over decades, the US has developed organizational capacity for resettlement of refugees. Unfortunately, with contemporary political decisions to sharply reduce the number of refugees, the infrastructure that has demonstrated some success at acculturating them is degrading and, in some cases, disappearing. In its absence, receiving communities rely on greater voluntary collaboration in areas of education, employment, health, housing and law enforcement.

The educational attainment of refugees spans from those with advanced degrees to those unable to read or write, as they had never attended a school. Variables such as gender, level of education, language proficiency and country of origin impact the individual experience as a refugee. Women likely will have different experiences than men; younger persons are liable to experience other interactions and paths to integration than elderly refugees. The internal and external push for economic self-sufficiency may postpone educational plans for adults and young adults.

In the education of children, educators often express a desire for greater parental involvement. A teacher may make a false inference that the parents do not value education. Olivos (2006) suggests that it may be a difference in what they prioritize. Refugee parents live and form their children in a bicultural environment: the culture of the home and the dominant culture where they have resettled. Educators benefit from an awareness of two factors. First, educators would do well to understand that their students come from "a rich social and cultural context of learning and cognition, even if it differs from that of the dominant culture." Second, educators need to understand racial and power dynamics. Structurally, much is already set against parents of the non-dominant culture. Administrators and teachers who pay attention to those places of tension with refugees can nurture a strong role for those parents who can transform and strengthen schools.

Resilience in matters of health requires attention to the elevated risks in the refugee community by attending to issues of access and language and by understanding the beliefs and health practices of the refugee community. Potocky-Tripodi's (2002) work on social work with refugees and immigrants distinguishes strategies for interventions at the macro (access to services), the meso (enhancing agencies' effectiveness) and the micro levels (clinical assessments).

Writing poignantly and powerfully about issues related to housing, Desmond (2016) rightly points to the centrality of housing in so many aspects of a person's life:

> The home is the center of life. It is a refuge from the grind of work, the pressure of school, and the menace of the streets. We say that at home, we can "be ourselves." Everywhere else, we are someone else. At home, we remove our masks.
>
> (p. 293)

A stable residence allows individuals and families to invest in their home and to deepen ties within the refugee community and to create relationships with the broader community. As well, educational outcomes improve with stable housing. The other side of the coin is that "[f]amilies who spend more on housing spend less on their children" (p. 299). Communities must attend to the challenges of securing housing, renovating dilapidated housing, adapting to residential overcrowding, and enforcing and mediating violations of housing code. The fragile peace within vulnerable communities can come undone explosively along racial and ethnic lines.

Many refugees have had negative experiences with law enforcement in their native lands, including corruption and violence. These experiences seed a natural mistrust toward law enforcement in the place of arrival. Some local law enforcement professionals favor being responsible solely for local laws, rather than enforcing federal immigration laws. In a 2008 study, the Police Foundation found that local law enforcement engaging in the enforcement of federal immigration laws caused significant harm to their relationship with the local community, including a telling quotation from one police chief: "How do you police a community that will not talk to you?" (Khashu, 2008, p. 36).

Not only does resilience require collaboration between service providers, perhaps more importantly it requires collaboration with, and empowerment of, the refugee community. Bringing those refugees otherwise excluded from power into the decision-making process often engenders better outcomes. A premise that non-refugees likely have a poor understanding of what the refugees need or want may, in fact, be a better starting point. Such a posture impedes a well-meaning person or organization from doing things that obstruct the refugees, and it empowers the refugees to help themselves.

The primary agents of refugee resilience are the refugees themselves. Rather than identifying what the receiving community assesses to be their needs, it seems wiser to find those places where the refugees have exercised initiative— for themselves and others—and invest in it. Community leadership that trusts and respects refugee families to lead their own change empowers further initiative.

Conclusion

The welcoming of refugees challenges the narrow interpretation of the receiving community's heritage and identity. Receiving communities can experience an escalation of conflict, xenophobia and racism, or thrive as they embrace their new demographic makeup, depending on what story is told. The world is increasingly interconnected and interdependent. Amid staggering and increasing numbers of refugees, resilience is born of overcoming racial, ethnic and religious differences through understanding, respecting and welcoming the stranger.

References

Desmond, M. (2016). *Evicted: Poverty and profit in the American city*. New York: Crown.

Hein, J. (2006). *Ethnic origins: The adaptation of Cambodian and Hmong refugees in four American cities*. New York: Russell Sage Foundation.

Khashu, A. (2008). *The role of local police: Striking a balance between immigration enforcement and civil liberties*. Washington, DC: Police Foundation.

Nelson, D. (2017). Pastors have the power to convene conversations. Retrieved from www.christiancentury.org/article/features/pastors-have-power-to-convene-conversations.

Olivos. E. M. (2006). *The power of parents: A critical perspective of bicultural parent involvement in public schools*. New York: Peter Lang.

Potocky-Tripodi, M. (2002). *Best practices for social work with refugees and immigrants*. New York: Columbia University Press.

Rawlence, B. (2016). *City of thorns: Nine lives in the world's largest refugee camp*. New York: Picador.

Rigaud, K., de Sherbinin, A., Jones, B., Bergmann, J., Clement, V., Ober, K., . . . Midgley, A. (2018). *Groundswell: Preparing for internal climate migration*. Washington, DC: World Bank.

United Nations (2018). *Global compact on refugees*. New York: United Nations.

United Nations High Commissioner for Refugees (2018). Retrieved from www.unhcr.org/en-us/figures-at-a-glance.html.

16 Resilience and Older People

Denise Tanner

Introduction

In the western world, older people are commonly perceived as suffering poor physical and mental health, placing heavy demands on scarce health and social care resources and "burdening" younger generations. Need, risk, dependency and burden more readily spring to mind than resilience. This chapter challenges negative constructions of older age and applies a sociological lens to understanding older people's resilience.

Although the concept of resilience is increasingly used within the field of gerontology, there is a lack of clarity in its definition and usage (Richardson & Chew-Graham, 2016). Windle (2011) distinguishes three key constituents: a significant risk or adversity that has to be negotiated, strengths or assets that counter its impact, and successful management of the difficulty. Resilience encompasses a number of interrelated dimensions. It can be seen as a process we invoke when trying to cope with stress and adversity, an outcome of the skills, resources and learning that are acquired through that process, and a resource that can be drawn upon again when facing future stress (Aldwin & Igarashi, 2012).

Of these, resilience as a *process* is highly relevant for older people, who face many losses as they age. These include physical and practical losses, such as loss of ability and mobility, roles and routines; there are also psychosocial losses, including loss of loved ones to bereavement and loss of identities, choices, opportunities, independence and control. These losses may prompt significant changes in living environments and daily lifestyles and also impact on psychological and emotional well-being, perhaps triggering or compounding depression and loneliness (Adams, Sanders, & Auth, 2004). Understanding processes of resilience involves examining the mechanisms by which individuals navigate or adapt to stresses or adversities they encounter.

Resilience is also an *outcome* of processes and strategies for managing loss and vulnerability. It is therefore logical that, rather than dwindling in later life, resilience may increase over the lifecourse, as new skills and abilities are learned with each challenge negotiated (Fry & Keyes, 2010). For example, there is strong evidence that older age is associated with more positive adjustment to chronic illness and disability than younger age (Rybarczyk, Emery, Guequierre, Shamaskin, & Behel, 2012) and that older people's sense of well-being may improve over time, despite an increase in their difficulties (Johnson & Barer, 1997). However, the common perception that resilience is about "bouncing back" from adversity may need moderating when applied to older people with chronic conditions; for them, resilience may be more about "keeping going" despite prolonged or increasing adversity, rather than returning to a previous state of well-being (Richardson & Chew-Graham, 2016).

If viewed as a *resource* that can be drawn upon in times of adversity, resilience may be depleted in later life, depending on the factors that serve a protective function for that individual. In practice, the factors central to resilience as a process, an outcome and a resource are interrelated. For example, social support from others may be instrumental across all three dimensions.

Successful Aging

Successful aging has been explained in terms of processes by which older people seek to maximize gains and minimize losses as they age. These processes require an ability to preserve continuity with interests, roles and activities that give life meaning and value alongside an ability to adapt to changing circumstances (Baltes & Carstensen, 1996). However, responsibility for aging successfully is placed largely on older people's own psychological and self-help strategies. There are risks of neglecting the role of social and economic contributors to experiences of aging, ignoring the diversity of meanings of "successful aging" and marginalizing those who cannot achieve it (Lloyd et al., 2014). The study of resilience is potentially more helpful as it encompasses those who may not fit these notions of "aging well" but who manage to retain a state of well-being despite, or sometimes because of, significant adversities (Wild, Wiles, & Allen, 2013).

A Lifecourse Perspective

The level of vulnerability and resilience that older people bring to their later years is influenced by their earlier lifecourse (Windle, 2011). For example, they may have experienced lifelong disadvantage through disability, discrimination or poverty that have adversely affected their life chances. Single life events may also have increased their vulnerability—for example, bereavement or family breakdown may have diminished their social support. It is therefore important to consider the strengths and resources but also the vulnerabilities that older people bring with them into later life. Although previous experience of coping with adversity may enhance their coping strategies, as mentioned earlier, losses encountered at various life stages may have depleted resources that are central to their resilience.

Older People's Perceptions and Experiences

The predominant conception of resilience as an attribute of an individual's personality implies responsibility and blame on the part of individuals who are seen as lacking resilience. An additional individualist construction that particularly affects older people is vulnerability. Ageist attitudes lead older people, particularly older women, to be perceived as "vulnerable" or "frail," physically and/or mentally. Being seen as vulnerable signals a need to be protected from risk, including risk that arises from one's own choices. However, vulnerability can more accurately be perceived as an attribute of situations or circumstances, and this may or may not accord with the self-perceived level of vulnerability of the person concerned. For example, an older woman perceived as physically frail may experience herself as strong and coping, while another, though objectively stronger physically, may experience herself as frail due to circumstances that trigger feelings of destabilization (Grenier, 2006). The significance of individual interpretations can be seen in relation to social support. While the availability of social support is often viewed as a protective factor, for older spousal carers of people with dementia, receiving support did not necessarily promote resilience. A key factor was the "fit" between the level and type of support that was available and the recipient's perceptions about what was needed. Support that generated feelings of dependency was experienced as unhelpful (Donnellan, Bennett, & Soulsby, 2017).

Much can be learned about older people's resilience from qualitative research that explores how they negotiate challenges and maintain a state of perceived well-being. This research belies negative stereotypes of old age rooted in assumptions of need, decline and burden, highlighting instead the strengths, resourcefulness and adaptability of older people. A New Zealand study (Wiles, Wild, Kerse, & Allen, 2012) found that, for community-dwelling older people, resilience was seen as related to personal characteristics, such as having a positive attitude, keeping busy and feeling young at heart, but also about external sources of support, including family and friendship networks, community resources and accessible services. The study highlighted the contextual and multidimensional nature of resilience; an older person might see him- or herself as struggling in one area, such as physical health, but strong in others, such as social support.

Resilience as Multidimensional

Resilience is therefore not a state of being/not being; rather, it is a wide-ranging concept, spanning multiple domains that can encompass elements of vulnerability. Janssen, Van Regenmortel and Abma (2011) explored the nature of strengths that contributed to the resilience of older people who were receiving long-term community care. They found that the sources of strength fell within three interlinked domains: individual, interactional and contextual. Strengths in the individual domain included beliefs about one's competence, the ability to exercise control and capacity to understand one's situation.

In the interactional domain, strengths related to empowering social relationships, including with professionals. Strengths in the contextual domain included access to resources and health and social care services, as well social policies that were supportive to long-term disability and old age. A systematic literature review on resilience in older people corroborated the importance of older people's personal resources and also highlighted the significance of environmental features, including community support, access to resources such as care services, and supportive societal responses (Van Kessel, 2013).

Resilience at the Community Level

Environments and communities can strengthen older people's resilience. The World Health Organization (WHO) supports age-friendly communities which facilitate the participation of older people, including fostering opportunities for reciprocity (WHO, 2007). Design features include accessible and affordable transport, accessible buildings, suitably adapted housing, social activities, adequate public toilets and adequate community support and health services. Similarly, dementia-friendly communities can help older people with dementia to continue living well within their local environment. Bailey et al. (2013) see resilience for people living with dementia as about "the ability to continue with established roles and activities that (re)affirm a sense of self" (p. 394). They highlight the importance of interactions between person and place in enabling people with dementia to sustain connections with their community, thereby maintaining social networks and an ongoing sense of self.

While communities facilitate older people's resilience, older people also contribute to community resilience (Wild et al. 2013). Community resilience refers to the ability of community members to take collective action to respond to or manage adversity. Community resilience has been found to be higher amongst people aged 61 to 75 than in younger age groups (Cohen et al., 2016).

Implications

Building older people's resilience needs to be viewed as an issue of health and well-being across the lifecourse, rather than confined to later life. Furthermore, building resilience requires holistic policy and practice developments that target intersecting levels of individuals, social networks, community and government/institutions. This is a radical departure from approaches to resilience that see it as matter of individual attributes and individual responsibility. Instead of the view that particular older people are "vulnerable" or "frail", it is helpful to reconceptualize them as people living in risky situations (Bailey et al., 2013). This widens the ambit of intervention and the attribution of responsibility; it also instigates conversations about how risks are understood and experienced by different parties.

A key message of this chapter is that, in order to build older people's resilience, we must first understand their lifecourse and perspectives about what gives their life meaning and value. As adversity plays a key part in definitions of resilience, we need to understand what each older person experiences as "adversity" as well as the strengths that enable them to negotiate it. Most studies adopt the researchers' definition of adversity, rather than engaging with older people's subjective experiences (Van Kessel, 2013). For practitioners, connecting with the individual older person will help them know when to intervene but also what type of support may be most helpful and how this can bolster existing strengths, strategies and resources.

The level and nature of older people's social relationships are closely linked with resilience, so attention needs to be given to facilitating and supporting their social networks and their participation in communities. Professionals need to consider the ways in which their own relationships with older people can act as protective factors with the potential to promote resilience (Van Kessel, 2013). Actively involving older people in initiatives, such as age-friendly and dementia-friendly communities, not only builds community resources for everyone but also gives older people opportunities to contribute to community resilience.

Conclusion

If resilience is about how we negotiate experiences of vulnerability (see Chapter 1 in this volume), it is readily apparent why resilience in later life is important. Older people have a great need for resilience if they are to cope with the multiple, recurring and overlapping losses that old age often brings. At the same time, efforts to build resilience in later life have to recognize the impact of lifecourse experiences, including inequalities, resources and coping strategies that older people bring to this phase of life. A challenge for those working to strengthen older people's resilience is to avoid romanticizing the individual survivorship of older people or minimizing the social, economic and physical challenges they face, while at the same recognizing their strengths and capabilities (Wild et al., 2013).

It will help this endeavor if resilience is understood as fluid and developmental, fluctuating over time in response to shifting vulnerabilities and strengths (Windle, 2011). It consists of multiple dimensions; at any particular time, an older person may feel resilient in one area but vulnerable in another. Furthermore, risks and protective factors comprise a number of interacting levels: individual; family, social and community; and societal. Action to build older people's resilience must not stop at individual strategies, such as improving physical and mental health, but must also encompass measures to strengthen social support within communities and wider action at the institutional level.

References

Adams, K. B., Sanders, S. and Auth, E. A. (2004). Loneliness and depression in independent living retirement communities: Risk and resilience factors. *Ageing & Mental Health*, 8(6), pp. 475–85.

Aldwin, C. M. and Igarashi, H. (2012). An ecological model of resilience in late life. *Annual Review of Gerontology & Geriatrics* 32, pp. 115–30.

Bailey, C., Clarke, C. L., Gibb, C., Haining, S., Wilkinson, H. and Tiplady, S. (2013). Risky and resilient life with dementia: Review of and reflections on the literature. *Health, Risk & Society*, 15(5), pp. 390–401.

Baltes, M. and Carstensen, L. (1996). The process of successful aging. *Ageing and Society*, 16(4), pp. 397–421.

Cohen, O., Geva, D., Lahad, M., Bolotin, A., Leykin, D. and Goldberg, A. (2016). Community resilience throughout the Lifespan—The potential contribution of healthy elders. *PLoS One*, 11(2), p. e0148125.

Donnellan, W., Bennett, K. and Soulsby, L. (2017). Family close but friends closer: Exploring social support and resilience in older spousal dementia carers. *Aging and Mental Health*, 21(11), pp. 1222–28.

Fry, P. S. and Keyes, C. L. M (Eds.) (2010). *New frontiers in resilient aging: Life-strengths and well-being in later life.* Cambridge: Cambridge University Press.

Grenier, A. (2006). The distinction between being and feeling frail: Exploring emotional experiences in health and social care. *Journal of Social work Practice*, 20, pp. 299–313.

Janssen, B. M., Van Regenmortel, T. and Abma, T. A. (2011). Identifying sources of strength: Resilience from the perspective of older people receiving long-term community care. *European Journal of Aging*, 8(3) pp. 145–56.

Johnson, C. and Barer, B. (1997). *Life beyond 85 Years: The aura of survivorship.* New York: Springer Publishing.

Lloyd, L., Tanner, D., Milne, A., Ray, M., Richards, S., Sullivan, M. P., . . . Phillips, J. (2014). Look after yourself: Active ageing, individual responsibility and the decline of social work with older people in the UK. *European Journal of Social Work*, 17(3), pp. 322–35.

Richardson, J. and Chew-Graham, C. (2016). Resilience and well-being. In C. Chew-Graham and M. Ray (Eds.), *Mental health and older people: A guide for primary care practitioners.* Switzerland: Springer, pp. 9–17.

Rybarczyk, B., Emery, E., Guequierre, L., Shamaskin, A. and Behel, J. (2012). The role of resilience in chronic illness and disability in older adults. *Annual Review of Gerontology & Geriatrics*, 32, pp. 173–88.

Van Kessel, G. (2013). The ability of older people to overcome adversity: A review of the resilience concept. *Geriatric Nursing*, 34, pp. 122–27.

Wild, K., Wiles, J. L. and Allen, R. E. S. (2013). Resilience: Thoughts on the value of the concept for critical gerontology. *Ageing & Society*, 33, pp. 137–58.

Wiles, J. L., Wild, K., Kerse, N. and Allen, R. E. S. (2012). Resilience from the point of view of older people: "There's still life beyond a funny knee." *Social Science & Medicine*, 74(3), pp. 416–24.

Windle, G. (2011). What is resilience? A review and concept analysis. *Reviews in Clinical Gerontology*, 21, pp. 152–69.

World Health Organization (2007). *Global age-friendly cities: A guide.* Geneva: WHO.

17 Recovering From Childhood Trauma

Vivienne Dacre

Resilience is a key issue for developmental trauma in children because it is a marker of post-traumatic recovery. This chapter examines the role of the protective environment in the promotion of resilience, as a countermeasure to the effects of trauma. It considers the importance and context of timely and informed interventions that promote resilience.

Resilience as a Counterbalance to the Impact of Trauma

When children are exposed to ongoing traumatic experiences, such as physical and sexual abuse, neglect, war, loss, domestic violence, it impacts their development profoundly. The impact is extensive because developmental change is rapid in childhood, more so than at any other time of life. Research into Adverse Childhood Experiences (ACE) has established that trauma impacts across the lifecourse producing compromised health outcomes and increases in offending (Felitti, Anda, & Nordenberg, 1998). ACE studies bring attention to the prevalence of traumatic experience across all socio-economic groups, cultures and societies (Bellisi et al., 2015). The effect of trauma on a child's neurological development has been widely publicized (Schore, 2009). Perry, Pollard, Blakley, Baker and Vigilante (1995) summarize this effect as affecting social, emotional, physical, cognitive and behavioral functioning.

The phrase "post-traumatic recovery or growth" is used to signal those markers that seek to prevent the negative trajectory of ACE outcomes. According to Steele and Malchiodi (2012), trauma-informed care involves reparative, restorative and resilience-enhancing practices. Resilience therefore is a marker of post-traumatic growth and an important counterbalance to the developmental impact of trauma. A resilience-focused approach shifts the focus from children's negative, problem-saturated narratives of trauma to a focus on children's strengths and opportunities for growth.

In sociological terms, trauma-informed care takes place within a context of a series of interconnecting relationships. Children with a history of abuse and trauma are often placed within a system of care, usually either family placement or residential care. There are distinctive features about residential childcare that translate into a particular way of working. The complexity of the residential environment provides a backdrop within which residential childcare workers seek to promote post-traumatic growth.

Residential childcare operates in a group context where teams of workers care for groups of children. According to Ward (2007), this way of working is distinctly different to care manager social workers based in offices. While social workers are part of a team, they are likely to each have a separate caseload. Residential workers, on the other hand, will practice in a public space, in the presence of colleagues and children, what they say and do observed and "on show."

Residential childcare workers are with children for a much longer time, with care provided 24 hours a day. By contrast, therapists are likely to meet with a child for a one-hour appointment once a week. Added to this, the residential workers' shift will involve them in a range of informal tasks (playing football, eating together) and formal ones (supervising family contact visit or taking part in a statutory placement review). According to Ward (2007, p. 16), "this can be experienced as quite stressful, especially for new or inexperienced workers."

Working in a group context requires teamwork. Mainey and Crimmens's (2006) research found that the three highest motivational factors for staff were teamwork, residents' progress and pride in the job. Respondents identified the main areas covered by teamwork as "stability, consistency, communication, support and leadership" (2006, p. 46). The study goes on to highlight that teamwork affects care quality. Teamwork helps the residential childcare worker to feel supported and provides children with a valuable experience of supportive relationships through adults working collaboratively. Group care provides opportunities for both a person-focused and group-focused perspective. This is particularly relevant to a residential setting where the worker is supported by an organization and positioned within a group of workers caring for a group of children.

Residential childcare is relationship based, and so the primary task of the team is to build trusting relationships with children who, based on their history of abuse, are likely to find it difficult to trust adults. How the boundaries of the relationship are managed is a complex issue for teams and organizations. Ethical debate about such things as love and affection can too easily become the subject of a policy document (Smith, 2009). An over-bureaucratic system of care can create a situation where the centrality of relationships is compromised and even discouraged. Staff teams can become anxious about responding to a distressed child without first seeking their permission to put a comforting arm around them. Smith (2009) highlights the difference between physical care and "caring care." Child development thrives on loving, affectionate relationships.

Residential childcare operates within a historical and political context, and debates are often focused on protection, rights and outcomes. This is the backdrop upon which trauma-informed care takes place within residential childcare. Tensions like regulation and resources are likely to affect care provision and how children experience opportunities for post-traumatic growth.

Felt Safety as a Prerequisite for Resilience

Prolonged exposure to frightening and abusive experiences can impact cortisol levels and key regulatory processes (Cicchetti, Rogosch, Gunnar, & Toth, 2010); "toxic stress" sensitizes the child to further stress. Therefore, even though a child has been removed from the source of fear and placed in a safe environment, they are unlikely to feel safe. Van der Kolk (2005) notes that children who have experienced trauma relating to their attachment figures may not develop the belief that help will be provided for them, should they require it. This illustrates the double impact of traumatic stress: the child is unable to regulate their own internal states or address their own panic, combined with an inherent belief that no one else can address their panic either.

A focus on decreasing stress and increasing support is needed to help the child begin to feel safe. Grotberg (1995) describes the core of resilience as the child not just being safe but also being able to perceive safety. Staff in residential care, for example, have the opportunity to offer such children an immersive experience. Cairns (2016) emphasizes the importance of the environment in focusing on safety, security and consistency, all tenets of a trauma-informed approach. Consistent and predictable nurturing experiences happen within relationships that give rise to opportunities for the development of resilience.

According to Woodier (2011), resilience emerges in a supportive context. When adults are helped to manage the distress of a child's anxiety and respond with care, then, as Nicholson, Irwin and Dwivedi (2010) argue, the child experiences a view of self that is "worthy of care" and thus an experience of a caring, rather than abusive, relationship. As such, the role of secure relationships is central.

Consistency is achieved when teams work together with a common approach to meet children's needs. Watson (2003) concludes that consistency is considered by residential workers to be the most essential ingredient for quality care and good outcomes. Consistency through stable relationships is one of the key factors that predict good outcomes for children recovering from trauma.

Consistency within placement, however, is difficult to achieve on two counts:

1. Children are frequently moved to different placements. Numerous studies (Hart, LaValle, & Holmes, 2015; Ward, Skuse, & Munrow, 2005) highlight that children change placements frequently.
2. Consistency is often hampered due to high staff turnover. Moses (2000) reported that residential workers chose to work in residential care for personal and ideological reasons, although many tended to view this choice as temporary due to seeing the working conditions (shift work, long hours,

low pay, low status) as not conducive to long-term employment. These findings are supported by Colton and Roberts (2007), who report that one of the contributory factors regarding high staff turnover is negative perceptions of the service. Children frequently moving placements and high staff turnover compromise consistency and impact the development of consistent and stable relationships.

Promoting Resilience

Children's homes are both a home for children who live there and a place of work. Therefore, unlike children who live with their families, children in residential care live in an environment where refrigerator temperatures are recorded, fire exits are monitored, and activities take place only following a risk assessment. These children are cared for by a group of adults, and a staff rota dictates the time spent in the children's presence. Therefore, there is an overlap of home, workplace and institution (McIntosh, Dorrer, Punch, & Emond, 2011). These factors contribute to the complexity of the task and provide both opportunities and potential barriers for developing skills and attributes of resilience.

A child's care plan is likely to include a range of support provided by various professionals from different disciplines. Therefore, consistency is most relevant in the planning and organization of any intervention. Gilligan (2009) recognizes two significant attributes that contribute to outcomes of resilience:

1. There needs to be an opportunity presented to the child.
2. This needs to be coupled with the readiness of the child to engage with the new opportunity.

Those adults closest to the child therefore need to be attuned to that readiness so that opportunities can be seized. The quality of relationships, coupled with the timeliness of new opportunities, are significant to a trauma-informed approach and the promotion of resilience.

Practice focus

Jay was ten years old and living in a residential group home. She displayed sexualized behavior, resulting in her moving through various other placements. Both parents were serving custodial sentences which included offences of sexual abuse against Jay. The team at the home worked hard to manage her sexualized behavior through kind, clear, supportive boundaries. In addition, she attended weekly individual direct work sessions focusing on sexual health and relationship education. These weekly sessions were carried out by a play therapist and supported by Jay's keyworker from the home. During a multidisciplinary team consultancy meeting, the care team discussed their concerns that Jay had been complaining of abdominal pains. The keyworker observed that she and her colleagues were tending to view these complaints as Jay's way of communicating her need for attention, rather than an indicator of a health concern. A medical examination confirmed that there appeared to be no particular concerns, but her condition would be monitored. Following the weekly sexual health and relationship education session, the play therapist transported Jay and the keyworker back to the home. Jay sat in the back of the car, allowing her space to process the direct work session before arriving back at the home. On one particular occasion the session had included information about the process of reproduction. While driving home Jay said from the back seat of the car: "So, does that mean my dad's sperm are no longer in my belly?" The workers confirmed that Jay was correct and reiterated the information from the session. Following this, staff observed that there were no further complaints of stomach pain.

It could be hypothesized that the opportunity for education enabled Jay to be less muddled about the consequences of her sexual abuse experiences. The opportunity through child-centered direct work promoted understanding, indicated by Jay's response on the journey home and further by the reduction of physical symptoms. As such, it liberated her from the worry about her "dad's sperm" being permanently present. The experience promoted resilience through her new understanding. The sexual abuse experiences were behind her, rather than constantly present and inside her.

This direct work was conducted in a planned way and at a stage of placement where Jay had already had plenty of time to settle into the life of the home and to build a trusting relationship with her keyworker and other members of the home and wider organization. In other words, the opportunity was provided at a time when Jay was able to make use of the opportunity. In this way, resilience is promoted through an experience of learning, thereby reducing the impact of traumatic experience. When the adults consistently focus on the child as a whole person it allows the child to have a belief that their experiences of trauma do not need to define them. In this example, sexual health and relationship education is provided as a protective factor, which promotes resilience for children traumatized through sexual abuse. However, it could only take place with interdisciplinary cooperation and support. A consistent approach includes processes of planning, communication, support and reflection.

Potential Barriers to Resilience

Timely and informed interventions promote resilience. Teams therefore need to resist pressure to move the child on too quickly—for instance, where a team considers that a child requires more socialization. This might be in response to support struggles with social interaction. However, if the child has not developed appropriate interpersonal skills, the child may inadvertently be put in situations where they are likely to fail. Many of the coping strategies a child with a history of trauma has utilized to survive, such as controlling behaviors, or their seemingly disproportionate responses to stimuli, can be confusing and frightening for their peers and therefore lead to further experiences of rejection. Thus, the child's opportunity to practice socializing becomes a source of further shame and confirmation of their negative self-view. A resilience-led approach allows adults to understand that the child cannot practice skills that they do not inherently possess. The focus therefore shifts to the adults using role modelling to demonstrate social skills and to provide a safe arena to make mistakes and learn from them.

Conclusion

The promotion of resilience through trauma-informed care will not only serve to assist children in coming to terms with their past lives, but also it will prepare them to cope with their futures.

References

Bellisi, M. A., Ashtoni, K., Hughesii, K., Fordii, K., Bishopi, J. and Paranjothyi, S. (2015). *Adverse Childhood Experiences and their impact on health-harming behaviors in the Welsh adult population*. Cardiff: Public Health Wales NHS Trust.

Cairns, K. and Cairns, B. (2016). *Attachment trauma and resilience: Therapeutic caring for children*. London: BAAF.

Cicchetti, D., Rogosch, F. A., Gunnar, M. R. and Toth, S. L. (2010). The differential impacts of early physical and sexual abuse and internalizing problems on daytime cortisol rhythm in school age-children. *Child Development*, 81, pp. 252–69.

Colton, M. and Roberts, S. (2007). Factors that contribute to high turnover among residential child care staff. *Journal of Child and Family Social Work*, 12, pp. 133–42.

Felitti, M. D., Anda, R. F., Nordenberg, M. D., Williamson, D. F., Spitz, A. M., Edwards, V., . . . Marks, J. S. (1998). Relationship of childhood abuse and household dysfunction to many of the leading causes of death in adults: The Adverse Childhood Experiences (ACE) study. *American Journal of Preventive Medicine*, 14(4), pp. 245–58.

Gilligan, R. (2009). *Promoting resilience: Supporting children and young people who are in care, adopted or in need*. London: BAAF.

Grotberg, E. (1995). *A guide to promoting resilience in children: Strengthening the human spirit*. Netherlands: Bernard von Leer Foundation.

Hart, D., LaValle, I. and Holmes, L. (2015). *The place of residential care in the English child welfare system research report*. London: Department of Education. Retrieved from www.gov.uk/government/publications/residential-care-in-the-english-child-welfare-system

Mainey, A. and Crimmens, D. (Eds.) (2006). *Fit for the future? Residential child care in the United Kingdom*. London: National Children's Bureau.

McIntosh, I., Dorrer, N., Punch, S. and Emond, R. (2011). "I know we can't be a family, but as close as you can get": Displaying families within an institutional context. In E. Dermott and J. Seymour (Eds.), *Displaying families: A new concept for the sociology of family life*. Basingstoke: Palgrave Macmillan, pp. 175–94.

Moses, T. (2000). Attachment theory and residential treatment: A study of staff client relationships. *American Journal of Orthopsychiatry*, 70(4), pp. 474–90.

Nicholson, C., Irwin, M. and Dwivedi, K. N. (2010). *Children and adolescents in trauma: Creative therapeutic approaches*. London: Jessica Kingsley Publishers.

Perry, B. D., Pollard, R. A., Blakley, T. L., Baker, W. L. and Vigilante, D. (1995). Childhood trauma, the neurobiology of adaptation, and "use-dependent" development of the brain: How "states" become "traits". *Infant Mental Health Journal*, 16(4). Retrieved from www.trauma-pages.com/a/perry96.php

Schore, A. N. (2009). Relational trauma and the developing right brain: An interface of psychoanalytic self psychology and neuroscience. *Annals of the New York Academy of Sciences*, 1159(1), pp. 189–203.

Smith, M. (2009). *Rethinking residential child care: Positive perspectives*. Bristol: Policy Press.

Steele, W. and Malchiodi, C. (2012). *Trauma-informed practices with children and adolescents*. East Sussex: Routledge.

Van der Kolk, B. A. (2005). Developmental trauma disorder: Towards a rational diagnosis for children with complex trauma histories. *Psychiatric Annals*, 35(5), pp. 401–8.

Ward, A. (2007). *Working in group care: Social work and social care in residential and day Care settings*. (5th Edn.) Bristol: The Policy Press.

Ward, H., Skuse, T. and Munrow, E. R. (2005). The best of times, the worst of times: Young people's views of care and accommodation. *Adoption and Fostering*, 29(1), pp. 8–17.

Watson, D. (2003). Defining quality care for looked after children: Frontline workers' perspectives on standards and all that? *Child and Family Social Work*, 8, pp. 67–77.

Woodier, D. (2011). Building resilience in looked after young people: A moral values approach. *British Journal of Guidance & Counselling*, 39(3), pp. 259–82.

18 Care Leavers and Resilience

Lorna Stabler

Leaving foster care, or "aging out," was the transition out of care in 2017 for around 20,000 young people who had experienced non-relative foster care in the U.S. (U.S. Department of Health and Human Services, 2018). In other words, they are those that are not adopted or reunited with their birth family but rather reach an age where the state is no longer legally responsible for their care. Leaving care tends to happen at a point described by Arnett (2000) as emerging adulthood. Care leavers are often expected to transition directly from childhood dependence to adult self-sufficiency (Propp, Ortega, & Newheart, 2003), unlike many of their peers living with family. For many care leavers, social support may be limited, and relationships with their family may be missing or stressful (Sinclair, Baker, Wilson, & Gibbs, 2005). In addition, they enter this period with more stressors and prior and present disadvantages, such as poverty, maltreatment and instability of living arrangements (Arnett, 2007; Courtney, Hook, & Lee, 2010).

Care experience is one of loss. Loss is inherent in entering care, and there is an increased likelihood that children in care will have experienced the loss of a significant adult to death. If we perceive leaving care as an additional loss—be that of the relationships developed with a foster family, residential staff, professional child welfare personnel, or as a loss of normality, structure and reassurance—then it is clear to see why this is a challenge that requires resilience to adjust to and recover from.

The grief associated with this loss can leave a young person feeling unable to rise to the challenge of adapting to their new situation, feeling a lack of control over the controllable. Having a sense of control is an important part of mental well-being, and also in making practical, necessary decisions associated with independent living. Moreover, young people can lack emotional support as they make these transitions in and out of foster families or systems of care, and experience enduring insecurities about the stability of their living arrangements (Kools, 1997). Understandably, aging out of foster care is a challenging location from which to enter and navigate adulthood.

"Resilience" is therefore predictably a term peppered throughout most literature pertaining to care leavers and is seen as essential to successfully "survive" this transition. While there is great work around promoting resilience for this group (for example, Schofield & Beek, 2005; Stein, 2008), often interest is shown towards those young people who have experienced foster care but nevertheless thrive "against the odds," such as high achievement in education (Gilligan, 2007; Cameron, 2007). This can promote a focus on narrowing down the individual characteristics that lead to resilience in this group and interventions that can support the development of these characteristics in others. This perceived individualistic focus of resilience has made it a contested concept in this area (Hunter, 2012).

Trends of poorer outcomes for individuals leaving care across countries with comparable social work systems (the USA, UK, Australia) indicate structural disadvantage, rather than just individual characteristics, when considering resilience (Stein, 2006; Munro & Manful, 2012). This has led to a growing focus on the sociological factors that impact on the lack of, need for and building of resilience in these young people. The rest of this chapter will look at three sociological concepts that can increase understanding of resilience and how it can be promoted for care leavers.

Social Capital and Support Networks

One way in which young people can better cope with the vulnerability associated with transitioning into independence is by drawing support from social networks. The extent and quality of support available from key individuals, groups or organizations can greatly impact a young person's ability to respond to situations of adversity. The social capital available to the individual—social resources available from friendships, family support, community involvement, membership of various organizations and associations (Lin, 2002)—will have great bearing on the support from which a young person can draw to move from vulnerability to a position of greater security, confidence and coping during the major life transition of leaving care. The availability of these supports, and a young person's ability to draw on them, can increase their resourcefulness, supporting the navigation of difficult situations, and preventing situations of adversity, as outlined in Thompson's (2016) framework for promoting resilience.

In exiting foster care, young people experience the loss of "normality" of day-to-day life and the support that this conveys. Leaving care often means leaving behind a family, a routine, a house and crucially a room that a young person has come to think of as their own in some way. At the same time, many young people experience an abrupt end to structural and institutional support from the state. The state, as corporate parent, is often unavailable or inconsistent in providing the ongoing financial, social and emotional support and nurturing offered by most families of origin. This coincides with a shift in other social support networks that are available in childhood, such as school. This concurrent loss of support and change in routines can have the impact of leaving a young person feeling an overwhelming sense of "normlessness" (Durkheim, 2002), causing a challenge to resilience.

More than just availability of supports, however, of issue is how or if care leavers draw on these resources to prevent situations of adversity. Despite the clear importance of these social networks for young people leaving care, the existence of supports does not necessarily guarantee that these will be engaged with (Samuels & Pryce, 2008). There are aspects of being in foster care that may challenge a young person's use of, or openness to, receiving or requesting support. How young people learn to cope with their circumstances prior to entering care and make sense of their often multiple placements and caregivers during care matters in how they view themselves and their connections to the world around them.

While care experience is different for each individual, trends can be explored. There are many reasons that young people can develop through their care experience a desire to not be reliant on others for support. Young people who have been subject to a number of placement moves during their time in care (the average is around four for those aging out of care, but it can be much higher—Stein, 2008) can be socialized to not ask for support so that they are seen as low maintenance or "the ideal foster child." This can be a strategy for reducing the likelihood of having to move again. However, young people seen as "being able to handle themselves" then receive less support in a system of finite resources where other young people are seen to need it more. For a care leaver, then, being independent is seen as being "successful" in this sense, and that success is then linked intrinsically to receiving less support.

In addition, support from the state can be linked with increased scrutiny. This is particularly pertinent if they want their own children. For many reasons, care leavers who have children, particularly if they have children when they are young, may experience a higher likelihood of child welfare involvement than the general population (Cashmore & Paxman, 2006). All too aware of the potential consequences of this, young care-experienced parents may be more resistant to asking for support, as it is associated with the risk of their child being removed from their care. This complex relationship with support therefore impacts on the resourcefulness of care leavers facing difficult situations and also on how care leavers make sense of themselves and their experience.

Meaning Making

Care leavers will often have experienced a great amount of loss and adversity in their lives and therefore can be led to interpret the world through this lens. This can have negative consequences for young people in terms of their ability to develop trusting relationships or feel stable and secure in their circumstances.

On the other hand, it can allow young people to take ownership of their experiences and their identity. As Samuels and Pryce (2008) outline in their qualitative work with young people, many associate independence and not asking for support with a sense of pride in having "survived" alone—what they term "survivalist self-reliance." This indicates the way in which young people's experiences of growing up without their family, or a support network, can shape their view of themselves and how they see others in relation to them. To make sense of their stories, and the loss that they have experienced, the attributes of being a survivor can allow young people to reinvent themselves in a positive light. Rather than the negative experiences that led to their entering care, or going through "the system," being incidents done to them, they are reframed as things that the young person survived—creating the identity of a strong, independent survivor. This ability to find positive meaning in adversity can be a source of resilience for care leavers.

Social expectations also have a role to play in shaping the narrative for care leavers. The media and other social institutions create a set of expectations for young people, and for family life, that do not reflect the experiences or the adversity faced by care leavers. Media representation of care leavers is usually either one of pity or of blame, highlighting negative life trajectories. These stories often emphasize the situation of self-reliance, which reinforces societal expectations of independence and autonomy of care leavers. In addition, the portrayal of "normal family life" is a norm by which care leavers can compare their own experiences of family and find themselves lacking. When care leavers do have a role in popular media, this is usually based on tropes of being "troubled youths," often with trauma that restricts their ability to integrate into adult life. This pessimistic depiction can discourage young people from being open about their care experience, restricting potential support. It can also reduce potential resilience by decreasing positive expectations of the future (Sulimani-Aidan, 2016).

Place in Society

As the grief associated with the loss involved in leaving care is not socially recognized, there are no mechanisms through which a cultural response can emerge to develop practices and processes through which care leavers can be supported in this transition. Increasingly, technology has facilitated networks and groups of care-experienced people who can share their own experiences and offer advice and support. This development in itself has the potential to provide a cultural model of how young people can respond to adversity and loss associated with leaving care. Crucially, it can provide examples and narratives that the young person can locate themselves within and help them to understand their experience and place in society.

Often, understanding our place in society supersedes our understanding of where we fit within our family and within our immediate community. Being legally removed from a birth family removes the feeling of a young person knowing their place and trusting in their membership within a set family unit. This is potentially even more pertinent for young people who have siblings who remain at home or return home while they do not. This can lead to children in care never really feeling at "home" in the foster family. Consequently, this can be a push for young people to leave care prematurely, even when there is an option to stay longer term. This can potentially explain some of the slow uptake of initiatives to extend foster care beyond adolescence.

Not having a "normal" role within a family can complicate relationships that young people have with birth families once they leave care. They can be more comfortable offering support or care to parents and siblings than the other way around, taking security from the role of provider, rather than reliance on someone else. This is developed from the narrative of independence and self-reliance used to make sense of their experiences. This, however, can leave young people leaving care out of sync with other young people, especially with the trend of young adults staying at home longer and receiving ongoing support from parents. This disconnect can result in care leavers feeling a sense of being eternally lacking.

Being alone, growing up without parental support, and without security in a family identity can later cause difficulties for young people in understanding their place in society. While having been disconnected from family, culture and community, they are also disconnected from the new environment and norms of foster care. Having a belief in your role in society, your reason for getting up and going about your day, is essential to resilience, as it necessitates moving past the current experience of adversity. Without this, despair and disconnectedness can increase the vulnerability of a young person and make them unable to "bounce back" from negative experiences or navigate the difficulties of day-to-day life. This increases the risk of young people experiencing repeated difficulties throughout their lifecourse. This highlights the need for stability for young people in care—both through connection with family and foster family, but also community and society more widely.

Conclusion

By taking a sociological perspective on transitioning out of care to independence, we can see that, to promote resilience for this group, a broad response is needed. To increase resources, and the resourcefulness of care leavers, it is not enough to offer after-care support. Practitioners, youth workers, foster carers and beyond need to work with young people in care to form a positive relationship with asking for support. A starting point for this would be not to reinforce the belief that independence is the same as not drawing on support. It is important to take a holistic lifecourse perspective to support young people to embed their experiences in a broader societal, developmental, theoretical and practice context to make sense of their place in the world and their relationships with others. One way of doing this is to nurture the development of care-experienced networks to form cultural responses to the loss associated with leaving care. More widely, more needs to be done to influence the media representation of care experience to show more diversity, positive examples of young people who have left care and a more "normalized" experience. Taking this broader societal approach has the potential to both promote resilience *within* care leavers and also strengthen responses to care leavers facing adversity.

References

Arnett, J. J. (2000). Emerging adulthood: A theory of development from the late teens through the twenties. *American Psychologist*, 55(5), pp. 469–80.

Arnett, J. J. (2007). Afterword: Aging out of care—Toward realizing the possibilities of emerging adulthood. *New Directions for Youth Development*, 113, pp. 151–61.

Cameron, C. (2007). Education and self-reliance among care leavers. *Adoption & Fostering*, 31(1), pp. 39–49.

Cashmore, J. and Paxman, M. (2006). Wards leaving care: Follow up five years on. *Children Australia*, 31(3), pp. 18–25.

Courtney, M. E., Hook, J. L. and Lee, J. S. (2010). *Distinct subgroups of former foster youth during young adulthood: Implications for policy and practice.* Chicago, IL: Chapin Hall Center for Children at the University of Chicago.

Durkheim, E. (2002). *Suicide: A study in sociology.* New York: Routledge.

Gilligan, R. (2007). Adversity, resilience and the educational progress of young people in public care. *Emotional and Behavioural Difficulties*, 12(2), pp. 135–45.

Hunter, C. (2012). Is resilience still a useful concept when working with children and young people? *Journal of the Home Economics Institute of Australia*, 19(1), pp. 45–52.

Kools, S. M. (1997, July). Adolescent identity development in foster care. *Family Relations*, 46(3), pp. 263–71.

Lin, N. (2002). *Social capital: A theory of social structure and action,* Cambridge, UK: Cambridge University Press.

Munro, E. R. and Manful, E. (2012). *Safeguarding children: A comparison of England's data with that of Australia, Norway and the United States.* London: Department for Education.

Propp, J., Ortega, D. M. and Newheart, F. (2003). Independence or interdependence: Rethinking the transition from "ward of the court" to adulthood. *Families in Society*, 84(2) pp. 259–66.

Samuels, G. M. and Pryce, J. M. (2008). "What doesn't kill you makes you stronger": Survivalist self-reliance as resilience and risk among young adults aging out of foster care. *Children and Youth Services Review*, 30(10), pp. 1198–210.

Schofield, G. and Beek, M. (2005). Risk and resilience in long-term foster-care. *British Journal of Social Work*, 35(8), pp. 1283–301.

Sinclair, I., Baker, C., Wilson, K. and Gibbs, I. (2005). *Where they go and how they get on.* London: Jessica Kingsley.

Stein, M. (2006). Research review: Young people leaving care. *Child & Family Social Work*, 11(3), pp. 273–9.

Stein, M. (2008). Resilience and young people leaving care. *Child Care in Practice*, 14(1), pp. 35–44.

Sulimani-Aidan, Y. (2016). Future expectations as a source of resilience among young people leaving care. *British Journal of Social Work*, 47(4), pp. 1111–27.

Thompson, N. (2016). *The professional social worker: Meeting the Challenge.* (2nd Edn.) London: Palgrave.

U.S. Department of Health and Human Services. (2018). *The AFCARS report.* 2017. Retrieved from www.acf.hhs.gov/sites/default/files/cb/afcarsreport25.pdf.

19 The Role of the School

Robert G. Stevenson

Schools in the United States are charged with educating the "whole child." The meaning of that charge has undergone many changes. At first, the school focused on skills needed in life, both by individuals and by society as a whole. The Three Rs of "readin', 'ritin' and 'rithmetic" were said to be the basics of an education for most. However, the charge expanded and continues to grow as more responsibilities are added. Schools now teach "values" and help students to develop their understanding of themselves and their place in society. Starting in 1972, schools even had courses to help students to deal with loss and grief (Stevenson, 1986; Stevenson & Stevenson, 1996).

The rationale for this was simple. Research by Gaudry and Speilberger (1971) and others has shown that student learning is impaired as anxiety increases. Major losses, such as the death of a loved one, certainly can have that effect. To help students reach their academic potential, they can use help in learning how to deal with anxiety. Ideally, such education begins in the home. Parents and family members are the first and most important teachers of children. They model coping behaviors as they try to cope with the losses and stress they encounter in life. In an ideal situation, young people can go to family members for information and support in time of crisis, building on a foundation established early in life.

Religious institutions can also be a source of such information. Diversity of religious beliefs, or lack of such a belief, in our pluralistic society makes it difficult to generalize about the impact of religion in the education of young people about loss and grief. The roles of family and personal spiritual values must both be taken into account when working with grieving individuals, especially in the aftermath of a major loss. When such education is offered in schools it is not done in isolation. Teachers must be conscious of the many influences in the lives of their students. Instructors need to demonstrate multicultural sensitivity so that cultural, regional and religious differences will be acknowledged if the needs of students are to be met. In fact, if a fourth R might be added to that basic three, I would see it as "resilience."

Resilience can be defined as "the power to recover readily or to spring back from stress, trauma or other negative conditions in life" (Gladding,

2006, p. 123). This "power" or ability is helped by knowledge and skills imparted to students by parents and in schools by counselors and teachers. Many of the topics now being addressed by schools certainly fall within this area: grief, bullying, social isolation, suicide and depression and self-esteem to name but a few. These issues and more can be seen as having a similar goal. That goal is to evaluate and then find ways to address the social and psychological needs of students. Helping students to cope with these needs can facilitate better academic performance and can benefit any student facing a group or personal crisis.

Two Types of Crisis: Group Crisis and Personal Crisis

Schools have developed crisis response programs that address two separate areas: group crisis and personal crisis. A group crisis often results from a disaster (or the threat of one). Disaster may be defined as a sudden calamitous event bringing great damage, loss or destruction *which impacts many people* (Merriam-Webster.com, 2018). However, such events may be experienced differently by different individuals. While all disasters can produce a group crisis, an individual may experience disaster both as trauma and as a cause of personal crisis. Personal crisis exists when a person believes that an event or situation is an intolerable difficulty that exceeds the person's current resources and coping mechanisms (James & Gilliland, 2001; Cox & Stevenson, 2018). What is important in determining a crisis is what the individual believes. It need not necessarily be seen as that difficult by others.

Emotions, such as those felt with grief, can impair short-term memory. If one believes the situation to be beyond their ability to cope, it will magnify the effect of those emotions. The emotions present in grief are typically loneliness, helplessness and hopelessness. They can be both painful and confusing, and they also take energy away from other matters (such as schoolwork). An added risk occurs if the person has feelings of worthlessness. That added emotion can increase the risk of suicide in a grieving individual. Looking at this emotional package, it does seem that the school needs to have plans and procedures in place to assist students who are coping with personal crises (Stevenson, 2002).

Evaluation and Criticism of Crisis Support

Positive criticism of crisis support in schools came from British researcher Sonja Hunt. (Stevenson, 1984) Dr. Hunt was an adviser at Fairleigh Dickinson University in New Jersey. The comments here are from a personal interview with Dr. Hunt in 1984, cited in my 1984 dissertation. She pointed out that there are events and processes in life that leave a distinct mark on an individual. Death is such an event, and grief is such a process. She cautioned that educators need to be aware of the possible consequences of their work before attempting instruction which could affect the grief process. She also asked educators to clearly identify why schools would be an appropriate place for such interventions and to be clear about their goals if attempting such interventions (Stevenson, 1984).

If schools are to undertake such a role, what qualifications are needed for those who will implement such a program? The Association of Death Education and Counseling (ADEC) has provided lists of "core knowledge" that include key ideas that have been identified by experts in the field. ADEC also offers a certification program for crisis educators and counselors, and the number of qualified faculty is increasing. The basic text for educator certification is the *Handbook of Thanatology, 2nd edition*. It contains a set of chapters by the leading people in the field and is intended to be an essential body of knowledge for the study of grief, death and dying (Meagher & Balk, 2013).

Looking Ahead

Those who try to look ahead and see what the future holds for schools and the role of helping students to cope with crises identify the need for a broader focus. In recent years, the broader concept of "loss" has come to replace "death" in many places in the curriculum. The belief is that, if psychological models can also be used in dealing with losses other than a death, perhaps the focus should be on loss in general, rather than a focus chiefly of the grief that follows death. Models are, after all, not "real." It is the person/client/student who is real, and models are only useful if they help that person and those who work with them to understand what they are going through. It is this approach that allows educators to provide students with skills to help them cope with personal crises. Issues such as "communication" (whether parent-child, student-student or student-teacher) are taking on a larger role in the curriculum. Students have repeatedly said that, once they spoke about one difficult, or "taboo," topic, such as a death for example, they were more able and more likely to speak about other topics that were taboo (Cox & Stevenson, 2018).

Shaping and telling personal stories have become a new method for dealing with personal grief, as it has in narrative therapy (where clients rewrite their life stories to help themselves understand their own lives). Robert Neimeyer speaks of *meaning reconstruction* through narratives following a death. He sees theories using narratives and stories as having some points in common: skepticism about a predictable trajectory for the grief process; increased emphasis on continuing healthy bonds with the deceased; increased emphasis on the meaning-making process in mourning; greater awareness of the impact of major loss on the individual's self-identity; increased awareness of the possibility of "post-traumatic growth," as one recovers and uses lessons learned in the process; and a focus on groups beyond the grieving individual—such as family or community (Neimeyer, 1998, 1999).

Implementing Crisis Support Programs in Schools

Students cannot be shielded from the reality of loss or from the presence of crises in their lives. School can play a positive role in preparing adolescents to cope with the reality of dying, death and grief. Such preparation started as what was called "death education." That narrow focus showed great application, and many of the programs now fall under crisis preparation, intervention and response. If a school wants to implement such a program, the following points can be important:

- The process of implementing crisis intervention procedures with a student (or a school) should be open, and continuous input should be sought from students, parents and community members.
- Instructors and counselors must be qualified, both academically and emotionally.
- Any curricula must be age appropriate and sensitive to the culture and background of individual students.
- Ongoing programs of evaluation and professional development must be established.
- For educators and counselors to be of the most value in a time of crisis, a crisis response plan needs to be developed.

Physical illness can strike an individual at any time. For that reason, society recommends and may even require immunization to lessen the pain and suffering caused by such illness; treatment after the fact is often more difficult. Death and grief can also strike at any time, as can a crisis. Experience has shown that it can help adolescents to face the pain and suffering such events can cause. It will not prevent pain, but it may help to moderate it, offsetting the pain that can be greater due to coming from fear of the unknown.

Contemporary Issues of Life and Death

In 1972 I designed and taught the first independent high school course on "death education." It was nine weeks in length (one marking period) but student interest soon had it expanded to a full semester (18 weeks). One major issue with the course was its title. Any title with the word "death" in it brought up concerns from a small but very vocal minority in the community. The final title was "Contemporary Issues of Life and Death." That allowed it to be listed as "Contemporary Issues" in the school catalogue of courses—dropping the word "death" from the title to save space. The change placated those distressed by the word "death" but allowed the course to continue. The parents gave the course virtually unanimous support. The opposition came chiefly from some with other agendas that did not consider either the ability of students to handle such an elective or the need to make it available to them.

The story of the course was shown in a BBC program titled *The Facts of Death*, produced by David Willcock (1989). In producing the show, David asked an interesting question. He wanted to know if this course was so popular because of the teacher or because of the topic. That is not a minor point. If it was simply the teacher, then the course would run for a time and then disappear when that professor moved on to some other course. If it was the subject, he felt, then the topic would remain after that teacher was no longer connected with the course.

Conclusion

The need for courses in secondary schools (and units for younger classes) that help to foster resilience among students is now well established. More educators are developing new units and courses every year, as the challenges to their work, and the new areas which need to be addressed by that work, continue to grow. Schools are now confirmed as a place where students can develop skills that will help them to be more resilient. The needs of students and society have certainly changed from the days when the role of the school was to prepare students by providing them with basic skills and a simple knowledge of their nation's history, so they could understand their place in it. Now, as the needs of society change, the role of the school will continue to evolve, and the goal of providing students with knowledge and skills to help them be more resilient and to contribute to their society will be in good hands.

References

British Broadcasting Corporation (1989). *The facts of death.* London: BBC Everyman Series.

Cox, G. R. and Stevenson, R. G. (2018). *Children: Surviving traumatic death.* Omaha, NE: The Centering Corporation.

Gaudry, E. and Speilberger, C. (1971). *Anxiety and educational achievement.* Sydney: J. Wiley and Sons, pp. 40–1.

Gladding, S. T. (2006). *The counseling dictionary: Concise definitions of frequently used terms* (2nd Edn.) Upper Saddle River, NJ: Pearson Education.

James, R. K. and Gilliland, B. E. (2001). *Crisis intervention strategies.* (4th Edn.) New York: Brooks Cole Thomson Learning. pp. 23–4.

Meagher, D. K. and Balk, D. E. (Eds.) (2013). *Handbook of thanatology.* (2nd Edn.) New York: Routledge.

Merriam-Webster.com (2018). *Merriam-Webster online dictionary.* Retrieved August 21, 2018, from www.merriam-webster.com/dictionary/disaster.

Neimeyer, R. A. (1998). *Lessons of loss: A guide to coping.* New York: McGraw Hill.

Neimeyer, R. A. (1999). Narrative strategies in grief therapy. *Journal of Constructivist Psychology,* 12, pp. 65–85.

Stevenson, R. G. (1984). *A death education course for secondary schools: "Curing" death ignorance.* Doctoral Dissertation, Teaneck, NJ: Fairleigh Dickinson University.

Stevenson, R. G. (1986). Measuring the effects of death education in the classroom. In G. H. Paterson (Ed.), *Children and Death*. London and Ontario: King's College, pp. 201–10.

Stevenson, R. G. (2002). *What will we do? Preparing a school community to cope with crises* (2nd Edn.) Amityville, NY: Baywood Press.

Stevenson, R. G. and Stevenson, E. (1996). *Teaching death education in schools*. Philadelphia, PA: Charles Press.

20 Building Resilience in Organizations: A Challenge for Leaders

What Happens If Leaders Get Sick?

Rozana Huq

Introduction

Leaders need a broader understanding of building resilience in the workplace. A narrow perception of resilience as being "patriarchal," "heroic," "powerful" or an "individual" trait is misleading. This chapter brings attention to a critical issue that must be addressed. Leaders need to identify key people in organizations who need to be trained and taught how to be resilient, because what happens if leaders get sick?

It argues that leaders should not hoard power but rather share power, making sure that employees in organizations (at least key people) are given the freedom to make decisions when needed. One of the ways leaders in organizations can enable people to be resilient is through empowerment, Huq's Model C, the roots of which lie in the community and social work models (Huq, 2008, 2015).

Resilience in this chapter is not only about the capacity of the leader as a resilient and individual force, but the collective strength of individuals who equally have the capacity to develop resilient skills to help the organization bounce back and continue to thrive through a culture of empowerment.

Resilience and Coping with Adversity: What Happens if the Leader Gets Sick? Who Is Resilient Enough to Hold the Fort?

The word "resilience" is associated with "adversity," "toughness," "hardship" in various settings with regards to individual, groups or communities when they are faced with difficult situations; being resilient can enable them to overcome the hardships and adversities they may face.

Most of the time this recovery is related to psychological factors—for example, developing a stronger mindset, self-efficacy and self-esteem (Maslow, 1943; Bandura, 1977; Kieffer, 1984; Conger & Kanungo, 1988; Huq, 2015). Although psychological factors play an important role in building resilience, in order to have a broader and comprehensive understanding in the organizational context, leaders also need to take into account other factors, such as sociological (Thompson, 2018), cultural (Morgan, 1986) and human factors and relationship building (Huq, 2008, 2015).

Being resilient is not easy, and sometimes leaders lack training or coaching in this area, and yet they have to cope and make tough decisions. In business, there are ups and downs, and when the organization is going through difficult times, such as market loss or a business negotiation falls through, it is comparable to a "grief" scenario. Employees in the workplace feel vulnerable. This gives rise to questions: What happens if the leader gets sick? Who is resilient enough to hold the fort?

An important issue is the power to rise to the challenge and deal with the adverse situation. But how is power distributed in organizations? Is it only the leader who holds the power to make important strategic decisions? Key people in the organization may want to make decisions, but they often do not have the power. Consequently, they feel powerless to deal with difficult situations while the leader is off sick.

This "powerless" situation is comparable to social work, where often clients and communities feel powerless and disempowered. There is a strong agreement in the social work literature that powerlessness is a common condition experienced by different groups in society—for example, women, older people and people from ethnic minority backgrounds. Frans (1993) explains how social movements in the 1960s and 1970s contributed to the "spotlight" (p. 312) on powerlessness. Thus, empowerment is viewed as a necessary response to powerlessness and regarded as both a process and goal. The postmodernist approach in social work is about "understanding of power inequalities and a commitment to the empowerment of powerless people" (Fook, 2012, p. 53).

Furthermore, with the advance in information technology, it is no longer the case that knowledge is held in one department or by any one person, therefore people are empowered in more ways than they realize. In the context of resilience in the organization, talent and skills for being resilient may often lie with the most powerless people—for example, employees in non-management positions or those who are in the front line dealing with customers on a day-to-day basis. They are probably the people who know to come up with the best solutions in times of adversity. It is important that leaders train and teach all employees to be resilient should they have to deal with adverse situations on their own.

Huq's Model C: An Employee Empowerment Framework as an Enabler to Build Resilience in Organizations

A kaleidoscope of themes of employee empowerment, Huq's Model C is a framework for implementing employee empowerment in organizations that has its roots in management and social work disciplines (Huq, 2015). Due to limited space, Huq's Model C cannot be explained here in detail. To give a bit of background, the findings of my research titled "An Investigation of What

Employee Empowerment Means in Theory and in Practice" (Huq, 2008) led to the creation of this model as a "Framework for Implementing Employee Empowerment," which is the backbone for building resilience in organizations.

Suffice to say that there is agreement in the management and social work literatures that empowerment is important in people's lives. Thus, Ripley and Ripley (1993, p. 29) emphasize: "Empowerment is critically important in enabling . . . businesses and organisations to survive in this ever-expanding national and international marketplace."

The seven themes in Huq's Model C came out of the multidisciplinary literature reviews of management and social work and from the findings of the qualitative interviews in my research—as to what is meant by employee empowerment and the experiences of people in the case studies who experienced it (Huq, 2015). These seven themes were viewed as significantly important by the interviewees in my research as their lived experience.

Below is a brief summary of these seven themes of employee empowerment to explain how employee empowerment can enable people to be resilient.

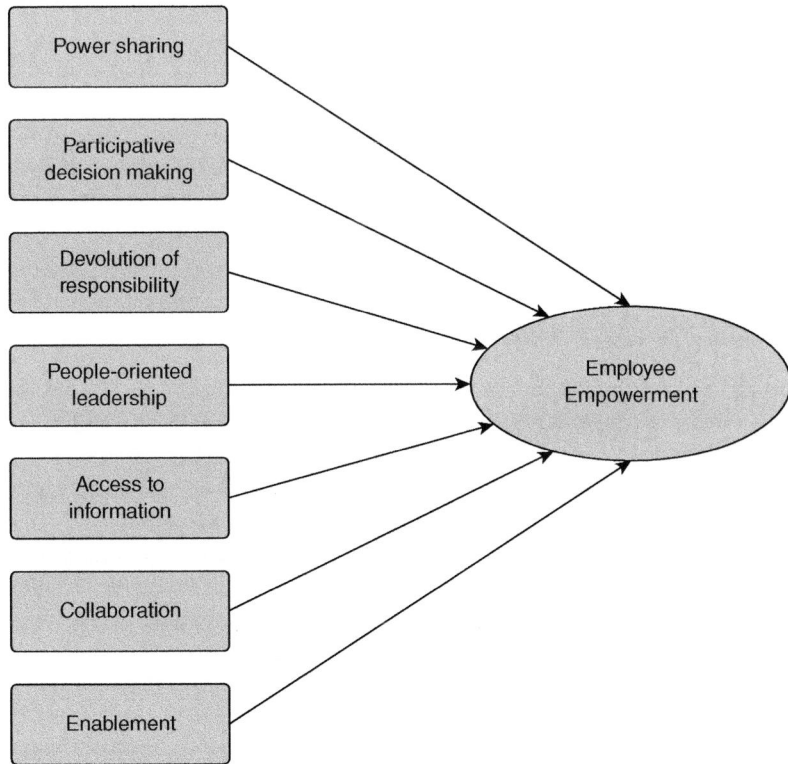

Figure 20.1 Framework for implementing employee empowerment

The Seven Themes of Employee Empowerment

Power Sharing

There is agreement in the literature that the distribution of power is more important than the hoarding of power (Kanter, 1984; Goski & Belfry, 1991; Greenberg & Baron, 2000; Huq, 2010, 2015).

Fincham and Rhodes (2005, p. 430) conclude that traditional organizational hierarchies are "structures of deeply entrenched power, and this has also proved to be a major constraint on work humanization." Often, people with power at the top, such as leaders or chief executives, are uncomfortable with changes and feel threatened by the fear of losing their control. Therefore, they fail to understand that the transformation of power actually helps to build dynamism and energy in organizations (Morgan, 1986; Huq, 2015).

Participative Decision Making

It is argued that one of the reasons for empowering employees is that employees are able to make decisions quickly, without looking for a leader's approval all the time. Hence, it makes sense that authority to make decisions and take action must increasingly be vested in those who are closest to the problem.

There is a growing realization that, in the complexity of the postmodern world, it is becoming less and less feasible to concentrate leadership and decision making solely at the top of the organization (Huq, 2017a). Similarly, with resilience it is becoming difficult for only leaders to take on the part of being resilient. In line with this, it is argued that one of the reasons for empowering employees is that they are able to make decisions confidently, which teaches them to be resilient.

Devolution of Responsibility

It is agreed in the management literature that the devolution of responsibility is also necessary in order to empower employees (Gandz, 1990; Wilkinson, 1998; Sahoo & Das, 2011).

If leaders empower non-managerial employees to take responsibility for decision making at the operational level, this frees up leaders to exercise their responsibilities at the strategic level. Nesan and Holt (2002, p. 201) observe: "In many cases, people like taking on responsibility, because they feel work becomes more meaningful."

A People-Oriented Leadership Style

One of the biggest challenges for empowered organizations concerns the role of leaders. How should leaders lead in an empowered organization? It is useful to note Ripley and Ripley's (1992) argument regarding the differences between a leader who is empowering and one who is not. They describe an empowering leader as having characteristics, such as being interactive, encouraging participation, sharing power and information willingly, and leaning towards a democratic, people-oriented leadership style. By contrast, the traditional authoritarian leader is predisposed to operate in command and control mode and is unwilling to share power and information.

In this sense, it needs to be pointed out that developing a people-oriented leadership style that supports employee empowerment is a significant part of the resilience-building process.

Access to Information

In order to be empowering, organizations need to make information available to individuals in a relevant way. Without access to information at the relevant time, people cannot make decisions or take responsibility (Huq, 2015).

Collaboration

Collaboration is a way of people working together to achieve common goals. This has resonance with social work where it is important that social workers collaborate equally with partners, stakeholders and clients (Adams, 2008; Kirst-Ashman, 2003; DuBois & Miley, 2005; Saleebey, 2013).

Enablement

The concept of empowerment in social work suggests both individual determination over one's own life and democratic participation in the life of one's community (Rappaport, 1987). At the practice level, although empowerment is viewed as a means whereby social workers, groups of people and/or communities are enabled to take control of their lives, the growth of the individual is also considered important.

Interestingly, this has resonance with the results of some studies in the management literature. For example, the conclusions of Conger and Kanungo's (1988) studies revealed that employee empowerment gives employees more control over their work. There is strong agreement that high levels of employees' control over decision making are associated with high levels of psychological well-being.

If all of the seven themes in Huq's Model C are implemented properly, then the resilience of people can be increased (Huq, 2015).

Conclusion

The need to build resilience in organizations is not just important for leaders; for a more sustainable resilient culture, organizations need to train and educate more than just their leaders. Key people and those in organizations who are willing and capable to learn how to be resilient need to be identified, and relevant training provided.

The reasoning behind the employee empowerment model is that people in organizations need to be empowered to develop their potential, and it gives them an opportunity to be creative and innovative Huq (2017b), and they develop a high self-esteem and self-efficacy leading to high resilience.

Feelings of empowerment are more likely to be found in a work group with an approachable leader who encourages the worth of the group—that is, their self-esteem—and facilitates group effectiveness, rather than a leader who does not.

There is also a noticeable change in employees' attitudes and expectations for a more meaningful way of life at work. According to Gandz (1990), a high level of educated human capital is being wasted, as people are not allowed to contribute their intelligence: "We have relatively highly educated human assets, many of whom are working and contributing at a fraction of their potential; the creative, innovative energy in this asset base is enormous" (p. 79). This has resonance with the authenticity of leaders to maximize the development of human potential individually and collectively (Thompson, 2016).

As Freire (1972) argues, it is about the development of critical consciousness and the ability to think against the status quo that enables people to act together, to change oppressive social conditions.

Leaders have a responsibility and commitment to the organization, employees, customers and stakeholders, and their resilience needs to go beyond the individual capacity to include key people who know how to be resilient and "hold the fort" should leaders fall ill or need to take a break for whatever reasons life brings forth. This, in turn, would lead to a more judicious utilization of human resources at all levels.

References

Adams, R. (2008). *Empowerment, participation and social work.* (4th Edn.) Basingstoke, UK: Palgrave Macmillan.

Bandura, A. (1977). Self-efficacy: Toward a unifying theory of behavioral change. *Psychological Review*, 84, pp. 191–215.

Conger, J. A. and Kanungo, R. N. (1988). The empowerment process: Integrating theory and practice. *Academy of Management Review*, 13(3), pp. 471–82.

DuBois, B. and Miley, K. K (2005). *Social work: An empowering profession.* (5th Edn.) Boston, MA: Pearson Education.

Fincham, R. and Rhodes, P. (2005). *Principles of organisational behaviour.* (4th Edn.) Oxford: Oxford University Press.

Fook, J. (2012). *Social work: A critical approach to practice.* (2nd Edn.) London: Sage.

Frans, D. J. (1993). A scale for measuring social worker empowerment. *Research on Social Work Practice*, 3(3), pp. 312–28.

Freire, P. (1972). *Pedagogy of the oppressed.* Harmondsworth, UK: Penguin.

Gandz, J. (1990). The employee empowerment era. *Business Quarterly*, pp. 74–9.

Goski, K. L. and Belfry, M. (1991). Achieving competitive advantage through employee empowerment. *Employment Relations Today*, Summer, pp. 213–20.

Greenberg, J. and Baron, R. A. (2000). *Behavior in organizations: Understanding and managing the human side of work.* (7th Edn.) Upper Saddle River, NJ: Prentice Hall.

Huq, R. (2008). *An investigation of what employee empowerment means in theory and in practice.* PhD thesis, Queen's University Belfast, UK.

Huq, R. (2010). *Employee empowerment: The rhetoric & reality.* Axminster, UK: Triarchy Press.

Huq, R. (2015). *The psychology of employee empowerment: Concepts, critical themes and a framework for implementation.* Abingdon, UK: Routledge.

Huq, R. (2017a, March). The impact of participative decision-making with regards to empowering employees. *International Journal of Business Administration and Management Research*, 3(1), pp. 6–8.

Huq, R. (2017b). Harnessing the power of innovation and creativity of people through employee empowerment. A framework for implementation, Huq's Model D. *European Journal of Business Research*, 17, pp. 45–56.

Kanter, R. M. (1984). *The change masters: Corporate entrepreneurs at work.* London: Allen and Unwin.

Kieffer, C. H. (1984). Citizen empowerment: A development perspective. *Prevention in Human Services*, 3 (Winter/Spring), pp. 9–36.

Kirst-Ashman, K. K. (2003). *Introduction to social work and social welfare: Critical thinking perspectives.* Pacific Grove, CA: Brooks/Cole, Thomson Learning.

Maslow, A. H. (1943). A theory of human motivation. *Psychological Review*, 50, pp. 370–96.

Morgan, G. (1986). *Images of organization.* Beverly Hills, CA: Sage.

Nesan, L. J. and Holt, G. D. (2002). Assessment of organisational involvement in implementing empowerment. *Integrated Manufacturing Systems*, 13(4), pp. 201–11.

Rappaport, J. (1987). Terms of empowerment/exemplars of prevention: Toward a theory of community psychology. *American Journal of Community Psychology*, 15(2), pp. 121–48.

Ripley, R. E. and Ripley, M. J. (1992). Empowerment: The cornerstone of quality: Empowering management in innovative organisations in the 1990s. *Management Decision*, 30(4), pp. 20–43.

Ripley, R. E. and Ripley, M. J. (1993). Empowering management in innovative organisations in the 1990s. *Empowerment in Organisations*, 1(1), pp. 29–40.

Sahoo, C. K. and Das, S. (2011). Employee empowerment: A strategy towards workplace commitment. *European Journal of Business and Management*, 3(11), pp. 46–55.

Saleebey, D. (2013). *The strengths perspective in social work practice.* (6th Edn.) Boston, MA: Pearson Education.

Thompson, N. (2016). *The authentic leader.* London: Palgrave.

Thompson, N. (2018). *Applied sociology.* New York: Routledge.

Wilkinson, A. (1998). Empowerment: Theory and practice. *Personnel Review*, 27(1), pp. 40–56.

21 Resilience at Work

Neil Thompson

Introduction

The world of work is a demanding one. Indeed, the very notion of paid work is based on the idea that demands will be made of employees in return for payment and possibly other benefits. However, it is unfortunately the case that there will often be situations in which the demands produce a level of pressure that is proving problematic for the employee concerned or even a whole group of employees. Workplace-based problems are therefore a matter that warrants careful consideration (Fevre, Lewis, Robinson, & Jones, 2013).

The concept of "workplace well-being" is one that has been receiving focused attention for quite some time now (Rath & Harter, 2010; Thompson & Bates, 2009). It is based on the principle that organizations that invest in making sure that their employees are not being harmed in their work are not only avoiding litigation and/or health and safety non-compliance charges, but also producing win-win outcomes. That is, they are creating a situation in which all stakeholders benefit. Employees have a better quality of life and are thus more productive and happy, and so employing organizations benefit from this, with lower sickness absence rates, lower staff turnover rates, less conflict, more learning and more creativity (Thompson, 2013). Consequently, customers, clients, suppliers and so on are also likely to benefit.

A commitment to workplace well-being can therefore be seen as a wise and productive step to take. How resilience fits into this picture is an interesting and important question to address, and that is what this chapter seeks to do—that is, to begin to clarify the role of resilience in the context of workplace well-being.

Workplace Problems

The workplace is a human environment. That is, although technology of various kinds will generally feature, at the heart of the workplace is human endeavor and therefore human interaction. Consequently, there will inevitably be tensions and problems from time to time (Fevre et al., 2013; Schnall,

Dobson, & Rosskam, 2009). This can include any of the following or any combination of them:

- *Stress*—adverse health and other consequences arising from excessive levels of work pressure (or a combination of work and personal life pressures);
- *Conflict*—some degree of conflict is, of course, inevitable and can be productive if well handled; however, unresolved or uncontrolled conflicts can do considerable damage to all concerned;
- *Bullying and harassment*—unfortunately, assaults on people's dignity are not uncommon in the modern workplace; they can have hugely detrimental consequences, including suicide;
- *Communication problems*—non-existent, ineffective or even counterproductive communication is frequently at the root of many problems in organizational life;
- *Loss, grief and trauma*—the workplace offers no immunity to the challenges presented by loss, especially traumatic loss—to what extent colleagues and the wider organization are sensitive and supportive will have a major bearing on the impact of the loss (Thompson, 2009); and
- *Discrimination*—equality and diversity policies and strategies will rarely, if ever, be successful enough to eradicate racism, sexism and other forms of discrimination, and so it would be naïve not to recognize the potential for discrimination to feature.

In my training and consultancy work I have long used what I refer to as the three Ps approach, as in the recognition that, where there are **P**eople, there will be **P**roblems, but there will also be **P**otential. I see my role as helping organizations to address the problems and realize the potential. This is where resilience can come into the picture.

Resilience in the Workplace

A key theme of this book, as highlighted in Chapter 1, is the need to understand resilience as a psychosocial phenomenon—that is, as one that needs to be understood in terms of sociological factors as well as psychological ones. One implication of this is that an adequate understanding of resilience needs to take account of contextual factors, and this will include the context of the workplace, of course.

Indeed, work settings are highly significant as part of the social context. This is because they have not only their own specific issues as a site of social interaction (a microcosm), but they also channel the wider social context in terms of what elsewhere I have referred to as the sociological SPIDER (social structures, processes, institutions, discourses, expectations and relations—Thompson, 2018) that form the macrocosm.

Resilience, as our ability to "bounce back" from adversity, will therefore be affected—positively or negatively—by various aspects of the workplace context. To explore some of these aspects, I am posing a number of telling questions that enable us to examine how resilience can be promoted through effective workplace well-being practices.

Are There Suitable Policies in Place?

Some organizations have generic well-being policies (possibly referred to as "Health and Well-being," "Wellness" or other such variations). Others will have specific policies around different areas—for example, a specific anti-bullying policy plus a health and safety policy that covers stress issues, and so on. Yet others will have no policies at all.

Policies can not only play an important part in making problems less likely to arise in the first place by giving all concerned clear expectations about what is expected, what is acceptable and what is not, but also provide a framework for addressing problems once they do arise. Policies can therefore provide a degree of confidence by offering a structured way of responding to issues that arise.

Are These Policies Real and Functional or Just Rhetorical?

Unfortunately, many organizations adopt a defensive approach to policy development. That is, they develop policies as a defense against criticism, rather than as foundations for developing best practice and achieving optimal results. In such circumstances, policies can easily become disengaged from actual working life. They can exist on paper or online but actually have no impact on working practices. They avoid senior managers or human resources professionals being open to criticism for not having policies in place but, of course, leave them open to criticism for having fairly meaningless, disconnected policies.

When this scenario arises the result is generally a mistrust of the upper echelons of the organization and potentially a cynical attitude towards the support that is mentioned in such policies. This, of course, is then likely to undermine resilience in some ways, with employees having little or no confidence in the support that is being rhetorically offered but which, in reality, is likely to be lacking. Social support through social connections plays a key role in mitigating stressful situations (Zautra, 2014), and so a perceived lack of support can undermine coping and resilience.

How Are Emotions Managed in This Workplace?

Workplaces will often be perceived as rational places of business, but this perception can be misleading, as emotions are just as prevalent here as they are in any other aspect of human life. How emotions are managed within a work setting will depend on a number of factors, not least the organizational culture—the habits, taken-for-granted assumptions and unwritten rules that form the bedrock of how people relate to one another within the organization concerned.

Some cultures will be emotionally open, in the sense that expression of feelings is encouraged or at least accepted, while others will be more closed, with disapproval featuring in any situation in which emotions are given free rein. This has significant implications for whether resilience is promoted or obstructed. Where people have been through difficult and distressing situations and have intense feelings to deal with, a culture that discourages emotional expression can be very problematic, whereas an emotionally open culture is likely to play a part in facilitating resilience.

Although emotions tend to be seen primarily as bio-psychological phenomena, we need to remember that they also have a significant social dimension (Turner, 2011). The social context in which life experience takes place will, of course, play a part in shaping that experience, including our emotional responses to it.

The social context will also influence how we interpret our experience, including those demanding aspects of life that give rise to the need for resilience. Park and Slattery (2014) propose that finding a thread of meaning in response to adversity is an important part of developing resilience. Meanings are, of course, rooted in the social context. As Illouz (2008) comments: "meanings differ in their ability to constrain definitions of reality: some meanings are more powerful and binding than others" (p. 9). She goes on to argue that "if culture matters, it is because of the ways it shapes and orients the meanings and interpretations with which we carry on our daily lives and make sense of the events that disrupt daily life" (p. 35).

This applies just as much to organizational culture as to any other cultural forms. We can therefore appreciate that both resilience and the threads of meaning that contribute to it are sociological phenomena. Consequently, if we want to develop an adequate understanding of resilience in the workplace, we need to incorporate cultural factors into our analysis.

Are There Appropriate Support Systems in Place?

Many organizations use the services of an employee assistance program (EAP) to offer confidential counseling and other such supportive services. Others rely on more informal ways of supporting staff through difficulties and their aftermath. Much depends on how flexible the organization can be—for example, by temporarily reducing workload expectations. However, a key factor is the extent to which the employers take seriously the core principle of human resources management—namely, that the most important resource is the human resource, the people. How committed are they to genuinely supporting their employees through difficulties? Sadly, many organizations have a "macho" culture that sees staff support as an unnecessary expense, thereby failing to appreciate the value of workplace well-being.

158 Neil Thompson

What Approach to Staff Supervision Is Adopted?

Approaches to staff supervision vary widely from organization to organization. Some employers take the word quite literally as "keeping an eye" on the supervisee. More enlightened approaches recognize that supervision can be a key factor in organizational success by focusing on how the process can help the supervisee to be the best worker they can be. This includes not only focusing on developmental issues but also providing support as and when required. This, then, would play a part in promoting resilience. Knowing that they have managerial support can help give employees facing adversity more confidence in rising to the challenges they encounter and in bouncing back as soon as reasonably possible.

One particular aspect of this is the extent to which supervision boosts confidence and helps people to feel valued. Fevre et al. (2013), in their important discussion of "troubled" workplaces, make the point that "the key predictor of the troubled workplace is that individuals feel that they do not matter" (p. 61). Conversely, we could argue, employees who feel that they do matter will be empowered by constructive supervision that strengthens their resolve and feeds a sense of security. We should therefore not underestimate the significance of supervision (Thompson & Gilbert, 2019).

What Is the Quality of Leadership?

Huq (Chapter 20 in this volume) emphasizes the importance of leadership in developing positive workplaces where resilience will be enabled to flourish. In my own work, I have stressed the value of understanding leadership as, in large part, a process of shaping culture (Thompson, 2016). This is because organizational cultures are very powerful, more powerful than individual managers. Consequently, if the culture is not a positive and helpful one, there is a need for the manager(s) concerned to work towards shaping the culture in ways that make it more of an asset than a liability.

Whether the culture helps or hinders the development of resilience will depend on a number of factors, not least the skills and commitment of those employed in leadership positions. However, it will also depend on the power issues the quotation above from Illouz touched on. Cultures are sites of power, and so the power dynamics and how they are handled by the individuals involved will also play a part, emphasizing once again the need for a sociological lens to complement psychological understandings.

Conclusion

Work takes up a major proportion of many people's lives, offering the potential for significant rewards and satisfactions. However, it also brings the potential for considerable problems, ranging from mild and minor to serious and severe. The challenges involved will often call for resilience. That is, the adversity involved will put us in a position where we can either "go under" or bounce back.

Which it is to be—under or back—is not, contrary to dominant conceptions of resilience, simply a matter of personal strength of character; it is much more complex on that. The highly significant range of social factors will also have a bearing—often a major bearing—on how things turn out. The sort of sophisticated understanding we require to do justice to the complexities involved therefore needs to take account of the social circumstances—including, of course, the workplace as a site of social relations.

This is a complex field of study, and this chapter has only begun to scratch the surface. However, I hope that it has done enough to highlight the need for workplace issues to be part of our understanding of the social context of promoting resilience. Work is such a central part of so many people's lives that the absence of any consideration of its import in seeking to make sense of—and promote—resilience seriously weakens any attempt to develop an adequate appreciation.

References

Fevre, R., Lewis, D., Robinson, A. and Jones, T. (2013). *Trouble at work*. London: Bloomsbury.

Illouz, E. (2008). *Saving the modern soul: Therapy, emotions, and the culture of self-help*. Berkeley: University of California Press.

Park, C. L. and Slattery, J. M. (2014). Resilience interventions with a focus on meaning and values. In M. Kent, M. C. Davis and J. W. Reich (Eds.), *The resilience handbook: Approaches to stress and trauma*. New York: Routledge, pp. 270–82.

Rath, T. and Harter, J. (2010). *Wellbeing: The five essential elements*. New York: Gallup Press.

Schnall, P. L., Dobson, M. and Rosskam, E. (Eds.) (2009). *Unhealthy work: Causes, consequences, cures*. Amityville, NY: Baywood.

Thompson, N. (2009). *Loss, grief and trauma in the workplace*. New York: Routledge.

Thompson, N. (2013). *People management*. Basingstoke, UK: Palgrave Macmillan.

Thompson, N. (2016). *The authentic leader*. London: Palgrave.

Thompson, N. (2018). *Applied sociology*. New York: Routledge.

Thompson, N. and Bates, J. (Eds.) (2009). *Promoting workplace well-being*. Basingstoke, UK: Palgrave Macmillan.

Thompson, N. and Gilbert, P. (2019). *Reflective supervision: A learning and development manual*. (2nd Edn.) Brighton, UK: Pavilion.

Turner, J. H. (2011). *The problem of emotions in societies*. New York: Routledge.

Zautra, A. J. (2014). Resilience is social, after all. In M. Kent, M. C. Davis and J. W. Reich (Eds.), *The resilience handbook: Approaches to stress and trauma*. New York: Routledge, pp. 185–96.

22 Promoting Resilience, Challenging Bullying

Andrew J. Vitale

Introduction

Just what is bullying? According to the website stopbullying.gov (a federal government website managed by the U.S. Department of Health and Human Services, Washington, DC), it is

> unwanted, aggressive behavior among school aged children that involves a real or perceived power imbalance. The behavior is repeated, or has the potential to be repeated, over time. Both kids who are bullied and who bully others may have serious, lasting problems.

An imbalance of power and repetition are key factors for bullying. That is to say, it involves the use of force by physical strength, lording things over another, or using one's place in the pecking line as a means to hurt or cause harm to another, causing the person who is being bullied to become withdrawn into submission. This can indeed cause lasting problems for both the bullied and the bullies.

This chapter explores different types of bullying and argues for a psychosocial approach to the relationship between bullying and resilience.

Types of Bullying

The U.S. Department of Health and Human Services shares that there are three types of bullying (stopbullying.gov): verbal, social and physical. It is worth exploring each of these in turn.

Verbal bullying includes both vocal and written behaviors of being rude, hateful or aggressive toward another. This can include calling people by nasty names, teasing or taunting, threats to actually cause physical harm, as well as comments of any sort that are inappropriate.

Social bullying involves issues of breaking down a person's reputation or relationship. This includes examples of intentionally leaving someone out, children telling their peers to ignore other children or saying bad things about them, public embarrassment and the willful spreading of rumors about another person.

Physical bullying involves such actions as kicking, punching, pushing, pinching, grabbing and the like. Although the website quoted speaks of children, these types of bullying also apply to adults. Indeed, the phenomenon of workplace bullying is a major problem in a wide variety of occupational settings (Thompson, 2019).

In the school setting, bullying can take place in any location (in the hallways, restrooms, playgrounds, classroom) and at any time (before, during or after the school day). Such instances tend to happen at times when no one in authority, such as an adult, is present. The bully can tease or taunt the other child who is seen as inferior to, or different than, the seemingly stronger child, although this is not always the case. The bullying actions of one child over and over again cause the person bullied to slowly break down their defenses, their sense of strength, even their sense of individuality, as usually no one comes to their aid for help, tearing at the very fiber of their being and sense of who they are as a person. This, of course, has significant detrimental implications not only for a person's general well-being but also for their spiritual well-being, our sense of who we are and how we fit into the world being a key part of our worldview and thus of our spirituality (Holloway & Moss, 2010).

When this happens, the person being bullied can either give into the bullying and thereby fall prey, or they can learn from repetition and positive feedback from others who have been on their side to fight back. This is where resilience comes into the storyline, a topic to which I shall return below.

A fourth type of bullying that is growing due to its availability in the digital age is cyberbullying. This is also known as online bullying. It has become more common, especially among teens. It is the bullying or harassing of others on social media sites. The 2010 data from the United States Department of Justice shares that more than one in five children in the United States has been bullied and that nearly 40% report having been assaulted by other youths (Office of Justice Programs). Bullying is considered to be a major public health problem according to the Center for Disease Control (CDC).

Bullying and Empathy

Consider the well-known saying: "When the going gets tough, the tough get going." After being beaten down time after time, do we stay down? Or do we rise to a new occasion and create a new means to bounce back from difficult situations? The quote would certainly suggest the latter, and that is the basis of resilience.

Empathy can be seen to be a significant factor in relation to bullying. When someone is bullied, they are beaten down, leading them either to become a bully in their own right or to learn from the experience and bounce back with empathy—"the ability to see another person's perspective and understand how they must be feeling" (Teresa Porath Centers, 2019).

As Roller explains, "Bullying is frequently the product of the environmental conditions of the child and results from a lack of empathy or understanding of how actions affect others." As I wrote in an earlier work, "bullying is a learned behavior." (Vitale, 2018, p. 79). Teaching empathy and mindfulness can be an effective way to counteract bullying in our schools, workplaces, homes and so on, and bring about resilience in our children—and ourselves.

Learning that our actions have consequences is part of the puzzle. Oftentimes children do not see the larger picture of how an action can cause harm to another; it is sometimes learning through wearing another's shoes, that the child comes to realize that this is not nice, fun and nor does it feel good—thinking that if I do not like this, the person who I am doing this to probably will not enjoy it either. So, we learn to empathize because we have been there, and it did not feel good, and we would not want to hurt another in that fashion. Adults too can relearn and re-educate themselves, if they so choose, to not bully others. Unfortunately, it is oftentimes only when that adult has been in the other's shoes, gotten physically hurt or felt the pain of bullying psychologically that they choose to change and become more empathic toward others.

The Social Context of Bullying

Having considered the different types of bullying and the importance of empathy as a means of reducing the incidences of bullying, I now want to examine bullying in its broader sociological context. The major focus of the literature on bullying is predominantly individualistic, and so my aim is to begin to offer an understanding of the need for a wider, contextual understanding of the phenomenon. To do this I will briefly look at three theoretical concepts, namely socialization, social hierarchy and conflict theory.

Socialization

Social groups act based on social norms (Thompson, 2018). These are the rules to follow in order to fit in, whether in a social group or society as a whole. Agents of socialization consist of family, friends, teachers, religious leaders, the media and the like. These teach us how to act in, or react to, situations in life. Socialization can lead some people to see bullying as the norm (this could also contribute to why hate groups in the United States have grown in the past few years; according to a recent report from the Southern Poverty Law Center—Beirich, 2019). When a person does not fit into what is held as "correct," whether that be by what they say, do or even what they choose to wear, they may be scolded, yelled at or looked down upon—all forms of bullying. This is where the socially significant issue of peer pressure comes into play. When someone is bullied, those watching can resist doing anything for fear of being bullied. No one wants to be excluded in society, so we go with the flow.

Social Hierarchy

Social hierarchy works like a pyramid, with the most powerful people on top as they are seen as the most important. At the bottom we find people with limited power and few resources. This presents an "us-versus-them" picture, as opposed to seeing all people as equal. This power hierarchy creates opportunities for abuse and exploitation, including bullying (especially workplace bullying). Bullies will generally make use of power structures to take their feelings out on others—for example, teasing, taunting, with the intention to hurt mentally, physically, spiritually. We therefore need to understand bullying as a reflection of wider social hierarchies and not simply as a characteristic of individuals.

Conflict Theory

Following on from the idea that social hierarchies play a significant part in bullying, we also need to recognize the importance of conflict. Conflict theory is based on the idea that social hierarchies give rise to conflicting interests between different social groups. For example, the pursuit of wealth by powerful, well-resourced groups can be seen to lead to poverty for certain sectors of society (the haves and the have nots, for example—Dorling, 2015a). Similarly, the use of property speculation to create wealth for some people can lead to homelessness for others (Dorling, 2015b).

Bullying in this light can been seen as a sociopolitical as well as an individual phenomenon. To fully understand bullying, we need to look at the bigger social picture, hence the idea that bullying is a psychosocial issue, not simply an individualistic matter. Developing resilience in response to bullying similarly needs to be understood in psychosocial terms.

Resistance and Resilience

The effects of bullying in all its forms place its victims at an "increased risk for depression, anxiety, psychosomatic complaints, such as headaches and stomachaches, as well as poor school adjustment" (FindaPsychologist, 2016). School phobia can also become an issue as a result of bullying, with potentially long-term adverse effects in terms of the undermining of educational and career progress.

People can be bullied due to the way they look, the way they act or what they like; being different from what the norm says can cause exclusion, loneliness and misery. Growing up being bullied, I can relate to the negative impact of it. As the child who drew the blue and red tree, instead of the brown and green tree as society teaches us, I was "on the bottom" because I was seen as different than the rest—in a social context where difference can so easily be interpreted as deficit. All of this was true until I learned that I do have power (that "lightbulb" of knowledge; the "ah-ha" moment)—the power to stop the violence and teasing. Yes, I fell down or, rather, was knocked down many times, but I *always got back up*. Looking back, this was the beginning of resilience within my personhood. Practicing mindfulness has also helped:

> The more you understand your own mind, the more you can understand the minds of others. If you come to understand your own body language, you can read the body language of others better. Mindfulness doesn't give you a crystal ball, but it tends to increase your empathy, your ability to put yourself in someone's shoes with greater understanding.
>
> (Healey, 2019)

All of this brings us to the point in question: Why do people engage in bullying? Bullying is a means to an end, to be in control of others, usually out of fear. Bullying is wrong, but if an individual speaks out against this, they run the risk of becoming an enemy of the bully. Eyes get turned toward you, and you gain first-hand lessons of what bullying is about for seemingly butting in where you don't belong. This is potentially one of the main reasons bullying is still so rampant in our world. There needs to be a more collective psychosocial approach to the problem, rather than a reliance on the courage of individuals when confronting a bully directly is such a risky and demanding undertaking.

By being on the receiving end of the bullying, and being able to get up again and again and again, we begin to learn and build our resilience, and by practicing mindfulness—using our attention, awareness, memory, retention and discernment—we can grow to become one who empathizes with others and who can, and will, stand up to those who bully and with those who are afraid or don't have a voice. History is filled with this storyline—those with a voice stand up for the voiceless and those on the fringes. Teaching the voiceless to speak out for themselves: that is how change begins. By moving away from a narrow, individualistic focus on bullying and on resilience, we prepare the ground for a more collective, empowering approach.

Lived experiences teach us empathy, if we are open to it. Empathy teaches us how to care for ourselves and others who are in similar shoes and paths. All of our falling and getting back up again—not seen as failure but as learning something new each time—grows resilience within each of us. Resilience and empathy offer us, along with motivation and internal fortitude, the ability to speak up for those who have no voice due to fear. Our example of strength and falling—and always getting back up again—teaches others about resilience. The quotation from Saint Francis of Assisi springs into my head as I type this: "Preach the gospel at all times. When necessary, use words." In actuality Saint Francis never said this. His actual words were far more nuanced: "It is no use walking anywhere to preach unless our walking is our preaching" (Arpin-Ricci, 2012). The very example of our lives is a model to show others truth by standing up against that which is wrong. Bullying encases the bullied into a box of fear. Speaking out against them through our learned experiences and resilience allows our feet to be firmly planted against injustice and offers hope to those who are hopeless.

Conclusion

In this chapter I have shown that bullying, whether in children's lives or in the adult world of the workplace, is a harmful experience. It has its roots not only in individual behavior but also in how people are socialized into respecting and accepting social hierarchies which, despite their potential for abuse and exploitation, are presented as natural and normal—even though the least powerful groups in society tend to lose out in any conflict of interest such hierarchies create.

But what I have also argued is that resistance and resilience are ever-present possibilities. Individually and collectively we can turn against the unfairness of bullying and make a contribution to a more humane and less unequal society. Will bullying prevail in our world? That question is really a matter for all of us. Let's take a stand.

References

Arpin-Ricci, J. (2012). Preach the Gospel at all times? *Huffington Post*, August 31.

Beirich, H. (2019). The year in hate: Rage against change. *SPLC—Intelligence Report*, pp. 39–61.

CDC. Preventing bullying. Retrieved from http://dc.gov/ violenceprevention/youth violence/bullyingresearch/fastfact.html.

Dorling, D. (2015a). *Injustice: Why social inequality still persists.* (2nd Edn.) Bristol, UK: The Policy Press.

Dorling, D. (2015b). *All that is solid: How the great housing disaster defines our times, and what we can do about it.* London: Penguin.

FindaPsychologist Staff (2016). Abuse, bullying, parenting, *The Wire*, June 28.

Healey, T. (2019). Train your mind to work smarter. *Mindful*, January 31.

Office of Justice Programs. *Children exposed to violence.* Retrieved from https://ojp.gov/ programs/cev.htm

Stopbullying.gov (2012). A federal government website managed by the U. S. Department of Health and Human Services, 200 Independence Avenue, S.W., Washington, DC.

Teresa Porath Centers (2019). Some people have to learn how to be empathetic. *Midland Reporter-Telegram*, February 20.

Thompson, N. (2018). *Applied sociology.* New York: Routledge.

Thompson, N. (2019). *Bullying and harassment in the workplace: A learning and development manual.* Brighton, UK: Pavilion.

Vitale, A. (2018). Bullying. In G. R. Cox and R. Stevenson (Eds.), *Children: Surviving traumatic death.* Omaha, NE: Centering Corporation, pp. 79–84.

23 Resilience and Spirituality

A Personal Perspective

Bernard Moss

In Chapter 1 it was argued that "resilience can be understood as largely a question of how we manage our experience of vulnerability" (p. 5) and that "resilience is generally characterized by people having a sense of purpose" (p. 7). In this chapter I explore ways in which the contemporary debate around spirituality can enhance and deepen our understanding of this crucial dimension of human well-being.

From the outset we need to recognize that, in discussing this subject, we are in what we might call "mysterious" territory. The societal and personal circumstances that provoke a sense of vulnerability in us are widely discussed in this book, and yet there remains a deep mystery to the sheer variety of our human responses. In the face of disaster, some people "go under"—they are overwhelmed; they lose hope; their whole *raison d'etre* is demolished; and emotionally, if not always physically, they lose the will to live. By contrast, others will "rise" above the "slings and arrows of outrageous fortune": they will seek to help others; they seem to find a level of courage and generosity of spirit that refuses to give in. Some people find their experience of discrimination, oppression and abuse so powerful and demeaning that they feel they will never ever be able to live life to the full: resentment, bitterness and even hatred become the keynotes of their existence. Others, by contrast, refuse to allow their hurt to be the determining feature of their humanity but instead ensure that they live in such a way that seeks to neutralize the hurt by expanding their capacity for generosity and kindness to others. The profound experience of grief and loss, which is a key theme in this book, evokes a similar kaleidoscope of responses: for some it is a deep descending path into a never-ending darkness of bewilderment and pain that even therapy and medication fail to relieve. Others discover the resilience and courage to move forward into a new phase of living. For some, the experience of grief and loss is underpinned by a deep faith and a religious hope; for others, any such faith or belief is irredeemably shattered. And perhaps the deepest mystery of all is that maybe none of us really knows, until it happens to us, how we will respond when our vulnerabilities are remorselessly exposed.

In this profoundly "mysterious" territory that deeply affects us all, the wide-ranging contemporary debate around spirituality provides something of a framework for a discussion about resilience, not least in its emphasis upon meaning and purpose and their significance for human well-being. Tantalizingly, however, somewhat like the term "resilience," spirituality is difficult to define. For some, spirituality is an intensely personal, even individualistic construct: it is what "makes them tick"; it is what gives meaning and purpose, enjoyment and fulfilment in their lives. For some, spirituality has a distinctive religious dimension to it: as members of a faith community they will understand their spirituality in terms of their religious devotion, their life of prayer and contemplation as they seek to align their lives to the will and purpose of the Divine Other. But there are other people who do not hold a religious worldview who, nevertheless, from a secular perspective insist that spirituality is important to their emotional well-being. Indeed, they would argue that to lose the term "spiritual" from their emotional vocabulary and experience would seriously undermine their humanity. The enrichments of joy and wonder, mystery and awe are gifts that can take us by surprise, whether or not a religious dimension is ascribed to them. Spirituality, in other words, both reflects and expands what it means to be fully human and invites us to reflect on the ontological challenges (the big "why?" questions) that challenge our capacity to be resilient.

Several attempts at defining spirituality suggest that a purely individualistic approach is inadequate. Lindsay, for example, talks about "a search for purpose and meaning, and having a moral dimension which reflects a concern with relationships to others, the universe and to some transcendent being or force" (2002, pp. 31–2). In a similar vein, Canda and Furman (1999) talk about

> the wholeness of what it is to be human—the spiritual relates to a person's search for meaning and morally fulfilling relationships between oneself, other people, the encompassing universe and the ontological ground of existence, whether a person understands this in terms which are theistic, atheistic, nontheistic or any combination of these.
>
> (1999, pp 43–3)

Admittedly, these quotations are drawn from a rich social work literature on spirituality but are nevertheless relevant to a much wider audience. These definitions suggest that spirituality invites us to reflect upon ourselves, our relationships to each other and to the planet, and what we understand our role and purpose to be. It provides a context for exploring some fundamental existential questions; and, in the context of this book, spirituality also raises sociological questions about our awareness of our obligations not only to ourselves but also "to the wider realm of families, community and society". (See Chapter 1, p. 7) Spirituality, if you like, is a

> sort of short-hand way of asking the important questions about ourselves—what makes us "tick"; what is important to us; what gives us a

sense of meaning and purpose in our lives. In short, it asks of people what is their world-view?

(Moss, 2005, p. 12; see also Holloway & Moss, 2010, Chapters 1 and 2)

From a sociological perspective, the worldviews that we choose, as well as the worldviews that are imposed upon us, play a crucial role in our individual and corporate resilience. Behind all political slogans lies a set of worldviews that not only compete for our allegiance: they also contain a threat to those who do not subscribe to them. Crusading zeal can often foster resilience to deal with setbacks and defeats along the way: the hope for future "victory" and the shared struggle provide a supportive context in which individual disappointments or even shared setbacks can be absorbed into the wider vision of what is being fought for. So long as you are part of the struggle, resilience is (almost) assured.

Ironically, this can work for both the oppressor and the oppressed. The "glorious dead" can be celebrated and honored by both sides in a conflict. The struggle against oppression and discrimination evokes passion and energy as people fight for their basic human rights against systems that undermine their basic humanity. Setbacks may have to be endured for the sake of the cause to which they are committed.

Two issues emerge from this brief discussion. First, what about those who fall through the net? Those who are rejected by, or who choose no longer to be associated with, "the cause"? How might their resilience be affected? And, second, is there an assumption here that spirituality is a morally neutral concept?

Becoming socially isolated for whatever reason is likely to undermine a person's capacity for resilience. In Chapter 1 attention was drawn to the important concept of "social capital" (Lin, 2002) as a "key sociological contributory factor when it comes to resilience" (p. 15). The fewer the social contacts available—family, friendships, social links, and so on—the more likely it is that resilience will be undermined, unless that person has such a strong sense of his or her intrinsic self-worth and value that they feel able to withstand all the undermining stressors to their well-being. Our own individual spirituality will raise key questions: Who am I? Why am I here? What are the purpose and meaning of my life? For many people, the responses they receive—if not actual answers to these questions—will come from a shared sense of community, rather than being self-generated. How a society deals with people for whom no such answers or responses are forthcoming remains one of the litmus tests of a civilized, compassionate community. Mental health services, care for homeless people and victims of oppression, asylum seekers, victims of natural disasters and international conflict: these are but some of the issues where we find the real challenge of how a community or society reaches out to provide hope, comfort and relief to people in great need, whose resilience has reached breaking point. In such circumstances, resilience is far less of an individual capacity and much more an offered gift from others. Other people's worldviews come into play at this point: How do we respond to people whose resilience has been powerfully "zapped"?

In his seminal work on resilience Rutter noted that

> for psychologically healthy adult development and relationships, people need to accept the . . . reality of the bad experiences they have had and find a way of incorporating the reality of these experiences into their own self-concept, but doing so in a way that builds on the positive while not denying the negative.
>
> (Rutter, 1999, p. 139)

In this brief discussion I am suggesting that spirituality provides something of a creative framework and opportunity whereby some of these key issues and questions can be explored. Just by posing these questions, arising, I would suggest, from a spirituality perspective, we need to return to the question of whether spirituality is a morally neutral concept. If there are as many "types" of spirituality as there are people to espouse them; and if there are as many "spirituality worldviews" as there are people to choose them, is this a moral free-for-all? Is there any way of discriminating between, let us say, people who belong to a far right political group who believe violence is an appropriate political activity and whose members feel that their involvement strengthens their sense of resilience, and (on the other hand) supporters of, say, Greenpeace, whose members may similarly believe that their involvement strengthens their resilience?

At one level perhaps, the answer has to be "yes." If spirituality is a lens through which we appraise our lives, who we are and how we achieve meaning and purpose, then a fundamental relativity is inevitable. We will all develop our individualized, or organizational, answers to the question about our spirituality, the implications of which will vary enormously. If spirituality is "what we do to give expression to our chosen world-view" (Moss, 2005, p. 12), then inevitably our far right members and the Greenpeace followers will reach fundamentally different decisions about what actions to pursue that express their chosen worldviews.

This would suggest, therefore, that underlying the discussion about our spirituality there has to be some sort of moral and ethical yardstick that poses this question: If this is your chosen worldview, then "so what"? In other words, how moral or ethical is the behavior that flows from your chosen worldview? To what extent does it foster and enhance human well-being and flourishing? To what extent does it respect and celebrate human diversity? To what extent does it foster and develop our resilience? To what extent does it offer the opportunities for resilience to those who are struggling and feeling overwhelmed?

These questions, of course, are deeply moral and ethical and which we would suggest need to be addressed to the spirituality discourse. In terms of this book, the importance of resilience remains paramount. If our spirituality—our chosen worldview—diminishes or undermines our resilience, then it deserves a penetrating critique.

From a practice perspective, I would suggest that you find the courage to explore these issues in whatever professional context you are working. It is not always necessary to use the term "spirituality"—indeed, some people may find this off-putting. But, some of the issues in the spirituality discourse may be easily framed. For example, you might want gently to ask: Is there anyone you turn to when you need help? Is there anyone you feel you can really rely on? What are the most important things in your life? What do you live for? Who do you live for? What gives you pleasure and enjoyment? What causes you greatest upset? Do you find yourself sometimes trying to pray? Do you have a religious faith or belief?

I began by suggesting that this area of resilience and spirituality is somewhat "mysterious." There are no easy "fixes," but without resilience our capacity to be fully human and to live life to the full would be severely diminished. I also argue that, left to our own devices, resilience would be seriously compromised: we can be deeply disempowered by other people, organizational cultures or by prejudice and oppression. Grief can overwhelm the strongest. But, our resilience can also be protected, enhanced and strengthened through the rich tapestry of social capital, and our engagement with the discourse around spirituality can deepen our awareness of who we are, the sense of meaning and purpose that are fundamental to our well-being and resilience, and the behaviors we choose to express our chosen worldview. Spirituality provides an opportunity to explore fundamental aspects of our humanity and, in doing so, has the capacity to enhance the precious gift of resilience in our moments of greatest need.

References

Canda, E. and Furman, L. (1999). *Spiritual diversity in social work practice: The heart of helping*. New York: The Free Press.

Holloway, M. and Moss, B. (2010). *Spirituality and social work*. Basingstoke, UK: Palgrave Macmillan.

Lindsay, R. (2002). *Recognising spirituality: The interface between faith and social work*. Crawlet: University of Western Australia Press.

Lin, N. (2002). *Social capital: A theory of social structure and action*. Cambridge UK: Cambridge University Press.

Moss, B. (2005). *Religion and spirituality*. Lyme Regis, UK: Russell House Publishing.

Rutter, M. (1999). Resilience: Concepts and findings: Implications for family therapy. *Journal of Family Therapy*, 21, pp. 119–44.

24 Resilience Through Meaning Making

Neil Thompson

Introduction

An emphasis on meaning making is nothing new. *The Meaning of Meaning*, the classic text of Ogden and Williams was published in 1927, and, of course, philosophers were exploring the significance of meaning for centuries, if not millennia, before that. It is now well established that, as human beings, we are meaning-making creatures—we live our lives through the stories we create, the constantly evolving narratives that shape our experience (Payne, 2006).

If we are to move beyond the idea that resilience is simply a personal characteristic, then we need to explore how it fits with this broader picture of meaning making, which is necessarily social in nature, and, indeed, sociopolitical, with power playing a key role. Beginning that exploration is precisely what this chapter aims to do.

The Meaning of Meaning

Meaning has been studied under various academic labels over the years—linguists discuss semantics; sociologists, anthropologists and cultural studies scholars write about semiotics; philosophers speak of hermeneutics, and so on. In addition, the literature relating to spirituality regularly references meaning and links it to having a sense of purpose and direction (see Chapter 23 in this volume). It is one of those slippery terms where we all know what it means, but it is exceedingly difficult to pin it down precisely. This is ironic, of course, as the struggle to make sense of the term is precisely a struggle around meaning itself.

We need to recognize that "meaning" is a broad term. It ranges from the meaning of a single word (or even a syllable or letter, as in "The S at the end of chairs *means* it is a plural noun") right through to the meaning of life and the philosophical and theological quests to establish whether or not there is a purpose to existence.

Meaning is not simply about language (meanings can be signaled nonverbally, for example), but it is clear that language is a strong linking thread across the broad field of the study of meaning and its role in social life. Language is, by its very nature, social, which is partly why we shall be examining the social nature of meaning below. Language is, in so many ways, what connects each of us, as individuals, to other individuals, to groups, communities and society as a whole (Thompson, 2018a). It is largely through language that culture operates, and, of course, culture is very much a part of how meanings work. Indeed, the question of what connects individuals to wider elements of the world is a key point to which we shall return below.

The Sociological Basis of Meaning

By drawing on my earlier work on PCS analysis (Thompson, 2018b), it can be helpful to understand meaning in terms of embedded layers. We each make sense of our lives at a *personal* level—what sociologists refer to as our biography. Bourdieu (1993) uses the term "habitus" to refer to the set of meanings that we each have and by which we create our own sense of identity—it is a sort of personal culture, comprising those assumptions that give us a sense of familiarity, security and being "at home" (*Heimlichkeit*, as Heidegger, 1978, called it).

This biography, though, does not operate in a social vacuum. It is embedded within a wider *cultural* framework, a set of meanings that define, and are defined by, the cultural context in which each of us lives. Part of that context is a set of discourses—that is, frameworks of meaning that we are exposed to through our upbringing and which are reinforced through the media and other social institutions (Thompson, 2018c). Renner explains the concept of discourse in the following terms:

> Following Ernesto Laclau and Chantal Mouffe's argumentation, a discourse represents a relatively stable arrangement of social meaning or a 'structured totality' in which meaning and social identities are temporarily arranged in a relational system of signification [Laclau & Mouffe, 2001].
>
> (2018, p. 79)

In this sense, our personal meanings (biography/habitus) are in large part shaped by the wider cultural context and the discourses that operate in that context.

But, these discourses do not operate in a social vacuum either. They are embedded within a wider context of *structural* power relations connected with the social divisions of class, race/ethnicity, gender and so on. Renner again offers a helpful explanation:

> Discourse theory considers discourses as powerful. Power here is understood not as the capability of agents, but as the potential of discourse to institute and naturalise a certain version of social reality while marginalising other possibilities [Epstein, 2008; Torfing, 1999]. Discursive power, thus, consists of a productive and repressive component, which represent two sides of the same coin.
>
> (2018, p. 80)

The two key terms here are "naturalize" and "marginalize." Discourses have the effect of making certain things seem "natural" or "common sense"—for example, a patriarchal discourse presents the caring role as one "naturally" better suited to women. Discourses also have the effect of marginalizing certain groups or categories of people. For example, a discourse that presents same-sex relationships as pathological serves to marginalize LGBT people from mainstream society; it presents them as "other" or "deviant"—difference is translated into deficit. Discourses—and therefore meanings—are very much about power. Meanings do not operate in some sort of power-free zone where relations of domination and subordination do not exist.

Using the conceptual framework of PCS analysis enables us to understand that personal meanings are not unconnected to wider society—they pass through sociopolitical "filters" at both cultural and structural levels, with all that this implies in terms of power relations and their influence on how individuals, groups and categories of people make sense of the world. Any attempt to understand meaning that disregards the wider social context is therefore not only inadequate in terms of explanatory power but also potentially oppressive in terms of the danger of discriminatory power relations being unwittingly reinforced or, at the very least, being allowed to operate unchallenged.

The Existential Basis of Meaning

Existentialism is concerned with ontology and phenomenology (Sartre, 2003). Ontology is the study of being and is concerned with what it means to exist, so clearly very much concerned with meaning. Phenomenology is the study of perception (phenomenon means "that which is perceived," and so that too is very much concerned with meaning).

Existentialism is premised on the idea that, as individuals, we do not have a fixed identity (or "essence"). Our lives are a constant process of identity creation based on an ongoing series of choices, the context in which those choices take place, and our reactions to that context. Consequently, the existentialist conception of identity, self or personhood is not that of a relatively fixed personality on a journey through life—rather, we *are* that journey. This means that we are constantly building, amending and rebuilding a "self-narrative"—a framework of meaning that gives our lives a shape, a perspective and a degree of coherence.

For the most part, we tend to manage this journey quite well, but not always. For example, existentialism offers an understanding of schizophrenia as a struggle to maintain a coherent sense of meaning and selfhood over time (hence the idea of a "shattered self"). Likewise, anxiety problems can be understood as part of the challenge of making our lives meaningful and satisfactory.

Frankl, a psychiatrist influenced by existentialist thought, put forward in his classic work the idea that we are constantly seeking and creating meaning (Frankl, 2004). From this premise he developed a therapeutic technique called "logotherapy" which is premised on negotiating meanings—an approach that has influenced modern-day narrative therapy (Denborough, 2014).

But, it is not just in the mental health field that meaning making can be disrupted. There will also be times of significant loss and/or trauma where we struggle to maintain a thread of meaning. It can even reach the point where we struggle to maintain a sense of who we are in such circumstances (a phenomenon known as "biographical disruption"). It is at such times, of course, that resilience becomes an issue, and so we can begin to see both meaning and resilience as existential phenomena, dimensions of what it means to be human, rather than just individualistic psychological matters.

Conflict is also a key issue. Gadamer (2013) wrote about the "fusion of horizons," by which he meant the complex dynamic interplay of different perceptions and perspectives. How I see the world at any given time may be very different from how you see the world, and both may be very different from how a third person sees it. So, while, as humans, each of us shares so much in common with other people, we need to recognize that there will also be myriad ways in which we differ, with conflict therefore an ever-present possibility. Existentially, managing conflict can be understood as a process of meaning making—for example, trying to develop a shared narrative that does justice to the differing perspectives involved. Conflict therefore raises the issue of resilience. This is because resilience can be understood as part of our response to adversity, and conflict, particularly conflict that is not well managed, can be a major source of adversity. We therefore need to give some thought to how meaning and resilience relate to one another, bearing in mind that both these concepts need to be understood sociologically and existentially.

Resilience and Meaning

If we understand resilience as picking ourselves up after adversity has knocked us down, it is not too difficult to see how meaning making fits into this picture. When we encounter adversity, we will be faced with the challenge of making sense of it, of incorporating an understanding of what has happened, and the pain and suffering associated with it, into our worldview.

If we take mental health crises as an example of such adversity, we can see how meaning and resilience are interconnected. The dominant approach to such matters is to see them as medical ailments, although this conception is being increasingly and vigorously challenged (see Chapter 8 in this volume). An alternative view to the medical model is to recognize the problems as *existential*, involving crises of meaning, immensely challenging experiences that undermine our sense of biographical continuity, stability and security. M. G. Thompson comments:

> The kind of pathology, or suffering, we are talking about is no more located in the mind or our behavior than it is in the body, because the kind of suffering we are concerned with is not mental, but existential: it

inhabits our *being*. As such, it concerns the manner in which we live our lives and the intelligence we bring to bear when trying our best to manage painful experiences. It is *where we live* that we develop these stratagems, not strictly speaking, in our thoughts and feelings.

(2017, p. 96)

Existential challenges involving adversity, whether mental health problems, as in the example given here, or other life problems, unsettle our biography and create difficulties for us in terms of retaining a self-narrative that enables us to feel safe and "at home" (*Heimlichkeit* again). The "bouncing back" of resilience can then be understood as the process of re-establishing a self-narrative that does not adversely affect our well-being—a narrative that is life affirming, rather than spiritually diminishing.

Engagement With the World

Another feature of existentialist thought that is relevant to the present discussion is that of engagement with the world. Despite the predominance of individualistic or atomistic understandings of human existence (especially in the western world), we are necessarily social beings. Sartre (2004) wrote of the "dialectic of subjectivity and objectivity," by which he meant that our private inner worlds (subjectivity) are necessarily connected with the wider social world (objectivity)—the two are inextricable. Trying to understand individuals without understanding their social context is going to result in, at best, partial success or, at worst, a gross distortion of the reality of the situation.

But, our connection to that wider world is not static; it is constantly changing, and so the meanings we rely upon are being perpetually renegotiated. Although meanings tend to be quite stable for the most part, they remain fundamentally fluid because of this process of constant renewal (autopoiesis, to use the technical term).

For example, if we return to our discussion of power, attempts to understand an individual's framework of meaning and their resilience without considering power dynamics are likely to omit potentially major considerations (such as the impact of sexist assumptions about women as sexual objects on the attempts of a rape victim to show resilience in recovering from the trauma involved).

Conclusion

Each of us lives in and of the social world. This has profound and far-reaching effects on how we make sense of our lives, of the world and our place within it. It is also highly relevant to our resilience, to our efforts to develop positive, life-affirming meanings in the wake of demoralizing experiences of adversity.

Within this social context we will encounter incidences of adversity, some minor, some quite major, but each, regardless of its magnitude, will challenge us to either go under, to be lesser persons because of that adversity, or to rise up again and reaffirm our being in positive terms, thereby creating the potential for growing and learning from the adversity—resilience at its best.

References

Bourdieu, P. (1993). *Language and symbolic power*. Cambridge, UK: Polity.

Denborough, D. (2014). *Retelling the stories of our lives: Everyday narrative therapy to draw inspiration and transform experience*. New York: W. W. Norton & Co.

Epstein, C. (2008). *The power of words in international relations: Birth of an anti-whaling discourse*. Cambridge, MA: MIT Press.

Frankl, V. (2004). *Man's search for meaning*. London: Rider.

Gadamer, H.-G. (2013). *Truth and method*. London: Bloomsbury Academic.

Heidegger, M. (1978). *Being and time*. Hoboken, NJ: Wiley-Blackwell.

Laclau, E. and Mouffe, C. (2001). *Hegemony and socialist strategy: Towards a radical democratic politics*. (2nd Edn.) London: Verso.

Payne, M. (2006). *Narrative therapy*. (2nd Edn.) London: Sage.

Renner, J. (2018). Producing the subjects of reconciliation: The making of Sierra Leoneans as victims and perpetrators of past human rights violations. In L. Odysseos and A. Selmeczi (Eds.), *The power of human rights/The human rights of power*. London: Routledge, pp. 78–96.

Sartre, J.-P. (2003). *Being and nothingness: An essay on phenomenological ontology*. New York: Routledge.

Sartre, J.-P. (2004). *Critique of dialectical reason. Vol. 1*. London: Verso.

Thompson, M. G. (2017). *The death of desire: An existential study in sanity and madness*. (2nd Edn.) New York: Routledge.

Thompson, N. (2018a). *Effective communication: A guide for the people professions*. (3rd Edn.) London: Palgrave.

Thompson, N. (2018b). *Promoting equality: Working with diversity and difference*. (4th Edn.) London: Palgrave.

Thompson, N. (2018c). *Applied sociology*. New York: Routledge.

Torfing, J. (1999). *New theories of discourse: Laclau, Mouffe and Žižek*. Oxford: Blackwell.

25 Continuing Bonds and Resilience

Charles A. Corr and Kenneth J. Doka

Introduction

- Carl was a beloved high school football coach. Although his wife, Marlene, was somewhat shy, she did enjoy her efforts to support her husband—baking goodies for his team and hosting an annual spaghetti dinner for the team, coaches and cheerleaders. At Carl's death, the community collected funds for a scholarship in his name. Now Marlene proudly administers the fund. Less introverted, she now manages the account, interviews applicants, works with a committee and presents the scholarship at an award ceremony. She enjoys this immensely and is proud to maintain the connection to her husband.
- Alisha mourns her husband. In the two years since he died, she thinks of him all the time. Before marrying later in life, Alisha was highly independent—living on her own, maintaining a job and driving. Since her marriage, she became highly dependent on her husband, Greg, who referred to her as "his little princess." As Greg was retired, he drove her back and forth to chores, even to her work. Now she no longer wishes to drive because "Greg did not believe women were good drivers." After his death, she no longer works or even socializes much.

In both of these cases, a grieving individual retains a bond with a deceased family member. In the first case, that bond seems to have facilitated the grief process and nurtured a sense of resilience. Yet, in the second case, the bond has become a shackle—deeply restricting Alisha's activities and impairing her ability to cope with her loss.

Understandings of grief have changed in recent years, both by recognizing continuing bonds as an aspect of the mourning process and by appreciating varied ways, including resilience, in which individuals respond to loss. This chapter explains these changes and explores how continuing bonds can both facilitate and complicate resilience within the mourning process.

Changing Paradigms of Grief

In recent years, significant changes to understandings of grief have included the following (Doka, 2011):

- Extending understandings of grief from reactions to a death of a family member to a more inclusive appreciation of loss;
- Recognizing personal pathways in grief versus universal stages;
- Identifying the multiple and multifaceted reactions that persons have toward loss and the ways that responses to grief are influenced by culture, gender and spirituality, instead of seeing grief solely as affect;
- Seeing possibilities of transformation and growth in mourning versus coping passively with loss;
- Recognizing more complicated variants and the necessity for careful assessment, rather than understanding grief merely as a normal transitional issue;
- Acknowledging that certain individuals show great resilience as they cope with loss and grief;
- Maintaining continuing bonds with the deceased versus relinquishing all ties.

This chapter focuses on the latter two changes, resilience and continuing bonds, and the relationship between them.

Continuing Bonds

Historical accounts of grief and mourning often argued that bereaved persons must sever ties with the deceased by withdrawing emotional energy from the person who has died in order to invest it elsewhere and go forward with a healthy life. This process of decoupling from a deceased person (decathexis) was seen by Freud (1917/1957) as the central process of mourning.

By contrast, Klass, Silverman and Nickman (1996) drew on research with bereaved children, spouses and parents, as well as on Eastern religions to demonstrate the importance for many bereaved persons and groups of efforts to maintain ongoing connections to the individual who has died. These connections involve the formation of continuing bonds with an internal representation of that individual. Such bonds are dynamic, not static. They involve negotiating and renegotiating the meaning of the loss over time. Continuing bonds develop in ways that allow the deceased to remain a transformed or changed but ongoing presence in the inner lives of the bereaved individual or group. Connections of this type "provided solace, comfort and support, and eased the transition from the past to the future" (p. xviii).

According to these authors, "the continuing bond has been overlooked or undervalued in most scholarly and clinical work" (p. xvii), and there has been "little social validation for the relationship people reported with the deceased or absent person" (p. xviii). Nevertheless, they believe continuing bonds involve new and altered relationships that reflect "the reality of how people experience and live their lives" (p. xix). Such ongoing connections are aspects of normal mourning processes and do not represent psychopathology. Stroebe and Schut (2005) have suggested that the key issue is whether continuing or relinquishing bonds to the deceased is helpful or harmful, in what ways or under what circumstances, and for whom. Doka (2011) added that continuing bonds can contribute in positive ways if they allow bereaved persons and groups to acknowledge their losses while also making possible continuing growth.

Bonds are maintained in a number of different ways. First, we always retain memories of the deceased. This is critical. Many bereaved individuals fear that as they cope with loss memories will fade, thereby exacerbating their sense of loss and impeding the grief process. Counselors should affirm to clients near the beginning of therapy that the goal of grief therapy is not to diminish memories of the deceased; rather they can find comfort in such memories as the pain of loss lessens. The amelioration of grief means that over time the intensity of the grief experience lessens and individuals function in ways comparable to (or perhaps even better than) they did prior to the loss. The fact that these memories are always retained is also a reason for subsequent surges of grief that may occur years after the loss. In fact, at the termination of a counseling relationship, it is helpful to suggest, and even identify, the significant life events or major transitions that might generate such surges.

Second, important attachments become part of one's own biography. We are influenced by many factors, such as birth order and family structure. The ways one interacted with others who are important also frame an individual's personality. In addition, significant attachments in one's life leave their legacies, and sometimes their liabilities, on the identity of the bereaved individual. Those legacies (and liabilities) can include everything from gestures of faith to the ways that one views self and relates to others and to the world.

Third, survivors retain spiritual ties such as the belief the deceased is or may be interceding for them and that they will be reunited in an afterlife. Most spiritual systems have beliefs and practices that strive to retain a connection, such as Roman Catholic Anniversary Masses or the Jewish "Mourners Kaddish"—a prayer said at the memorial service as well as for 11 months following the death. In fact, Klass acknowledged that in traditional Chinese worship, the veneration of one's ancestors was a common practice reinforcing a continuing family bond throughout generations.

Moreover many reports of extraordinary experiences have come from some bereaved persons who have sensed the continued presence of the deceased in their lives or have from time to time received after-death communications. Most often, these individuals have found comfort in these extraordinary or paranormal experiences (LaGrand, 1997, 2006). One challenge in mourning is to decide what such experiences might mean and to find ways to integrate them into healthful, ongoing living. This is another way a continuing bond is retained.

Finally, increasing numbers of bereaved persons have been using the internet and social media, particularly Facebook, to provide death notifications and to continue ongoing relationships with the deceased. They visit the Facebook page of the person who died, commenting there on pictures, posting memories and talking directly with the deceased (Pennington, 2013). Some have undertaken to "keep alive" the digital identity and/or the Facebook page of a deceased person (McEwen & Scheaffer, 2013).

Continuing bonds can be applied to groups and communities—even nations. For example, in the opening case of Carl, the deceased coach, his school community endowed an ongoing scholarship as act of remembrance. Communities may name parks, streets or buildings after individuals or may erect memorials in their honor. Even nations may honor ties with deceased or heroic leaders through such things as naming cities, building monuments or creating holidays.

Resilience

Defining Resilience

Resilience is derived from the Latin term *resilientem* meaning "inclined to spring back or resume its original form." The term originally derived from physics and referred to the ability of a substance to absorb some form of tension and then bounce back to its original shape. For example, a resilient rubber band might be sorely stretched, but then once released it reverts to its original form and retains all the former capabilities prior to the original stretch. While the term was originally a characteristic of objects, it soon began to be applied to individuals. Resilient individuals were seen as those persons who could bounce back from tragic and adverse conditions with little consequence.

In recent years, Bonanno (2009) has emphasized that many bereaved individuals are highly resilient to loss, experiencing even significant losses with comparatively few manifestations of grief and returning to life with little consequence. Bonanno's work may be seen as a corrective to early studies of grief that often stressed the significant range of difficult grief reactions and poor outcomes that can follow loss.

While perhaps not going as far as Bonanno, we can define resilience in grief as the ability to face a loss with relatively limited manifestations of grief that do not seriously interfere with one's ability to quickly resume, with little ill effects or disruption, key social roles in ways similar to before the loss.

Factors Supporting Resilience

Several factors have been identified as promoting resilience (see Doka, 2016). Some of these factors are situational. Resilient grievers tend to have fewer losses or other significant stressors in their lives. Generally the deaths they experienced were neither sudden nor traumatic—offering survivors an opportunity to say "goodbye" or deal with any yet unresolved issues. Other factors are sociological in nature. Resilient grievers tend to have positive relationships with others and receive effective social support within their intimate networks of family and friends. In addition, they live in communities with resources such as bereavement services.

There also are personal and psychological factors that support resilience. Resilient grievers have good psychological health—including no history of depression and anxiety. Generally they have social and adaptable temperaments and are valued by others. Resilient grievers tend to be optimistic. They look at adverse events, such as losses, as challenges and are optimistic and hopeful that they can surmount these tests and learn and grow from such experiences. They have an inherent sense of control that empowers response to crisis—believing there is something that they can do even in the most adverse circumstances. And though they recognize they cannot control the fact of loss, they believe they can have some control over the ways they respond to their losses. While hopeful, resilient grievers also maintain a positive yet realistic view of self—acknowledging their own flaws and seeking help when necessary.

Finally, resilient grievers have an intrinsic spirituality or underlying philosophy that helps them accommodate the loss within their view of the world. And perhaps most importantly for this chapter, resilient grievers maintain a positive relationship with the deceased and often invoke positive memories of the deceased when experiencing distress.

Resilience and Continuing Bonds

Certainly the ability to use such positive memories is one way that maintaining a continuing bond with the deceased facilitates resilience. For example, in one of the opening cases, Marlene's tie to her late husband and his coaching work, has led not only to opportunities for her to create a legacy to Carl but also has empowered her to grow as a person throughout her work. Here ongoing ties have supported resilience—allowing a survivor opportunities to cope and to grow from her grief.

Yet there may be times when continuing bonds are maladaptive—inhibiting resilience. Field and his associates (Field, 2006; Field, Gao, & Paderna, 2006) found that bonds that try to maintain physical proximity to the deceased, such as excessive use of the deceased's possessions or attempts to "freeze" life at the point of the death are problematic because they contain an implied denial of the deceased or of the death.

There may be other cases of maladaptive bonds as well. For example, as in the case of Alisha, one may have made promises to the deceased that are no longer viable. Such promises, as Alisha's not to drive, may impair adjustment to the new reality.

One other aspect of continuing bonds that can be problematic are challenges to the post-mortem identity of the deceased. For example, one may find that a beloved grandparent was a war criminal or that a loving father had multiple affairs and children with other women (Doka, 2019). Challenges to the memories of such individuals can invoke relational traumas and impair adaptation and resilience.

Clinical Implications

The acceptance of continuing bonds and their relationship to resilience has modified therapeutic approaches to grief. Earlier, it was indicated that it is often useful to frame the beginnings and termination of therapy—first as clinicians reassure clients that they will always retain a bond with their clients and, at termination, as they acknowledge moments that this bond may, in the future, possibly cause surges of grief.

This has also modified approaches to grief counseling. The first edition of Worden's classic book on *Grief Counseling and Grief Therapy* (1982) described the fourth task of mourning as "to withdraw emotional energy and reinvest it in another relationship" (p. 15). However, in his fifth edition, Worden (2018) acknowledges continuing bonds by reframing this task as "to find a way to remember the deceased while embarking on the rest of one's journey through life" (p. 50).

Similarly, the *Dual process model of grief* (Stroebe & Schut, 1999) affirms that grieving involves oscillating between two major processes—acknowledging the loss and adjusting to life now changed by the loss. Inherent in that model is the recognition that one has to decide in what ways the relationship with the deceased continues. This is consistent with clinical work emphasizing that grieving individuals have both to look back—acknowledging the legacies and liabilities of the past relationship with the deceased—even as they look forward to adjusting to a now-changed existence.

All of these clinical approaches affirm a basic point. Clinicians should assist grieving individuals in acknowledging the bonds they retain with the deceased and in understanding how these bonds can both facilitate and complicate their resilience and adjustment to the loss.

Conclusion

This chapter has explained theories about continuing bonds in bereavement and has shown how such ongoing connections may or may not support resilience among bereaved persons and groups. When individuals and groups are confronted by the death of someone who is significant to them, whether that may involve sudden or anticipated losses, their typically responses include grief reactions and mourning responses. When survivors are challenged by the finality of death, most bereaved persons and groups seek to cope with their losses and their grief by engaging in mourning practices. These may include traditional funeral or memorial rituals, as well as spontaneous activities designed to give vent to grief and to honor the memory and legacy of the deceased person. Such memorial activities often extend into the future, thereby forming the foundation for and acknowledging the ongoing connections with the deceased. This can occur on an individual level or even at a community or national level. For example, communities of various types may erect a roadside memorial, endow a scholarship, name a building or recall the legacies of the deceased in various other ways. Each of these can come to constitute a continuing bond with that person, and such bonds can encourage resilience in the communities or even nations involved so as to enable them to engage in ongoing forms of productive living.

References

Bonanno, G. (2009). *The other side of sadness: What the new science of bereavement tells us about life after loss.* New York: Basic Books.

Doka, K. J. (2011). Introduction: Beyond Kübler-Ross: New perspectives on death, dying and grief. In K. J. Doka & A. S. Tucci (Eds.), *Beyond Kübler-Ross: New perspectives on dying, death, and grief.* Washington, DC: Hospice Foundation of America, pp. iii–xvii.

Doka, K. J. (2016). *Grief is a journey: Finding your path through loss.* New York: Atrium.

Doka, K. J. (2019). Changes in post-mortem identity and grief. *Omega: Journal of Death and Dying*, 78, pp. 314–26. doi: 10.1177/0030222817693157.

Field, N. P. (2006). Unresolved grief and continuing bonds: An attachment perspective. *Death Studies*, 30, pp. 739–56. Retrieved from https://doi.org/10.1080/07481180600850518.

Field, N. P., Gao, B. and Paderna, L. (2006). Continuing bonds in bereavement: An attachment theory based perspective. *Death Studies*, 29, pp. 277–99. Retrieved from https://doi.org/10.1080/07481180590923689.

Freud, S. (1957; originally, 1917). Mourning and melancholia. In. J. Strachey (Ed. & Trans.), *Standard edition of the complete works of Sigmund Freud*, Vol. 14. New York: Basic Books, pp. 237–60.

Klass, D., Silverman, P. R. and Nickman, S. L. (Eds.) (1996). *Continuing bonds: New understandings of grief.* Washington, DC: Taylor & Francis.

LaGrand, L. E. (1997). *After-death communications: Final farewells.* St. Paul, MN: Llewellyn.

LaGrand, L. E. (2006). *Love lives on: Learnings from the extraordinary encounters of the bereaved.* New York: Berkley Books.

McEwen, R. N. and Scheaffer, K. (2013). Virtual mourning and memory construction on Facebook: Here are the terms of use. *Bulletin of Science, Technology & Society*, 33, pp. 64–75. doi:10.1177/0270467613516753.

Pennington, N. (2013). You don't de-friend the dead: An analysis of grief communication by college students through Facebook profiles. *Death Studies*, 37, pp. 617–35. doi:10.1080/07481187.2012.673536.

Stroebe, M. and Schut, H. (1999). The dual process model of coping with bereavement: Rationale and description. *Death Studies*, 23, pp. 197–224. doi:10.1080/074811899201046.

Stroebe, M. and Schut, H. (2005). To continue or relinquish bonds: A review of consequences for the bereaved. *Death Studies*, 29, pp. 477–94. doi:10 .1o80/07481180590962659.

Worden, J. W. (1982). *Grief counseling and grief therapy: A handbook for the mental health practitioner*. New York: Springer.

Worden, J. W. (2018). *Grief counseling and grief therapy: A handbook for the mental health practitioner*. (5th Edn.) New York: Springer.

26 The Dual Process Model and Resilience

Amy Y. M. Chow

Stage theory (Kübler-Ross, 1969; Bowlby, 1980) is commonly used to describe the process of bereavement. It holds a basic assumption that grief progresses through particular psychological phases. This assumption has been challenged and said to be an oversimplification of the chaotic process (Silver & Wortman, 2007; Stroebe, Schut, & Boerner, 2017). Though bereavement is an individual experience of losing an intimate and significant other through death, it happens in the social context in which familial, cultural and societal values play a role (Thompson & Cox, 2017). Bereavement is also a complex process, with fluctuations that cannot be captured solely by stage theory. The death of a significant person ripples secondary stressors that demand adaptions as well, a phenomenon that stage theory is not adequately equipped to cover. Further theories have emerged in the past two decades, addressing the gaps of stage theory in describing bereavement experiences. One of them is the Dual Process Model (DPM) as proposed by Stroebe and Schut (1999).

The Dual Process Model of Coping with Bereavement

DPM, as reflected by its name, consists of two processes: loss-oriented (LO) coping and restoration-oriented (RO) coping. LO coping refers to the focusing on, evaluating and processing of the loss experience by the bereaved persons. Putting the deceased person as the center, this coping includes memorializing, ruminating, searching and yearning for the deceased. RO coping, on the other hand, focuses on the adjustment to accommodate the secondary stressors induced by the death. It is comprised of analysis of the stressors and the corresponding plans, as well as the action towards adjustment of the world without the deceased (Stroebe & Schut, 1999, 2010). DPM has a third core component which captures the dynamic nature of the process: oscillation. The bereaved person shifts between the two types of coping, and this contributes to successful coping. This oscillation juxtaposes the confrontational and avoidance coping of cognitive stress theory, which flexibly addresses the different challenges and stressors in bereavement.

The Dual Process Model in Social Context

Compared with the other theories in bereavement, DPM puts more emphasis on the social context. The introduction of RO coping acknowledges the role of secondary stressors in bereavement, as well as the importance of the respective ways of coping with the stressors. This extension of emphasizing the adjustment has been explicitly valued in recent years, even by the American Psychiatric Association (APA). The updated version of the *Diagnostic and Statistical Manual on Mental Disorder*, version 5 (DSM-5) introduces a new bereavement-related disorder: Persistent Complex Bereavement Disorder (PCBD). Other than the criteria of symptoms, a necessary condition is that "the disturbance causes clinically significant distress or impairment in social, occupational, or other important areas of functioning" (APA, 2013, p. 790). A similar condition is present in the criteria for Major Depressive Episode as well (APA, 2013). The recently published 11th edition of the *International Classification of Diseases* (ICD-11) has less elaborated concerns of symptoms for Prolonged Grief Disorder criteria at the same time. Symptoms are presented as examples of intense emotional pain, with the specific demands of a number of symptoms. Instead, there is this requirement: "the disturbance causes significant impairment in personal, family, social, educational, occupational or other important areas of functioning" (Killikelly & Maercker, 2018, p. 3). These aspects of functioning, as mentioned by both manuals, are context related and are not limited to the personal level but encompass the social, familial, educational and occupational levels. RO coping of DPM is addressing these levels of functioning comparably. While the medicalization of grief has been strongly challenged by a range of social scientists and clinicians alike, the recognition of the importance of incorporating a consideration of the wider social context is to be welcomed.

More than a decade after the introduction of the model, Stroebe and Schut (2010) highlighted the possibility of cultural differences in coping as well. As proposed by Klass and Chow (2011), bereavement is experienced within a cultural framework. Culture prescribes the appropriate form, dosage and duration of coping. It sometimes even polices the expression of grief through different cultural standards of "abnormal" grief reaction. For example, Chinese culture favors restoration-oriented coping. As reflected by the common condolence statement "*Jié āi shun biàn,*" which literally means "stop grieving and adjust to the change," Chinese culture emphasizes the importance of moving on and discourages the emotion expression. As mentioned by Stroebe and Schut (2010), the Muslim community in Egypt favors loss-oriented coping. Bereaved persons of this community usually gather to share openly their grief and memories of the deceased.

The American Psychiatric Association (APA) also acknowledges the influence of cultural values and norms in bereavement. The DSM-5 removes the exclusion of bereaved persons from Major Depressive Episode and Adjustment Disorder. Yet, there is a clear statement for the diagnosis of Major Depressive

Episode: "This decision inevitably requires the exercise of clinical judgment based on the individual's history and the cultural norms for the expression of distress in the context of loss" (APA, 2013, p. 161). Similarly, for the diagnosis of Adjustment Disorder, it states: "when the intensity, quality, or persistence of grief reactions exceeds what normally might be expected, when cultural, religious, or age-appropriate norms are taken into account" (APA, 2013, p. 286). Lastly, a new diagnosis of Persistent Complex Bereavement Disorder is introduced. This diagnosis also takes cultural, religious and age-appropriate norms into account. Likewise, the criteria for prolonged grief disorder in ICD-11 specifically stated that "grief reactions that have persisted for longer periods than are within normative period of grieving given the person's cultural and religious context are viewed as normal bereavement responses and are not assigned a diagnosis" (Killikelly & Maercker, 2017, p. 3).

Aside from the significant influence of the larger cultural community on bereavement, the DPM of coping is situated in the family level of the bereaved person as well. Stroebe and Schut (2015) developed their DPM into the DPM-R, with the inclusion of individual-level and family-level coping. They believe intrapersonal dynamics and the interpersonal family dynamics in bereavement are mutually influencing one another. Incorporating the wider social context, the DPM-R refines the two types of coping into two levels: individual and family. A death in a family brings new challenges, as the role performed by the deceased member is usually no longer available. The family has to juggle a new form of functioning and search for a new equilibrium. Complicated by the different pace and values of individual family members, the disparities in coping and oscillations induce further stressors and tensions to the family. Each bereaved family member has to review his or her values in coping and preferences of use of LO and RO coping as well as the contextual factors affecting the choices of types of coping. At the same time, these have to be done at familial level as well.

Resilience Through the Lens of the Dual Process Model

DPM is about coping, and resilience is about the ability to cope in recovering from challenges (Cox & Thompson, Chapter 1 in this volume). Resilience can be viewed as the desired outcome of DPM coping. DPM enriches the understanding of resilience. To achieve resilience, the balancing of vulnerability between "too vulnerable" and "feeling invulnerable" or "vulnerable enough" is crucial. This balancing emulates the oscillating process of DPM between LO and RO coping. LO coping focuses on the loss and is more related to the awareness of vulnerability. The awareness of incapacity of bringing back the deceased, as well as the experience of grief and the permanent loss of the deceased, are all increasing the awareness of the vulnerability of human beings. The RO coping focus on handling the secondary losses emphasizes invulnerability and the ability to adjust to the changed world. Literally, the word "restoration" shares common essence with "resilience" too. The concepts of restoration and resilience in bereavement are conditions counteracting the "eligibility" of Prolonged Grief Disorder, Persistent Complex Bereavement Disorder and other forms of bereavement-related disorders. With restoration and resilience, the bereaved person is being able to function well socially and occupationally.

While resilience shares common threads with DPM in coping and oscillation, another related concept, "coping flexibility," sheds light on the understanding of resilience. Instead of a generic coping strategy, flexibility in coping is found to be correlated with the desirable outcome of adjustment in facing losses as well as crises and therefore is more helpful in achieving resilience. Coping flexibility means applying the appropriate coping strategy in the right context. The prerequisite is the awareness and ability of adopting different coping strategies, as well as the ability to differentiate the appropriate context. Fu, Chow, Li, and Cong (2018) further augmented the concept of resilience with delineation of aspects of coping, namely cognitive, behavioral and emotional. In addition, in defining emotional flexibility in facing loss, there are three sublevels: the tuning of negative emotions, the tuning of positive emotions and the communications of emotions. This new typology of coping adds two further dimensions: tuning (experiencing and avoiding) and communication (expressing and suppressing). This refined categorization supplements the LO coping and RO coping in DPM, offering more detailed choices in coping.

Dual Process Model Intervention in Practice

Inspired by the DPM, Caserta, Utz, Lund, Swenson and de Vries (2014) developed "Life After Loss" (LAL), a group-based intervention that incorporates the oscillations between LO and RO coping. Contrary to the expected result, there was no treatment effect between the LAL group participants and those in the comparison group who focused on LO coping only. They believed that probably "one size does not fit all" and concluded that individual-based intervention addressing specific RO-related challenges with appropriate coping skills might be more effective. Individually tailored intervention can accommodate a wider range of circumstances and the corresponding needs (Caserta, Lund, Utz, & Tabler, 2016), which is parallel with the concept of coping flexibility. Chow et al. (in press) translated and amended the LAL group intervention to fit the Chinese context. By contrast, the experimental intervention was found to be superior to that of the LO-focused comparison group. Chow and Xiu (in submission) further investigated the mechanism of change and found that RO-coping and oscillation played an important role in contributing to the positive outcome.

Promoting Resilience Through the Dual Process Model

While current bereavement care mainly accentuates working on the grief reactions or the prevention of complications in the reactions, the Dual Process

Model propounds attention to the importance of adjustment and functioning. Complementing the work in memorializing the deceased, reviewing the loss experience or building a continuing bond with the deceased, one has to take care of restoration-oriented tasks that emerge from the secondary losses associated with the bereavement. A balanced and flexible share of attention in addressing the LO stressors and RO stressors is equally important, if not more so. Coping is individualized and context relevant.

This understanding inspires the development of bereavement care or care for those who are facing different types of losses. Firstly, instead of addressing the feelings towards the death, the deceased or the loss, supporters should also attend to the adjustment and functioning involved in facing the changed world. A balanced and dynamic process of drifting between the different coping approaches to these two types of demands will help to reach resilience. Secondly, the RO coping is individualized and context relevant. Supporters have to be aware of the subjective perception of concerns about adjustment issues, with the cultural, religious and familial values and preferences taken into account. Thirdly, coping is not only limited to behavioral coping but extends to cognitive and emotional coping. It can involve adopting "approach or avoidance" and "expression and suppression" strategies. Fourthly, coping can be trained. Through education, coaching and sharing, the coping repertoire can be expanded, which in turn increases the likelihood of achieving resilience. Fifthly, coping needs internal and external resources. While educating the grievers, supporters should also aim at improving resources at the same time. This can also be done as a preventative, rather than remedial, intervention.

Conclusion

Losses and deaths are natural life experiences. Though they induce intense grief reactions that need to be dealt with, they can also be life lessons to be learned. With appropriate coping and resources at an appropriate pace, alternating between the acceptable dosage of approach and avoidance, one can become more resilient in facing future challenges. There is no single formula or "one-size-fits-all" mode of pathway; the process is individualized, shaped by the personal and familial experiences and cultural context.

References

American Psychiatric Association, APA (2013). *Diagnostic and statistical manual of mental disorders: DSM-5*. (5th Edn.). Washington, DC: American Psychiatric Association.

Bowlby, J. (1980). *Attachment and loss*. London: Hogarth Press & Institute of Psychoanalysis.

Caserta, M. S., Lund, D., Utz, R. L. and Tabler, J. L. (2016). "One size doesn't fit all"— Partners in hospice care, an individualized approach to bereavement intervention. *Omega*, 73(2), pp. 107–25.

Caserta, M. S., Utz, R., Lund, D., Swenson, K. L. and de Vries, B. (2014). Coping processes among bereaved spouses. *Death Studies*, 38(3), pp. 145–55.

Chow, A. Y. M., Caserta, M., Lund, D., Suen, M. H. P., Xiu, D., Chan, I. K. N. and Chu, K. S. M. (in press). Dual-process bereavement group intervention (DPBGI) for widowed older adults. *The Gerontologist*.

Chow, A. Y. M and Xiu, D. M. (in submission). Mechanism of dual process bereavement intervention: The mediating role of change in loss-oriented coping, restoration-oriented coping and oscillation on change in grief outcomes.

Fu, F., Chow, A. Y. M., Li, J. and Cong, Z. (2018). Emotional flexibility: Development and application of a scale in adolescent earthquake survivors. *Psychological Trauma: Theory, Research, Practice, and Policy*, 10(2), pp. 246–52.

Killikelly, C. and Maercker, A. (2018). Prolonged grief disorder for ICD_11: The primacy of clinical utility and international applicability. *European Journal of Psychotraumatology*, 8. Retrieved from www.ncbi.nlm.nih.gov/pmc/articles/PMC5990943/.

Klass, D. and Chow, A. Y. M. (2011). Culture and ethnicity in experiencing, policing, and handling grief. In R. A. Neimeyer, H. Winokuer, D. L. Harris and G. Thornton (Eds.), *Grief and bereavement in contemporary society*. New York: Routledge, pp. 341–53.

Kübler-Ross, E. (1969). *On death and dying*. New York: Macmillan.

Silver, R. C. and Wortman, C. B. (2007). The stage theory of grief. *The Journal of the American Medical Association*, 297, pp. 2692–4.

Stroebe, M. and Schut, H. (1999). The dual process model of coping with bereavement: Rationale and description. *Death Studies*, 23(3), pp. 197–224.

Stroebe, M. and Schut, H. (2010). The dual process model of coping with bereavement: A decade on. *Omega*, 61(4), pp. 273–89.

Stroebe, M. and Schut, H. (2015). Family matters in bereavement: Toward an integrative intra-interpersonal coping model. *Perspectives on Psychological Science*, 10(6), pp. 873–9.

Stroebe, M., Schut, H. and Boerner, K. (2017). Cautioning health-care professionals: Bereaved persons are misguided through the stages of grief. *Omega*, 74(4), pp. 451–3.

Thompson, N. and Cox, G. R. (2017). *Handbook of the sociology of death, grief and bereavement: A guide to theory and practice*. New York: Routledge.

27 The Role of Pastoral Care

Bernard Moss

> Pastoral care is familiar with the notion that staying with the questions is as important as finding answers.
>
> (Holloway & Moss, 2010, p. 129)

In this chapter we will explore ways in which resilience is an essential attribute of good pastoral care.

Exploring Pastoral Care

The importance of pastoral care is very familiar across many different disciplines and organizations, not least in the area of care for people who are dying or who have been bereaved. It is in some ways a "catch-all" phrase intended to capture the ways in which people reach out in care and compassion to others in moments of intense emotional and spiritual pain. It is perhaps a "first-level" response where pastoral carers could find themselves trying to offer support in moments of crisis or beyond, as a precursor in some instances to more specialist counseling, therapeutic or medical help that only skilled professionals are able to provide.

Having said that, pastoral care is more than offering a friendly shoulder to cry on. It is often offered in the name of, or on behalf of, a particular organization that has a moral or even statutory duty of care towards those entrusted to them. Within the wider sphere of education, for example, pastoral care is a key responsibility of each school or college. Also, various listening or befriending services often seek to provide a level of pastoral care in their local communities.

When it comes to pastoral care for end-of-life moments, faith communities are good examples of organizations that seek to offer pastoral care to their congregations, and within their neighborhoods, to support people in their times of need, especially if the funeral service has taken place in their place of worship.

The practice, experience and understanding of what pastoral care means, therefore, are rich, varied and diverse, as readers of this chapter will readily acknowledge. Within this complexity, however, it is important to recognize that all such organizations that offer pastoral care, whether they be secular or religious, will have a basic set of values and principles that underpin the pastoral care they offer, principles that include valuing and respecting the individual they are caring for, being non-judgmental, respecting the person's dignity, working within agreed boundaries of confidentiality and safeguarding guidelines, and having clear lines of accountability and oversight/supervision within their organization. Pastoral carers also need to be skilled in active listening and to ensure that they do not allow their own personal "baggage" (including their personal beliefs and prejudices) to get in the way of what the other person needs at the time. Pastoral care, as we have stated, is much more than offering a shoulder to cry on; it is a skilled activity in its own right.

The importance of resilience for pastoral care cannot be overemphasized, especially when focusing on the area of death, dying, bereavement, grief and loss. To offer pastoral care, in whatever capacity and on behalf of whatever organization, secular or religious, is to be exposed to a range of intense feelings and emotions. As a pastoral carer you will be expecting the person you are caring for to be deeply upset and distraught even as they face their own death, the life-threatening illness of someone close to them whose days are numbered, or the loss of someone whose death has just shaken them to the core. As a pastoral carer you will expect this, to a greater or lesser extent. What may come as a disconcerting shock to you, however, is the extent to which you yourself are distressed by this encounter with the big issues of death, dying and bereavement. The many-faceted strands of loss that interweave throughout all our lives can be powerfully stimulated when we meet it in others. And the last thing you want to happen in such situations is for your own pain to intrude upon the pain of the person you are seeking to comfort and support. To cope with such moments requires resilience.

Becoming a Wounded Healer

One author who has provided a perceptive insight into what resilience might mean for us is Henri Nouwen (1972), who talks about the concept of the "wounded healer." Nouwen argues that every single one of us, just by living our human lives, will experience pain and hurt, rejection and betrayal, grief and loss. Indeed, these painful but potentially life-enhancing (as well as often life-diminishing) moments make us who we are and who we are constantly becoming. How we deal with these experiences is crucial to our well-being and is a hallmark of our personal resilience. Often this involves a struggle with meaning making, as we grapple with whatever worldviews we have chosen to hold and with the extent to which our painful experiences resonate with or contradict the views we hold about ourselves and the world. In this sense, we all carry wounds. The implication of becoming a wounded healer as a pastoral carer involves two dimensions: first, our ability to be aware of the wounds we carry and how these have shaped our lives; and second, the ways in which these wounds deepen our awareness and sensitivity to the wounds of others.

The greater our resilience the more capable we will be of recognizing our own wounds, of refusing to foist their impact upon others whom we are seeking to care for, and of deepening our willingness and ability really to listen to the pain of others.

To foster that resilience as wounded healers also changes, albeit subtly, the relationship we have as pastoral carers with the people we seek to support. It is so easy to develop a mindset whereby we think we have "got it all together" and are going to someone for whom it is "all falling part"; we are the powerful one going to help those who are weak and needy. To some extent, of course, this has some truth in it: unless we are resilient enough, we can easily add to other people's burdens, rather than share them. But the concept of the wounded healer is a powerful reminder that much of this territory is our common shared humanity. Not only do we hope through our attentive listening and compassionate care that we will release and strengthen the resilience of the person we are seeking to help; by some strange "alchemy" we can find ourselves encouraged and strengthened by this shared process. Resilience fosters resilience, and the healer becomes healed.

Being a Fellow Traveler

This insight is captured in the fellow traveler model of pastoral care (Holloway & Moss, 2010, p. 111ff). The metaphor of life being a journey is so widely used now that it risks losing its potency. But, in pastoral care there is a sharing of someone else's journey, and for a short, or maybe longer period of time, the pastoral carer is a fellow traveler with the person they seek to support. And, rather than being an experienced mountain guide leading a complete novice through tricky terrain, the fellow traveler in this situation is offering to share the journey side by side for a while, to see what the journey brings, to explore what the scenery is like and to negotiate together the unexpected, as well as expected, obstacles on the way. The fellow traveler will rejoice when his or her companion grows in confidence and begins to take the lead, eventually to say they will go on ahead solo for a while and then report back. Such are the rewards of resilience.

Staying with the Questions

We began with the observation that "pastoral care is familiar with the notion that 'staying with the questions is as important as finding answers.'" And it is to this aspect of resilience, especially in the face of death, dying and bereavement that we must now turn.

Being a fellow traveler will necessarily involve listening not only to a person's pain, but also to some of the powerful, indeed existential, questions that the other person begins to fling out. Death and dying, terminal illness and major disasters inevitably throw up a whole series of questions that have dogged or enhanced (depending on your point of view) moral philosophers and theologians, and indeed politicians, for ages: *What sort of world are we liv-ing in? What sort of society have we created? How can this be allowed to happen? Why has this happened? What have I done to deserve this appalling heartbreak? How can people treat each other in such an awful way? Why, oh why, do some people behave so abusively towards innocent members of our community?*

The great "why" questions abound thick and fast, and pastoral carers will encounter them implicitly or explicitly as part of their work. The temptation to offer slick or easy answers (they may be heartfelt by the person offering them, but they are likely to be received in a different way by others) can be very strong, but often the complexity of shared human living precludes such responses.

Sociologists play an important role in developing our awareness and under-standing of the complexity of social groups and human societies and the pressures and forces that can impact powerfully upon human behavior. The sociological imagination encourages us, even at moments of distress, to stay with the questions and to develop an awareness of the complexity of human behavior, individually and communally. But this requires resilience. It requires a willingness to be open to even greater complexity and, dare we say it, confu-sion. A child knifed down in the street in front of passive onlookers by a young teenager under the influence of an illegal substance, who in turn has been egged on by a peer group, raises a whole battery of sociological questions wider than individual accountability, however crucial that dimension is.

Thompson (2016) provides important insights into how we can better understand these complex issues. When discussing the powerful and at times destructive power of discriminatory, oppressive behavior, he draws careful dis-tinctions between Personal, Cultural and Structural perspectives (PCS analy-sis). In the example above of the child being knifed, there are clearly personal, individual aspects to the behavior of the assailant. But what do we make of the peer group phenomenon of a knife-carrying culture; of the reluctance, perhaps fear even, of getting involved to intervene in violent situations; or of how safe our communities are? And what societal and structural issues are at work here, in how young people are regarded, trained or neglected and how social hous-ing, unemployment, welfare provision and other major social issues impact upon certain localities? Someone offering pastoral care to that bereaved family will be faced with the immediate agony of bereaved parent(s), but some of the wider painful questions arising from PCS analysis will inevitably have to be faced. And to do that requires resilience, not least because to tackle some of the wider issues will require a far wider range of responses and political action than individual pastoral care.

Reducing resilience to a personal characteristic disregards these important wider issues and sets the scene for a judgmental and potentially discriminatory approach to people who struggle to achieve resilience in incredibly trying cir-cumstances. Clearly, this is not a good starting point for anyone offering pastoral care. So, even in the highly personal, one-to-one world of pastoral care, we need to be alert to the significance of wider sociological factors (Thompson, 2018).

Further Thoughts on Resilience

Admittedly, all of this gives to our discussion about resilience a greater degree of complexity than perhaps you had expected. Or, rather, it enriches and deepens our understanding of resilience by taking it beyond being an attribute of the pastoral care worker into a much wider framework. Resilience is not a precious gift owned by a few to share with the less fortunate. Resilience is a potential and a capacity within each and every one of us, and it can be fostered and deepened by a variety of factors, including how our self-worth is enhanced, what sense of meaning and purpose we have in our individual and shared lives, what contribution we feel we can make to the welfare and well-being of others, and how our emotional and intellectual well-being is sustained and nurtured by our chosen worldview.

Resilience can also be diminished, of course, especially in times of personal crisis and distress. Grief and loss can undermine the very factors which, a moment ago, we suggested are important in enhancing and developing our well-being. When things and people upon whom we have come to rely are taken away from us, our foundations can crumble. When we are faced with major loss and grief, the worldview, which has given our life meaning and purpose, be it secular or religious, could well disintegrate, and we are left feeling shallow and unsupported in a cold and lonely universe . . . or that is how it could feel at least. To be able to share that level of angst with someone as a pastoral carer is very demanding.

It is also important to think about how organizations (large or small), local communities, local government, businesses and indeed much wider aspects of our various societies may or may not be resilient in terms of providing for people's welfare and well-being; their cultural, recreational, religious or spiritual needs; and the systems that can be put in place to support people when they encounter hard times. One of the hallmarks of good leadership at whatever level it is exercised is the extent to which resilience is encouraged and fostered in the communities they serve and the extent to which a clear direction and purpose is established with a strong value base underpinning it.

Practice Perspectives

We have covered a wide range of issues in this chapter, albeit briefly, and have raised some important questions about resilience and pastoral care. We hope that we have encouraged you first of all to reflect on your own resilience, how it is fostered and nurtured, what potential threats there may be to it and, importantly, how you have responded to and dealt with (if that is the best phrase to use) issues of loss and grief in your own life. This will give you important insights into who you are, how resilient you are and how you might be better able to help and support others.

We hope that the terms "wounded healer" and "fellow traveler" will have given you some insight into how to develop your own role within pastoral care.

And we hope that we have helped you to appreciate some of the wider complex issues that are the context for each and every one of us, especially as we face grief and loss, and to appreciate and foster resilience in a variety of different ways in your own communities.

But, most of all, we hope that your own commitment to becoming more resilient will enrich the lives of the people you seek to help and will foster greater resilience in them too.

References

Holloway, M. and Moss, B. (2010). *Spirituality and social work*. Basingstoke, UK: Palgrave Macmillan.

Nouwen, H. (1972). *The wounded healer*. New York: Doubleday.

Thompson, N (2016). *Anti discriminatory practice: Equality, diversity and social justice*. (6th Edn.) London: Palgrave.

Thompson, N. (2018). *Applied sociology*. New York: Routledge.

28 Promoting Resilience in Social Work

From the "Comfort of Strangers" to Community Empowerment and the "Management of Risk"

Paul Stepney

I am having a lunchtime break from working in the university library and have boarded the 3T tram that passes nearby and follows a long circular route around the city of Helsinki. On a cold fall day the tram attracts a diverse clientele and offers a snapshot of the world as it is, rather than how we might like it to be. When in Helsinki I often take this tram, so today, rather than gaze at the city sights, I look around and exchange a few words (in English and broken Finnish) with some other passengers—new migrants from Syria keeping warm, mother comforting her disabled child, older person wanting to speak and two homeless people begging. It soon became clear that, behind the wide diversity of human experience, the people I talked to all had something in common—they were trying to maintain a sense of dignity while confronting loss and were showing resilience in the face of adversity. In this chapter I want to critically examine and unpack the concept of resilience and explore how it might be promoted in social work.

The call for everyone to show "greater resilience" has become a fashionable response to adversity and loss in popular discourse. It is now routinely voiced by the sports coach to his or her players after another defeat, the politician under pressure from voters, parents seeking to improve their children's learning, teachers preparing students for exams, managers extolling staff to meet government targets, so on and so forth. In fact, the "call for resilience" is now commonly used by influential figures in many fields faced with the task of explaining how disappointing performance that failed to match expectations can be improved upon. This makes resilience a keyword in the social sciences, but one that has become inherently slippery and intellectually messy.

Raymond Williams (1983), in a classic study first published in 1976, identified a large number of socially significant *keywords* and explored the ideological meanings they conveyed which helped to define our culture. For example, keywords, such as "community," "family" and "welfare" reflected socially ordered priorities that still have resonance today. They tell us something about who we are, how we got here and where we might be heading.

Resilience, although not one of Williams's keywords, has certainly become a contemporary buzzword, alongside empowerment, social inclusion and well-being. It is therefore hardly surprising that it has entered the lexicon of the policy maker and social worker.

In social work the term "resilience" has historical significance. It emerged at a time when the focus of a practitioner's gaze was beautifully captured by the notion of social work as "the comfort of strangers" (Webb, 2007). This was in recognition that care and support will increasingly be met by "the services of strangers" rather than family members—a legacy of 19th-century social policy (Clarke, 1993, p. 5). In recent times resilience has become a key ingredient of empowerment approaches (Lee, 2001), informing the strengths perspective (Saleebey, 2006), and is now deployed with community-based methods that balance protection with prevention in the "management of risk" (Webb, 2006; Stepney, 2014). This reflects social work's professional culture, as well as the way ideas about coping and self-reliance have gained wider currency in both policy and practice. Such ideas are then communicated to clients and held up as a model for self-improvement.

Resilience can be defined as the successful adaptation to stressful life events (Rutter, 1993) and the ability to withstand adversity, recover from disruption and return to previous levels of functioning (Gilligan, 2000). It has become a complex and culturally sensitive, multifaceted construct (Ungar, 2004). As the subtitle of this volume indicates, resilience is a response to adversity, vulnerability, loss and grief. And, while these are clearly important in social work, the emphasis in this chapter will be more on sociological factors. These are not only relevant to helping clients cope with adversity and loss, but they also relate to wider issues of social disadvantage, inequality and change.

Research suggests that there is an underlying social gradient in factors relating to resilience. According to Garrett (2015), poor health, educational disadvantage and deprivation all exacerbate vulnerability across the lifecourse. Factors which increase resilience in children and help them cope with adversity, such as secure attachments, sociability and learning problem-solving skills, are often undeveloped in children from disadvantaged backgrounds. The structural adversity, vulnerability and multiple risks that socially disadvantaged children face make resilience building important if children are to manage key turning points and transitions in their lives (Garrett, 2015). But, some disadvantaged children get by, so other psychosocial and environmental factors are at work (Ungar, 2004).

The issue of resilience also applies to staff. Stress resilience has become a key requirement for emotional well-being in social work practitioners. Research with trainee social workers has shown that resilience is a protective factor that can help practitioners "buffer stress" associated with the constant flow of demanding and potentially traumatic events (Kinman & Grant, 2011). Individual and organizational factors found to enhance resilience included keeping control, remaining optimistic, having realistic expectations, having social support, expecting the unexpected, successfully managing emotions and maintaining clear boundaries between work and home (Grant & Kinman, 2014; McFadden, Campbell, & Taylor, 2015). In another study with early career practitioners, exercising control, coping strategies, social support and emotional self-advocacy were found to be key, along with reflective supervision and support (Kinman & Grant, 2017). This helps explain why some staff thrive, while others struggle in similar work environments.

It is instructive to note how the term "resilience" has emerged in policy making. According to Garrett (2019) there is a danger of resilience becoming another term to be re-worked by those on the political right pursuing a neoliberal agenda. At a time of resource constraints, blaming clients for having insufficient resilience can justify harsh, "tough love" policies designed to push claimants off benefits and into jobs (p. 6). Hence, the political context remains important, and we must guard against the term being used as an instrument of welfare regression. If we can liberate resilience from the jaws of adaptation and compliance, then it can become aligned with resistance and linked to empowerment and the development of critically reflective practice (Thompson & Stepney, 2018).

Resilience Linked to Empowerment

Lee (2001) suggests that empowerment is neither a theory nor a process but more a variety of conceptually coherent social work approaches and frameworks for practice (p. 32). Consequently, seeing empowerment as an overarching theoretical framework means that it can be applied to work with any client group to promote resilience. To illustrate how this might work we will now look at three brief practice examples—in mental health, child protection and community social work.

Practice Focus 1

At the mental health center, an impromptu discussion developed at the "well-being" group as clients were asked to say something about themselves. Mary said that she had recently lost her job and now felt anxious about everything. Frank explained that he had PTSD and hadn't worked since leaving the army. Jean had received counseling for depression, but now the negative thoughts had returned. Sonia said she was trying to get over losing her mother and just wanted to talk. Terry didn't want to say anything other than he was glad to be here (by a roundabout route from his bedsit, so no-one saw him) and could bring his dog.

During the coffee break Jema, the social worker, and Rosi, a student on placement, reflected on the session. They had made a promising start with everyone participating, so after coffee they would introduce group rules about confidentiality and respect. However, Jema felt they needed to offer the group something positive to take away. It was agreed Jema would introduce the idea of resilience linked to empowerment, what it was and how these qualities could be developed. They would then use resilience exercises as the focus for future sessions to address specific problems and help group members regain control over their lives.

Focusing on resilience and empowerment is known to be an effective way of helping group members tackle problems of social isolation and loss (Leonardsen, 2007). A group work approach offers clients a good blend of encouragement, structure and support. Using resilience linked to empowerment can also be used in child protection as the second practice focus illustrates.

Practice Focus 2

Venus was a single mother with two children, Sergio, four, and Clara, 18 months, living in a run-down inner-city neighborhood. She had mounting debts, health problems and was struggling with the children after her partner left. When Sergio turned up at the nursery with a bump on his head and Venus missed a developmental appointment with the nurse, the family was referred to Children's Services.

Kirsti, the social worker, visited and found a chaotic home situation with Venus struggling and the children running wild. Venus said that the bump on Sergio's head was the result of his falling in the street (confirmed by a neighbor), but she admitted that "things were getting difficult . . . with the kids out of control." Venus said she wanted to put things right and "was willing to try anything to prove I'm a good mom." She had few friends and no family nearby.

Kirsti went back to the office to discuss the case with her manager. It was agreed that Venus required intensive help and support (plus light-touch child protection) in partnership with nursery and health colleagues. The aim would be to empower Venus to become more resilient, regain control and exercise better care of the children. Hence, a dual prevention and protection plan was drawn up, written in clear language, to ensure that everyone was on the same page. The plan had targets for improvement and weekly monitoring to ensure progress— promoting resilience and empowering Venus to improve the children's welfare.

Social workers in children's services have many cases like this, where the child protection role is paramount. However, protection can usually be enhanced through prevention strategies of client empowerment, promoting resilience and offering family support. This is consistent with a community social work (CSW) approach, creating new informal networks of support, as the final practice focus shows.

Practice Focus 3

Social workers from the Adult and Children's teams came together to discuss common problems among their clients in the neighborhood. Two issues quickly emerged: first, the need for a family support group for single parents, like Venus, with young children; second, a group to tackle social isolation and loneliness among older people. With support and a small budget from the team manager, a CSW group of two social workers from each team was established to take the idea forward. The plan quickly gained support from health professionals and community members.

Two months later the social workers with two health colleagues, having consulted clients, were planning the first session of each group. It was agreed that the family support group would concentrate on helping parents develop greater resilience to cope with their children's behavior and teach simple behavioral strategies. The social workers from the adult team, with feedback from older people, similarly decided to focus on promoting resilience. They planned to experiment with reminiscence therapy, as a way of unpacking the concept of resilience, sharing experiences and developing mutual support and trust.

Later, when the team manager asked for a progress report (and what the budget had been spent on), the social workers were able to report significant progress. CSW endeavors to help clients and community members develop qualities of resilience in the long haul of achieving community change. The social workers had concentrated on developing qualities, identified from research, that would enhance client resilience: creating a network of informal support, developing problem-solving skills, managing emotions and retaining optimism when something went wrong, gaining confidence and control of their lives.

Conclusion

Resilience has become a crucial construct not just to help clients cope with adversity and loss, but to help social workers to manage their professional lives (Grant & Kinman, 2014). Social work is an intellectually and emotionally demanding profession, and developing resilience is essential if we are to promote it in our clients and the wider community.

From the international literature we know that many of the everyday problems clients face have both psychosocial and structural causes. That is why resilience linked to empowerment is not only a good way of helping clients regain control and cope with individual problems, but it also enables us to address culturally sensitive issues of disadvantage, inequality and social justice. This is one of the strengths of social work that was highlighted in each practice focus.

The spirit of resilience informing social work as the "comfort of strangers" remains a potent symbol and orientation even in an age of marginality characterized by the "management of risk." The notion of resilience linked to empowerment will help practitioners create a vision of achieving progressive change, even in the most daunting situations when all seems lost.

References

Clarke, J. (1993). The comfort of strangers. In J. Clarke (Ed.), *A crisis in care? Challenges to social work*. London: Sage, pp. 5–22.

Garrett, P. M. (2015). Questioning tales of "ordinary magic": Resilience and neoliberal reasoning. *British Journal of Social Work*, 46(7), pp. 1–17.

Garrett, P. M. (2019). Welfare words, neoliberalism and critical social work. In S. Webb (Eds.), *The Routledge handbook of critical social work*. Abingdon, UK: Routledge, pp 3–14.

Gilligan, R. (2000). *Promoting resilience: A resource guide on working with children in the care system*. London: British Association of Adoption and Fostering.

Grant, L. and Kinman, G. (Eds.) (2014). *Developing resilience for social work*. London: Palgrave Macmillan.

Kinman, G. and Grant, L. (2011). Exploring stress resilience in trainee social workers: The role of emotional and social competences. *British Journal of Social Work*, 41, pp. 261–75.

Kinman, G. and Grant, L. (2017). Building resilience in early career social workers: Evaluating a multi-model intervention. *British Journal of Social Work*, 47, pp. 1979–98.

Lee, J. A. B. (2001). *The empowerment approach to social work practice: Building the beloved community*. (2nd Edn.) New York: Columbia University Press.

Leonardsen, D. (2007). Empowerment in social work: An individual vs. relational perspective. *International Journal of Social Welfare*, 16, pp. 3–11.

McFadden, P., Campbell, A. and Taylor, B. (2015). Resilience and burnout in child protection social work: Individual and organizational themes from a systematic literature review. *British Journal of Social Work*, 45, pp. 1546–63.

Rutter, M. (1993). Resilience: Some conceptual considerations. *Journal of Adolescent Health*, 14(8), pp. 626–31.

Saleebey, D. (2006). *Strengths perspective in social work practice*. Boston, MA: Allyn and Bacon.

Stepney, P. (2014). Prevention in social work: The final frontier? *Critical and Radical Social Work*, 2(3), pp. 305–20.

Thompson, N. and Stepney, P. (Eds.) (2018). *Social work theory and methods: The essentials*. New York: Routledge.

Ungar, M. (2004). *Nurturing hidden resilience in troubled youth*. Toronto: University of Toronto Press.

Webb, S. (2006). *Social work in a risk society*. Basingstoke, UK: Palgrave.

Webb, S. (2007). The comfort of strangers: Social work, modernity and late Victorian England. *European Journal of Social Work*, 10(1), pp. 39–54.

Williams, R. (1983). *Keywords*. (2nd Edn.) New York: Norton.

29 An Exhibition on Resilience for a Time of Grief

Wendy Bowler

Two days after the catastrophic events of September 11, 2001, when terrorists flew hijacked planes into the Twin Towers in New York, the Pentagon in Washington and a field in Pennsylvania, the *New York Times* published a long article about the power of the arts to assuage loss and grief. It compiled the ideas of the newspaper's critics on the artworks that might resonate with readers' experiences ("The expression of grief," 2001). It goes without saying that these were traumatic events: in one morning 2,977 people died, and in Manhattan many thousands were forced to evacuate as the skyscrapers imploded and sent apocalyptic dust clouds coursing through the city streets. All the rest of us could do was bear witness.

It was a democratic article in its inclusion of all forms of art: theater, literature, art, television, classical music, jazz, popular music, photography, dance and film. We read, for example, of Laurence Olivier's cries in *Oedipus Rex* at the Old Vic in post-war London ("A rendering scream that spoke for all"); of various poetry, including "Thou has drunken the dregs of the cup of trembling" from Isaiah; of Martha Graham's dance *Lamentation* (1930); of Rembrandt's self-portraits showing mourning as "a state of mind" not a time-limited event, plus Picasso's "cry of outrage" in *Guernica* (1937); of Elton John's "Candle in the Wind," as revised for Princess Diana's funeral; and—from jazz music—the tradition of the two-part New Orleans funeral march (the blues on the way there and "the joys" on the way back).

From Homer to Eric Clapton, the salient point was that, as human suffering was ubiquitous, the list of works expressive of trauma, loss and grief could go on and on. As to the question of why produce an arts review, the justification was that "art in all its forms has girded us to go on grieving and living." We needed art. New York's paper-of-record was publishing a guide to indicate how culture and the arts could be of service (a compassionate act). We might tweak the basic premise to state that art both *girds us* in grief and *enables us* to continue living before asking, do these aspects relate to resilience, and, if so, how does this work?

When we question the role of the arts we are talking about the multifaceted concept of culture. Sociologists who study culture and the arts work to interpret symbolic representations of the world—not out of a strict interest in an art object's content, form and historical context, but as a manifestation of subjective and social life. One influential framework is the cultural anthropology of Clifford Geertz, for whom culture is "the pattern of meanings embodied in symbols [by which people] communicate, perpetuate, and develop their knowledge about and attitudes towards life" (1973, p. 89). Cultural theorist Raymond Williams determines three broad usages in which culture is a general process, a particular way of life and a word describing "the *works and practices of intellectual and especially artistic activity*" (1983, p. 89; emphasis added).

To understand the capacities of culture I suggest we first look at the nature of aesthetic experience. When we engage in the arts through art making, art therapy or as a member of an audience, we are adopting an "aesthetic perspective" or attitude that shifts our perception of reality away from the dominant concerns of the everyday (Geertz, 1973, p. 110; Wolff, 1996, pp. 74–7). This argument, bearing on phenomenology and extending Immanuel Kant's "disinterestedness," gives the aesthetic its own "intentionality," based on the "bracketing of this experience" from everyday reality (Wolff, 1996, p. 74). Common sense similarly speaks of the benefits of bracketing in grief, through "taking time out" to socialize, go to work, just have a rest, and so on.

Geertz perceives people as moving easily and frequently between "radically contrasting ways of looking at the world" through making cognitive shifts which he likens to philosopher Kierkegaard's "leaps of faith" (p. 120). For example, similar to the child's transition into the play world is "the radical change in our attitude if, before a painting, we permit our visual field to be limited by what is within the frame as the passage into the pictorial world" (Geertz, quoting Schütz, 1962, p. 120; Wolff, 1996, p. 75).

Significantly, we might appreciate resilience to be something that starts with this "leap" out of the daily tumult (temporarily) and into another sphere of life—a different "province of meaning" (ibid.)—such as the "world of art." I think the common meaning of resilience as a "bouncing *back*" is problematic when there has been a death; more helpful is the sense of "leaping" from the Latin root *(re)silire*. "Salience," a related word, is also useful, this being the "starting point" of something: the *punctum salient* (Online Etymology Dictionary, 2019). These meanings bear an affinity with the foregoing description of the aesthetic perspective.

Catastrophic events seem to split time, as terms such as "pre-" and "post-9/11" suggest. Before my own family's schism in time, I spent five years interpreting the media's "tragedy" of September 11 for a doctoral thesis, using Nietzsche's *The Birth of Tragedy*. I interpreted a sequence of images that exemplified the shock, terror, pathos and profound sense of individual and communal loss. I became aware that I was approaching these news shots as art, giving them the time and consideration usually reserved for pictures in a gallery, in trying to determine their meaning. Art was suffering's consolation, for Nietzsche.

Then came May 3, 2012, the day my 18-year-old son, Jesse, was killed in a car fire with two other young men. Minutes before the crash he had evidently climbed in the back seat of his mate's vehicle after a shift at work. The event turned our family of four into a highly vulnerable threesome and began an interminable process of learning to cope with states of trauma, chaos and profound grief. On the day of the funeral I said in my tribute that, despite my years of study, I had known nothing about tragedy. There is no doubt that the death of a child opens up tragedy's "hole of meaningfulness" (Reiss, 1980, p. 302), a term that takes on an awfully graphic meaning once you have had to view your own son's grave. It was an image that seared itself in memory and necessitated a barely conscious search for beauty as an antidote: the perpetual arrangement of flowers, visits to places of natural beauty and opportunities to re-engage with art.

An Imaginary Exhibition

We have considered the aesthetic perspective, but what of the traits of the creative work of culture? To take a metaphorical page from the *New York Times*, what follows is a necessarily subjective review of works in an imagined thematic exhibition (they could also be pictures in a book, or images on PowerPoint or Instagram). It is a version of my daughter's "grief playlist," but in place of music and songs helping to create a safe (aesthetic) space in which to hear the chiming of mutual loss and grief, the form is visual art on imaginary "playwalls."

Rather than sorrow and despair, I suggest we begin with anomie and alienation, psychosocial states that are underrated aspects of grief and which point to the "problem of meaning" (Weber, 1968, p. 506; Geertz, 1973, p. 104). To try to discover (recover) resilience we need to understand this pair, for example, through an engagement with *Evening on Karl Johan Street* (1892) by Munch, the Norwegian painter of *The Scream*. It represents a crowd of people pressed together and walking along a city street. They have owl-eyed, vacant stares as if living without purpose beyond the impulse to keep moving and, despite being shoulder to shoulder, are utterly separate, like atoms. It is a scene that resonates with my "post–May 3" life of walking in the city without aim, leaving one place and not having a clue what to do next. It was a feeling of being radically "out of step" with the crowd and of falling in a hole. These people were coldly "detached from and indifferent to [my] needs" (Yinger, 1964, pp. 158, 171).

The Munch would pair well with *Nighthawks* (1942), American artist Hopper's portrayal of alienated people sitting in a downtown diner at night. We could then fast forward 60 years to 2001 and the 9/11 "dust people" images documenting the anomic terror of ordinary workers fleeing Manhattan: a man vacantly standing with his briefcase and suit jacket, completely caked in dust (Shannon Stapleton/Reuters); a woman turned ghostly white by the dust (Stan Honda/AFP). We would be left with the South Tower ruin (Gary Miller, *NY Post*/Rex), a shot that blurs the boundaries of documentary photography and photo-art through its desolate appeal to the "tragic sublime" (Bowler, 2012).

The question arises: why view such disturbing scenes if you are already suffering? You have to pick your days, but then I see resilience as depending on knowing what you are dealing with. This might be called the homeopathic approach of *facing grief* by finding art that "shows how it is": identifying "models" for, and of, this aspect of life (Geertz, 1973, p. 93). Nevertheless, we are ready for an antidote, and here I would design a "Sunflowers and Starry Nights" wall for Van Gogh's expressive works. It would be ablaze with color in the form of paintings of flowers, trees, fields, orchards and starry skies, and be a testament to the beauty of nature—as to one man's extreme creativity in the loneliest of times. We would feel refreshed, particularly when standing before the pulsating *Country Road in Provence by Night* (1890): a world away from Munch's claustrophobic street. It would bring the whole place back to life.

Next, we would turn to recognize the creative power of a mourning community in the form of panels from the AIDS Memorial Quilt: "the largest piece of community folk art in the world" (NAMES Project, 2019). A wall label would explain the significance of the panels' equal dimensions, three feet by six feet, the size of the burial plots denied to so many victims (ibid). Beside these would come two unassuming felt works made by women of my art therapy group (through Road Trauma Support Services Victoria): *The Forever Tree* (2013) and *Life After the Fall* (2017), a flowing piece of felted silk chiffon symbolizing grief as a turbulent turquoise river. The exhibition enhances the power of these handworks when they are also seen to defiantly counter Munch's anomie.

Finally, we approach the "heart" of the exhibition: images from the rich theme within western visual culture of the Mother-and-Child, as steeped in the Christian story. I think of the iconic form of the Pietà, meaning both pity and piety, in which Jesus's body is held by the Madonna. Although the *Rome Pietà* is best known, I would highlight Michelangelo's *Rondanini Pietà* (1564) for the capacity of his unfinished work to suggest "becoming" (Tolnay, 1966, p. 25)—as bereavement and self-identity after trauma are states of becoming. Comparing this to other works by Michelangelo, we could concur that his Madonnas are "solitary sibyls" who foresee the catastrophe of the Crucifixion. (A biographical note would add that the artist lost his own mother at age six [ibid, pp. 7–8, p. 13].) After this I would choose Raphael's *Borghese Entombment* (1507) to study the collapsed Mother and supporters on the right side, plus the preparatory drawing *Study of Skeletal Forms and Female Heads* (1506–7) depicting Mary as a skeleton (Whistler & Thomas, 2017, p. 117). In these she is a dead weight just like her son.

When I was introduced to this painting two decades ago, it was put to me that we should be attending to the tableau on the left: the bearer party carrying Jesus's heroic-looking body to the tomb. The Mother was lost in grief and of no use to us, a harsh interpretation that I now obviously resist. A wall label could provoke argument on the question of how contemporary society and culture deal with death and bereavement: in my view, by preferring to deny both the pathos associated with the end of life and the validity of grief. They are seen as purely personal (not social or cultural) matters, best kept behind the closed doors of people's bedrooms and their psychotherapists' offices.

From here we would enter the "world" of Kollwitz, the German interwar artist whose work generously offers intimate views of poverty-stricken mothers and children, people confronting death and bereavement, and of the artist herself as an aging, mourning woman. To study the drawing of a young child's sleeping face in *Head of a Child in its Mother's Hands* (1900) is to reconnect with feelings of maternal love and loss (of the physical touch of one's child). The poignancy of Kollwitz's art increases when you learn that her son Peter died in Belgium in 1914 as a soldier in the "Great War." Her large bronze *Pieta* (1937–38), situated in Berlin's New Guardhouse since German reunification, is a powerful symbol of, and for, all women bereft of their children due to war and dictatorship. I would emblazon on our gallery wall Kollwitz's words: "I accept that my art has a purpose. . . . People are so desperate and in need of help" (as seen in *Käthe Kollwitz: Art and Life*, 2018, Art Gallery of Ontario).

We would finally shift from the centers of western culture to receive a lesson in resilience from some "remote masters" of Australian Indigenous art. Like the Van Gogh wall, color and vibrancy would be the saving features. But I would also highlight paintings by the late Rover Thomas related to the massacres of Indigenous people from the time of colonization. *Ruby Plains Killing 1 & 2* (1990) are "our *Guernica*" in the eyes of Australian writer Nowra (1998, p. 99). In the first version, curving lines of landscape defined by chains of white dots lead the eye to a small tree trunk housing a single white dot: a human head (ibid). In the second, the hollow log contains several dots/heads. The point is to bear witness. It is art of determination and vitality, constituents of a resilient response to radical social displacement and to intergenerational trauma and grief.

What this imagined or idealized exhibition has tried to do is identify art's capacity to confront, console and inspire people in times of travail. Culture bears an onerous responsibility in this regard, but like the New Orleans jazz funeral it can also serve up "the joys" for the way home. Artworks, in the broadest sense, may be our homeopathic remedies and antidotes, helping to gird and enable us, and restore equilibrium in the worst of times. So, what is resilience? I see it as the spark of human creative endeavor; the "leap" large or small; the work of someone trying to make meaning after trauma and tragedy had taken meaning away.

References

Bowler, W. (2012). Seeing tragedy in the news images of September 11. In J. C. Alexander, D. Bartmanski and B. Giesen (Eds.), *Iconic power: Materiality and meaning in social life*. New York: Palgrave Macmillan, pp. 85–99.

Geertz, C. (1973). *The interpretation of cultures*. New York: Basic Books.

Nowra, L. (1998). Blackness in the art of Rover Thomas. *Art and Australia*, 35(1), pp. 94–9.

Reiss, T. (1980). *Tragedy and truth*. New Haven, CT: Yale University Press.

'Resilience' + 'Salience'. *Online Etymology Dictionary*. (2019, January). Retrieved from www.etymonline.com/word.

Schütz, A. (1962). *Collected papers I: The problem of social reality*. M. Natanson (Ed.) The Hague: Martinus Nijhoff.

The Expression of Grief and the Power of Art. (2001, September 13). *The New York Times*, pp. E1–5.

The Names Project AIDS Memorial Quilt (2019, February). Retrieved from www.aid squilt.org.

Tolnay, C. de (1966). The historic and artistic personality of Michelangelo. In *The Complete Work of Michelangelo*. New York: Reynal and Company, pp. 7–71.

Weber, M. (1968). *Economy and society: An outline of interpretive sociology*. New York: Bedminster Press.

Whistler, C. and Thomas, B. (2017). *Raphael: The drawings*. Oxford: Ashmolean Museum.

Williams, R. (1983). *Keywords: A vocabulary of culture and society*. London: Fontana.

Wolff, J. (1996). *Aesthetics and the sociology of art*. (2nd Edn.) Ann Arbor: University of Michigan Press.

Yinger, J. M. (1964). On Anomie. *Journal for the Scientific Study of Religion*, 3(2), pp. 158–73.

30 Compassion and Resilience

Darcy L. Harris

In the past decade, there has been a surge in research exploring what is termed "prosocial psychology" (Gilbert, 2019). This term covers a wide range of actions meant to benefit one or more people other than oneself, including behaviors such as helping, comforting and demonstrating kindness and cooperation (Batson & Powell, 2003). Included in the interest of prosocial psychology is the study of compassion.

Compassion is often misunderstood and frequently associated with formal religious beliefs and practices. It is also believed to be, at times, the cause of distress, as in the notion of *compassion fatigue* (Figley, 1995). By contrast, recent research suggests that compassion might be a source of hardiness, resilience and well-being (Gilbert, 2009). This research also points to a relationship between compassion and resilience, indicating the cultivation of compassion may be related to enhanced resilience. This chapter focuses upon the role and interrelationship of compassion and resilience within individuals and organizations, and at the overarching community and political levels.

We start with clarification about what compassion is and how it differs from other prosocial constructs. Following this exploration, we examine the components of compassion, including a discussion about how compassion and resilience relate to one another. Finally, we explore the role of compassion and resilience at the individual, community and governance levels.

Compassion

Paul Gilbert, founder of compassion-focused therapy (CFT), defines compassion as a sensitivity to the suffering of self and others, with a commitment to try to alleviate or prevent it (Gilbert, 2009). According to CFT, there are two key factors that underpin compassion. The first involves developing the ability to notice, turn towards and engage with suffering (as opposed to avoiding or dissociating from it). It is normal to wish to avoid engaging with distress and suffering; however, a compassionate stance overrides this instinctual aversion and opens the door for a choice (and the strength) to face suffering directly without trying to avoid or pull back when confronted with painful situations. This "being with" suffering is often referred to as "distress tolerance" (Gilbert, 2009). This requires practice to develop the skills and techniques that strengthen one's ability to stay fully present in situations where distress and suffering occur and, in so doing, that enhance a sense of sustainable well-being, even when in these difficult scenarios (Gilbert & Choden, 2013). The second aspect involves the motivation to relieve or prevent the cause of suffering. It is interesting to note that a motivation is different from a feeling, implying intentionality and focused behavior.

Gilbert's definition is shared by most researchers who study compassion and its components. For instance, Jazaieri et al. (2013) state that compassion is

> a multidimensional process comprised of four key components: (1) an awareness of suffering (cognitive/empathic awareness), (2) sympathetic concern related to being emotionally moved by suffering (affective component), (3) a wish to see the relief of that suffering (intention), and (4) a responsiveness or readiness to help relieve that suffering (motivational).
>
> (pp. 1117–8)

Halifax's (2013) descriptions of compassion is very closely aligned with these, adding the dimension of insight and discernment to recognize situations where relief of the suffering may not be possible, but human presence and comfort may still provide benefit.

Terms that are sometimes used interchangeably with compassion include "empathy," "kindness," and "sympathy." The main differences are in the attentional and motivational components of compassion. Specifically, like empathy, compassion includes the empathic attunement and understanding of another's feeling state, but empathy does not necessarily involve a motivation or intention to relieve pain or distress. Likewise, kindness and sympathy are also viewed as prosocial predispositions, but there is no expectation that being kind or sympathetic includes the intention of directly addressing the source of the suffering in order to alleviate the distress. The intention to transform suffering is one of the main features that distinguishes compassion from other prosocial inclinations (Halifax, 2013).

Components of Compassion

Most of the research in compassion describe it as an entity by itself that therefore cannot be cultivated or enhanced. However, there are components of compassion that can be strengthened through various types of training, thereby increasing overall compassionate capacity. In general, such training refers to the systematic acquisition of knowledge, skills or competences; it can take the form of focused work on a specific component, such as engaging in a mindfulness meditation program to enhance focus and develop the ability to regulate emotion (Borneman & Singer, 2013). Halifax (2012) identifies the following components in compassion:

1. The ability to focus attention.
2. The ability to regulate emotion and tolerate distress.

3. The ability to discern the situation, including its cause and potential for remedy.
4. Insight into the "big picture" perspective, which includes the understanding that not all suffering can be relieved.
5. The ability to consider a response to suffering that best serves the individual who is in distress or the situation as a whole.

One of the key mental features that arise when all these components are activated is equanimity. Equanimity "is characterized by a calm, even, balanced state of mind; it is also supported by the realization of the truth of impermanence and holding things in equal regard" (Halifax, 2013, p. 220). Halifax suggests the importance of engaging in contemplative practices (including mindfulness) to develop insight and the ability to focus attention. In her GRACE model (Halifax, 2014) of compassionate response, specific steps in responding with compassion are described:

G—Gather attention and focus on what is presenting itself to you in the moment.
R—Recall your intention; this taps into your motivation to relieve suffering.
A—Attune to self and others in the situation, which includes empathic attunement.
C—Consider what will serve. The emphasis here is not necessarily upon "doing something" but in making an informed choice regarding how to best approach the suffering/distress in the situation.
E—Engage with the situation and enact the most reasoned response, given all of the factors that come together uniquely in the moment. This section also includes consciously ending the encounter to keep from carrying the distressful aspects of it with you.

Levels of Compassion

Thus far, the description of compassion has been focused mostly on the interpersonal level, between individuals. However, compassion can be applied at the *intrapersonal level* (self-compassion), as well as the *community level* (for example, compassionate organizations) and at the *political/structural level* (compassionate cities). Each of these is discussed in turn.

Self-Compassion

While compassion is generally considered in terms of social relationships in various settings, Neff and her associates recognized that a major block to training individuals in the components of compassion were their critical, negative and judgmental views of themselves. It was discovered that it is difficult, if almost impossible, to extend true compassion to others if that same motivation does not extend inwardly to how an individual views him- or herself

(Neff & McGehee, 2010). Despite an emphasis in psychology on enhancing self-esteem to improve relationships and well-being, such attempts didn't necessarily correlate with increases in prosocial behavior; in fact, high self-esteem was often described as counterproductive, characterized by increased prejudice against people perceived as different, the need to engage in ego-defenses to protect self-esteem, and narcissistic and self-centered attributes, including a decreased concern for others (Damon, 1995; Neff & Vonk, 2009). In response to this awareness, researchers turned to the concept of self-compassion.

The definition of "self-compassion" is related to being touched by the suffering of others, opening one's awareness to others' pain and not avoiding or disconnecting from it so that feelings of kindness toward others and the desire to alleviate their suffering emerge. Likewise, self-compassion involves being touched by, and open to, one's own suffering, not avoiding or disconnecting from it, generating the desire to alleviate one's suffering and to view oneself with kindness. Self-compassion also involves offering non-judgmental understanding of one's pain, inadequacies and failures so that personal experiences are seen as part of the larger human experience (Neff, 2003).

When faced with experiences of suffering or personal failure, self-compassion entails three basic components:

1. self-kindness—extending kindness and understanding to oneself, rather than harsh judgment and self-criticism;
2. common humanity—seeing one's experiences as part of the larger human experience, rather than seeing them as separating and isolating; and
3. mindfulness—holding painful thoughts and feelings in balanced awareness, rather than over-identifying with them (Neff, 2003).

Self-compassion also represents a balance between concern with oneself and concern with others, a state that researchers are increasingly recognizing as essential to optimal functioning (Blatt, 1995). This balance does not stem from pitting concerns with oneself against concerns for others and finding some sort of compromise. Instead, it recognizes that all individuals should be treated with kindness and caring, and that a compassionate attitude toward oneself is needed to avoid falsely separating oneself from the rest of humanity (Neff, 2003).

Compassionate Organizations

While compassion is usually considered in the context of individuals responding to each other, the concept of compassionate organizations has also been receiving attention. In an organization, suffering comes in many different forms, which may include lack of respect for colleagues, pressure to meet unrealistic workloads and failure to value the contributions and accomplishments of workers. A growing number of organizations now recognize the importance of the workplace culture in promoting the well-being of those who work within them, and attention is turning to the consideration of compassion as an organizational construct. Kanov et al. (2004) state that "compassion is . . . an essential, yet often overlooked, aspect of life in organizations," citing that "although organizations are frequently portrayed as sites of pain and suffering, they are also places of healing, where caring and compassion are both given and received" (p. 809). They identify the terms "collective noticing," "collective feeling" and "collective response," all of which are fostered within an organization whose policies and practices positively acknowledge responding to difficulty and/or vulnerability with compassion as an organizational priority. Workplace policies and leadership that acknowledge shared humanity demonstrate the values of respect and dignity, and those that promote both physical and psychological health and safety foster organizational compassion. For organizations in which dealing with human pain is a persistent and central part of their mission (for example, in healthcare, firefighting and social services) this form of collective compassion capability may be particularly important for sustained organizational effectiveness and resilience (Seppala, Hutcherson, Nguyen, Doty, & Gross, 2014).

Compassionate Cities

The concept of a compassionate city or community was initially discussed in the context of the argument for the provision of humane end-of-life care within given geographical areas. The pain and suffering from terminal illness needed to be addressed at a level that would provide the necessary groundwork for compassionate care to be available in community settings (Kellehear, 2013). More recently, the concept of compassion has been extended into political structures and governing bodies. The *Charter for Compassion* was developed in 2009 under the direction of Karen Armstrong and the non-profit TED (Technology, Entertainment and Design) group. The intention of the charter was to be a global "summons to compassionate action" (Armstrong, 2011, p. 22), with The Golden Rule ("do unto others as you would have them do unto you") as the guiding principle. Its aims were to create a global compassion movement, reminding people of the ethic of compassion within their own traditions, and to provide guidelines for the practice of compassion (see https://charterforcompassion.org/).

Since the charter's introduction, similar charters have been drafted to serve as guidelines over large sectors of community involvement. Examples of these include The International Charter for Human Values in Healthcare (Rider et al., 2014) and The Children's Charter for Compassion (Kohler-Evans & Barnes, 2015). Another example of compassionate community engagement is The Compassion Games (http://compassiongames.org), which originated in Louisville, Kentucky. The mayor asked citizens to perform acts of service in the community during a one-week period. During that week, more than 90,000 acts of service were recorded (Kohler-Evans & Barnes, 2015).

Finally, and perhaps the most important aspect of compassion at the governance level, is the role of citizen participation in electing leaders who have

214 Darcy L. Harris

the courage to enact legislation to address the suffering that results from issues such as poverty, inequality, racism, healthcare and safety for all citizens (Harris, 2016).

Conclusion

As stated, the concepts of compassion and resilience are inherently related to each other. The presence of compassion, along with the perspective and intention that accompanies it, nurtures resilience that is manifest in both the response to, and the outcome of, situations where there is suffering and/or distress. Just as the components of compassion can be cultivated and experienced intrapersonally, interpersonally, organizationally and politically, resilience can also be manifest at these same levels.

In closing, as we consider the relationship between compassion and resilience, we can be directed to the image created in the process of *Kintsugi*, or what is termed "gold-joining" in the Japanese aesthetic tradition (Buetow & Wallis, 2017). In this practice, the broken pieces of an accidentally smashed pot are carefully picked up, reassembled, and then joined back together with lacquer that has gold powder mixed into it. Rather than trying to hide the damage, the point is to render the cracks as obvious but aesthetically pleasing. Metaphorically, the gold in the cracks emphasizes that what is broken has merit on its own. The tender and painstaking process of reshaping and repairing the bowl after it was damaged is representative of the compassionate response to brokenness. The ability of the bowl to once again hold all types of liquids represents resilience.

References

Armstrong, K. (2011). *Twelve steps to a compassionate life*. London: The Bodley Head.

Batson, C. D. and Powell, A. A. (2003). Altruism and prosocial behavior. In T. Millon and M. J. Lerner (Eds.), *Handbook of psychology: Personality and social psychology*, Vol. 5. Hoboken, NJ: Wiley, pp. 463–84.

Blatt, S. J. (1995). Representational structures in psychopathology. In D. Cicchetti and S. Toth (Eds.), *Rochester symposium on developmental psychopathology: Emotion, cognition, and representation*, Vol. 6. Rochester, NY: University of Rochester Press, pp. 1–34.

Borneman, B. and Singer, B. (2013). A cognitive neuroscience perspective: The ReSource model. In T. Singer and M. Bolz (Eds.), *Compassion: Bridging practice and science*. Leipzig: Max Planck Institute for Human Cognitive and Brain Sciences, pp. 178–88.

Buetow, S. and Wallis, K. (2017). The beauty in perfect imperfection. *Journal of Medical Humanities*, pp. 1–6. Retrieved from https://doi.org/10.1007/s10912-017-9500-2.

Damon, W. (1995). *Greater expectations: Overcoming the culture of indulgence in America's homes and schools*. New York: Free Press.

Figley, C. R. (1995). *Compassion fatigue: Toward a new understanding of the costs of caring*. In B. H. Stamm (Ed.), *Secondary traumatic stress: Self-care issues for clinicians, researchers, and educators*. Baltimore, MD: The Sidran Press, pp. 3–28.

Gilbert, P. (2009). *The compassionate mind: A new approach to the challenges of life.* London, UK: Constable & Robinson.

Gilbert, P. (2019). Explorations into the nature and function of compassion. *Current Opinion in Psychology*, 28, pp. 108–14.

Gilbert, P. and Choden. (2013). *Mindful compassion.* London, UK: Constable-Robinson.

Halifax, J. (2012). A heuristic model of enactive compassion. *Current Opinion in Supportive and Palliative Care*, 2(6) pp. 228–35.

Halifax, J. (2013). Understanding and cultivating compassion in clinical settings: The A.B.I.D.E. compassion model. In T. Singer & M. Bolz (Eds.), *Compassion: Bridging practice and science.* Munich, Germany: Max Planck Society, pp. 208–26.

Halifax, J. (2014). GRACE for nurses: Cultivating compassion in nurse/patient interactions. *Journal of Nursing Education and Practice*, 4(1), p. 121.

Harris, D. L. (2016). Care for the caregiver: A multi-layered exploration. In D. Harris and T. Bordere (Eds.), *Handbook of social justice in loss and grief: Exploring diversity, equity, and inclusion.* New York: Routledge, 251–64.

Jazaieri, H., Jinpa, G. T., McGonigal, K., Rosenberg, E. L., Finkelstein, J., Simon-Thomas, E., . . . and Goldin, P. R. (2013). Enhancing compassion: A randomized controlled trial of a compassion cultivation training program. *Journal of Happiness Studies*, 14(4), 1113–26.

Kanov, J. M., Maitlis, S., Worline, M. C., Dutton, J. E., Frost, P. J. and Lilius, J. M. (2004). Compassion in organizational life. *American Behavioral Scientist*, 47(6), pp. 808–27.

Kellehear, A. (2013). Compassionate communities: End-of-life care as everyone's responsibility. *QJM: An International Journal of Medicine*, 106(12), 1071–5.

Kohler-Evans, P. and Barnes, C. D. (2015). Compassion: How do you teach it? *Journal of Education and Practice*, 6(11), pp. 33–6.

Neff, K. (2003). Self-compassion: An alternative conceptualization of a healthy attitude toward oneself. *Self and Identity*, 2(2), pp. 85–101.

Neff, K. and McGehee, P. (2010). Self-compassion and psychological resilience among adolescents and young adults. *Self and Identity*, 9(3), pp. 225–40.

Neff, K. D. and Vonk, R. (2009). Self-compassion versus global self-esteem: Two different ways of relating to oneself. *Journal of Personality*, 77, pp. 23–50.

Rider, E. A., Kurtz, S., Slade, D., Longmaid III, H. E., Ho, M. J., Pun, J. K. H., . . . Branch Jr, W. T. (2014). The International Charter for Human Values in Healthcare: An interprofessional global collaboration to enhance values and communication in healthcare. *Patient Education and Counseling*, 96(3), pp. 273–80.

Seppala, E. M., Hutcherson, C. A., Nguyen, D. T., Doty, J. R. and Gross, J. J. (2014). Loving-kindness meditation: A tool to improve healthcare provider compassion, resilience, and patient care. *Journal of Compassionate Health Care*, 1(1), p. 5.

Index